ARISTOPHANES &

THREE CON

Peace

Money, the God

Samia

Translated by Douglass Parker

Edited, with Introductions and Notes, by Timothy J. Moore

Hackett Publishing Company, Inc.
Indianapolis/Cambridge

17 16 15 14   1 2 3 4 5 6 7

For further information, please address
  Hackett Publishing Company, Inc.
  P.O. Box 44937
  Indianapolis, Indiana 46244-0937

www.hackettpublishing.com

For information regarding performance rights, please email us at
Permissions@hackettpublishing.com.

Interior design by Elizabeth L. Wilson
Cover adapted by Elizabeth L. Wilson from a design by Deena Berg
Interior art adapted by Chris Williams and Deena Berg from originals by Douglass Parker
Composition by William Hartman

Library of Congress Cataloging-in-Publication Data
Three comedies : Peace, Money, The god, Samia / Aristophanes and Menander ; translated
by Douglass Parker ; edited with introductions and notes by Timothy J. Moore.
    pages cm
  Includes bibliographical references.
  ISBN 978-1-62466-185-3 (pbk.) — ISBN 978-1-62466-186-0 (cloth)
1. Aristophanes. Peace. 2. Aristophanes. Plutus. 3. Menander, of Athens. Samia.
I. Parker, Douglass. II. Moore, Timothy J., 1959– III. Aristophanes. Peace.
English. 2014. IV. Aristophanes. Plutus. English. 2014. V. Menander, of Athens.
Samia. English. 2014.
  PA3465.A1 2014
  882'.01—dc23   2014006754

ARISTOPHANES & MENANDER

THREE COMEDIES

Peace

Money, the God

Samia

Contents

Preface

Upon his death in 2011, Douglass Parker left unpublished completed translations of three Greek comedies: Aristophanes' *Peace* and *Money, the God,* and Menander's *Samia*. By happy coincidence, these three unpublished comedies also provide one example each of the three periods scholars generally use in distinguishing the periods of ancient Athenian comedy: Old, Middle, and New. The present volume therefore offers both new translations by a master translator of three delightful comedies and a useful introduction to Greek comedy for students, performers, and others.

With the exception of two very short passages (see below), all three of these translations were completed and revised long before Douglass Parker's death, and each had been performed on several occasions. Always the perfectionist, Douglass was determined to revise each of the plays further. Working with the texts, however, I found that very little revision was necessary. I have kept the translations unchanged with the following exceptions:

> 1. Douglass left untranslated *Peace* 775–818, a set of obscure insults, and 1305–1317, an odd bit of dialogue. I have noted the lacunae in the text and have included my own prose translations of the two passages in Appendix A.
>
> 2. I have corrected some typos and made some changes in spelling for greater consistency between the plays.
>
> 3. I have added a number of explanatory notes. These notes are for readers interested in details and are not necessary for a basic understanding of the plays. As he makes clear in the lecture found in Appendix B, Douglass wanted his translations to be performable and therefore sought to include all necessary explanation in his translations. Throughout the volume, all notes are mine (not Parker's) unless otherwise noted.
>
> 4. I have access to two separate typescripts of *Money, the God* and *Peace* and three of *Samia*. For the most part these typescripts differ only in formatting and very minor details, and it is not always clear which version is the latest. I have therefore either chosen one version without comment or noted some minor divergences in the notes.
>
> 5. Yana Zarifi-Sistovari also kindly provided me the performance script for the Thiasos Theatre Company's presentation of *Peace* at the University of Texas at Austin in April 2001. Working with Douglass, Zarifi-Sistovari and her colleagues abbreviated the translation in order to have a shorter production, and they also made some other changes. In a few passages where I thought the script shed important light on Douglass' approach to performance of his translations or to his conception of *Peace,* I have noted the performance script's variants in the notes. Douglass' own program notes for this production are preserved on the website of the Thiasos Theatre Company (http://www.thiasos.co.uk/supplement-pages/aristophanes-peace.html).

Douglass was a great lover of the word processor's ability to produce varied fonts and images. As much as possible, the fonts and graphics he used have been replicated in this edition.

I received help from many in preparing these translations for publication. Deena Berg's work in gathering Douglass' papers and in polishing Douglass' illustrations for this volume has been invaluable, as has William Levitan's guidance over Douglass' literary legacy. Yana Zarifi-Sistovari and Jamie Masters provided priceless information from their work with Douglass in performing his *Peace* and *Money, the God,* and Yana also let me use her text of Douglass' *Samia.* Andrew Faulkner shared with me a video of the production he directed of *Money, the God.* In preparing electronic versions of Douglass' typescripts I received valuable help from Stott Parker, Michael Whisenhunt, and my graduate assistants Daphne McWilliams and James Prothro. Funds for James and Daphne's work were provided by the John and Penelope Biggs Distinguished Professorship in Classics in the College of Arts and Sciences at Washington University in St. Louis. Douglass' own work on these translations was supported by a fellowship from the Guggenheim Foundation. Elizabeth Scharffenberger provided the text of Douglass' 1988 Constantine Lecture at the University of Virginia. The staff at Hackett, especially Brian Rak and Liz Wilson, and copyeditor Lori Rider have been of great help. My thanks also to Douglass' children, Stott Parker, Clark Parker, and Alison Parker, for permission to publish these translations.

I am very happy to have the opportunity here to acknowledge my own debt to Douglass Parker. As translator, colleague, mentor, friend, guest lecturer in numerous classes, and fellow performer in a long series of dramatic readings, he has enriched my life for many years, and it is a great honor and pleasure to be able to work with his translations.

General Introduction

Ancient Greek Comedy: Old, Middle, and New

These three comedies translated by Douglass Parker offer us examples of each of the three periods into which scholars generally divide the comedies of Ancient Athens. From the time comedy began in the late sixth/early fifth century BCE through the beginning of the fourth century BCE, playwrights such as Aristophanes (c. 448–c. 388 BCE) produced what is known as Old Comedy, of which Aristophanes' *Peace* (421 BCE) is a typical representative. A number of features in comedy appear to have changed by the second decade of the fourth century, so that Aristophanes' last plays, especially *Money, the God,* his very last play (388 BCE), are considered to belong to the next period, called Middle Comedy. By the last quarter of the fourth century, the style now known as New Comedy had replaced its predecessors. Just as Aristophanes is the only surviving playwright of Old and Middle Comedy, Menander (c. 342–c. 292 BCE) is the only writer of New Comedy whose plays, including *Samia* (probably c. 314 BCE), have survived. Between these three periods of comedy there was both much continuity and radical change.

An element of fantastic wish fulfillment lies at the heart of all Greek comedy. At the opening of most Old Comedies the comic hero (or, occasionally, heroine) has developed an absurd plan. During the course of the play the plan is fulfilled in spite of various kinds of opposition, and then the hero and others celebrate the plan's fulfillment. In the process they often expel interlopers who oppose or want to take unfair advantage of that fulfillment. The plays often end in a marriage, a vestige of the fertility rituals from which comedy began. Thus in *Peace* Jack the Reaper devises a plan to fly to Mount Olympos on a cockroach to persuade Zeus to end the Peloponnesian War. When he gets to Olympos, he rescues the goddess Peace from captivity so that the war can end. He then returns to Athens and celebrates, excluding a war-mongering dispenser of oracles and several weapon makers from the festivities; as the play concludes he marries Peace's attendant, the goddess Lady Bountiful.

Middle Comedy, at least as represented by *Money, the God,* involved similar fantastic plans fulfilled: Khremylos has the god Money cured of his blindness, then he celebrates his own new wealth along with others, but he excludes an informer from the celebrations. Instead of a wedding, *Money, the God* ends with the festive reinstallation of Wealth at the temple of Athena. There is, however, a conspicuous difference between the plot of *Peace* and that of *Money, the God.* Jack the Reaper's plan involves specifically the state policy of Athens (it ends her war), whereas the plan fulfilled in *Money, the God* is more closely associated with the private realm. Middle Comedy appears to have been as a rule less involved with Athenian politics and more concerned with the universal.

This move away from public policy went farther in New Comedy, where the element of wish fulfillment remained but became domestic. The plans of New Comedy nearly always involve love: a young man desires a woman (either a wife or the total attention of a prostitute), and obstacles to the union of the man and woman are overcome in the course of the play. Hence when *Samia* begins Moschion wants to marry Plangon, and after various confusions threaten to prevent the marriage, the play ends with their wedding. New Comedy thus laid the foundation for the love-centered comic plot that has remained standard through the modern era.

Accompanying the political plots of Old Comedy was biting political satire. In a practice known as *onomasti komoidein* (producing comedy by name), Aristophanes and his contemporaries ruthlessly ridiculed individual Athenians. Throughout his career, for example, Aristophanes took every opportunity to remind a certain Kleonymos he had dropped his shield and fled from battle; and Aristophanes' verbal war against the demagogue Kleon led to a suit for libel (which Aristophanes won) and continued even after Kleon was dead. *Onomasti komoidein* continued in Middle and New Comedy, but, as *Money, the God* and *Samia* show, it played a less central role in Middle Comedy and occurred only occasionally in New Comedy.

As even a cursory reading of *Peace* makes clear, Old Comedy reveled in obscenity, both sexual and scatological. The obscenity comes in part, no doubt, from comedy's origins in fertility rituals, and from the freedom of expression brought by the plays' festive context. It should also be remembered that standards for public presentation of the sexual and the excretory, and especially for the erotic portrayal of women, vary widely between cultures. Those standards in ancient Athens were very different from our own. The text of *Money, the God* would suggest that the obscenity was toned down somewhat in Middle Comedy. It should be noted, however, that some of Aristophanes' earlier plays also feature less obscenity than *Peace* (see Parker's thoughts on this in Appendix B), and that *Money, the God* may not be representative of its period in this respect. By the time of New Comedy, we can be more confident that the obscene element of comedy had been subdued. *Samia* includes references to matters as shocking as rape and incest, but obscenity brings very little of the play's humor.

Throughout its history Greek comedy existed in close symbiosis with tragedy. The playwrights of Old Comedy interacted a great deal with contemporary tragic playwrights, especially Euripides. Thus in *Peace* we find an extensive parody of Euripides' *Bellerophon,* which many in his audience would have recently seen on stage. By the time of Middle and New Comedy the great age of Greek tragedy had passed. Tragic parody remained important, but it was primarily a response to a familiar tradition rather than to contemporary literary controversies. Hence we find characters of *Money, the God* using the style of tragedy to make their language sound "high-falutin'," and in *Samia* both Demeas and Nikeratos cite mythological stories they would know from the tragic repertoire.

The plays of all three periods of Athenian comedy were performed at festivals in honor of the god Dionysos (the Greater Dionysia and the Lenaia) in the Theater of Dionysos on the slope of the Acropolis. The theater sat as many as seventeen thousand spectators on benches (first made of wood, and later of stone) in a semicircle around the *orchestra,* or dancing place, where the chorus performed. To each side of the *orchestra* was a parodos (side entrance) used by the chorus and sometimes the actors as well. In most plays the parodos to stage right leads to the harbor at Piraeus or to the countryside, the one to stage left to the agora and other destinations within the city. Originally actors probably performed in the *orchestra* along with the chorus, but by the time of

Peace some sort of raised stage was probably used, and some evidence suggests that by the time of *Samia* the stage was raised high above the *orchestra*. Behind the *orchestra* and stage was a building known as the *skenê*, the front of which provided a backdrop. In Old Comedy the *skenê* could represent a variety of places: the action of *Peace* occurs both in front of Jack the Reaper's house and on Mount Olympos. Middle Comedy was known for its mythological burlesques, so some plays may have kept their exotic settings. The action of *Money, the God*, however, all occurs on the street in front of Khremylos' house. That setting on a city street had become standard in New Comedy, where the action of virtually every play occurs in front of one, two (as in *Samia*), or three houses.

All actors—or at least all speaking actors—on the Athenian stage were male. It is not certain whether females could play mute roles. The nude females shown sometimes in Old Comedy, such as the goddess Jamboree in *Peace*, were thus probably male actors in body suits, but they may have been actual naked women.

The rules governing performances of Greek tragedy determined that only three actors performed all roles in each play. Comedy appears to have sometimes allowed a fourth actor. The limitation on the number of actors remained throughout the history of Athenian comedy: using the same actor for multiple roles, four actors could perform all the speaking parts of *Peace, Money, the God*, or *Samia*, except perhaps for some very minor parts.

All Greek comedies included a chorus as well. Unlike the actors, who were professionals, the chorus members were amateurs in the fifth century, though professional singers may have been employed later. In the time of Aristophanes there were twenty-four chorus members. Whether the number of comic chorus members changed over time, as happened in tragedy, is unknown, but some of the most important differences between Old, Middle, and New Comedy involve the role of the chorus.

In Old Comedies the chorus sings and dances an elaborate set of songs. They enter early in the play singing a song called the parodos. Often they offer some kind of opposition to the play's hero when they first enter but are soon won over. They then remain on stage throughout the rest of the play, and their songs provide the play's essential structure. Those songs include stasima, in which the chorus comments on the action in the play or other things; syzygies, pairs of metrically equivalent scenes and songs; and the parabasis, in which the chorus addresses the audience directly, often explicitly in the name of the playwright. Thus in *Peace* the chorus enters and sings the parodos when Jack has reached Olympos. Jack must persuade them not to indulge in premature celebration before Peace is rescued. They sing syzygies with Jack, Hermes, and Xanthias; a second parodos when Jack has returned from Olympos; a stasimon before the final scene; and two parabases, one praising Aristophanes and asking for victory, one celebrating peace.

By the time of Middle Comedy the chorus' role appears to have been reduced. *Money, the God* has no parabasis. The chorus does seem to have remained present through most of the play and to have danced and sung in between scenes throughout the play, but the only long choral song preserved in the play's text is the parodos. The choruses of New Comedies sang and danced in four interludes, but texts of New Comedies preserve no words sung by the chorus. Whether or not they remained in the *orchestra* between their songs is unknown. Two features of the chorus, however, remain constant. One is their initial opposition to a character: Karion and the chorus sing insults to each other in the parodos of *Wealth,* and characters such as Demeas in *Samia* describe the chorus as a group of drunken revelers whom the character wants to escape. The other constancy is the chorus' structural importance. Though their words are not preserved, the choral interludes of *Money, the God* provide important divisions between the play's scenes, and the four choral interludes of *Samia* create the five-act structure that appears to have been standard in New Comedy.

The choruses sang and danced to the accompaniment of the aulos, a two-piped double-reed instrument somewhat similar to two oboes being played simultaneously. The aulos player entered with the chorus and remained with them in the *orchestra*. Actors also sang. In *Peace,* for example, Jack, his daughters, and Xanthias sing while Jack departs on the cockroach; Jack, Hermes, and the chorus alternate between speaking and singing as they rescue Peace; and Jack celebrates his success in song. Karion exchanges sung verses with the chorus in the parodos of *Money, the God,* and the *agon* (debate) between Khremylos and Poverty was probably sung to accompaniment. The lively fourth act of *Samia* and the play's last verses were probably sung to accompaniment as well.

In all Greek comedy, both actors and chorus members wore masks. By the time of New Comedy an elaborate system of mask types had developed. Audience members would know something about entering characters from the kinds of masks they wore, and playwrights such as Menander could play against the expectations produced by the masks.

Costumes of Old Comedy included tights, comic padding, and large phalloi. The phalloi and padding probably went out of use during the period of Middle Comedy, and New Comedy appears to have had costumes closer to those worn in everyday life. Costumes of New Comedy, like masks, varied to indicate different character types.

Douglass Parker

Douglass Parker (1927–2011) was one of the twentieth century's leading translators of ancient Greek and Roman comedy. In the 1950s and 1960s Parker, along with translators such as William Arrowsmith and Richmond Lattimore, created a new style of translation, lively and modern while remaining true to the ancient texts, which opened the door to ancient literature to countless students, readers, and audiences. Parker's 1964 translation of Aristophanes' *Lysistrata* is arguably the most read and most performed translation of any ancient drama. He also published translations of Aristophanes' *Acharnians, Wasps,* and *Congresswomen,* Plautus' *Menaechmi* and *Bacchides,* and Terence's *Eunuch* and *Phormio,* as well as translations of and works on authors ranging from Ovid to Johannes Sapidus to Tolkien.

As an appendix to this volume, I include the text of a lecture Douglass Parker gave at the University of Virginia in 1988: "A Desolation Called *Peace:* Trials of an Aristophanic Translator." Here, in his usual self-deprecating and humorous way, Parker offers us a glimpse into his approach to translating ancient comedy.

Further Reading

Greek Comedy

Csapo, Eric, and William J. Slater. *The Context of Ancient Drama*. Ann Arbor: University of Michigan Press, 1994.

Green, Richard, and Eric Handley. *Images of the Greek Theatre*. Austin: University of Texas Press, 1995.

Hughes, Alan. *Performing Greek Comedy*. Cambridge: Cambridge University Press, 2012.

Konstan, David. *Greek Comedy and Ideology*. New York: Oxford University Press, 1995.

Pickard-Cambridge, Arthur Wallace. *The Dramatic Festivals of Athens*. 2nd ed. revised by John Gould and David M. Lewis. Oxford: Clarendon, 1988.

Rusten, Jeffrey, ed. *The Birth of Comedy: Texts, Documents, and Art from Athenian Comic Competitions, 486–280*. Baltimore: Johns Hopkins University Press, 2011.

Sandbach, F. H. *The Comic Theatre of Greece and Rome*. New York: Norton, 1977.

Old Comedy

Dover, Kenneth J. *Aristophanic Comedy*. Berkeley: University of California Press, 1972.

Henderson, Jeffrey. *The Maculate Muse: Obscene Language in Attic Comedy*. New Haven, CT: Yale University Press, 1975.

MacDowell, Douglas M. *Aristophanes and Athens: An Introduction to the Plays*. Oxford: Oxford University Press, 1995.

Platter, Charles. *Aristophanes and the Carnival of Genres*. Baltimore: Johns Hopkins University Press, 2007.

Reckford, Kenneth. *Aristophanes' Old-and-New Comedy. Volume 1: Six Essays in Perspective*. Chapel Hill: University of North Carolina Press, 1987.

Revermann, Martin. *Comic Business: Theatricality, Dramatic Technique, and Performance Contexts of Aristophanic Comedy*. Oxford: Oxford University Press, 2006.

Segal, Erich, ed. *Oxford Readings in Aristophanes*. Oxford: Oxford University Press, 1996.

Silk, M. S. *Aristophanes and the Definition of Comedy*. Oxford: Oxford University Press, 2000.

Slater, Niall W. *Spectator Politics: Metatheatre and Performance in Aristophanes*. Philadelphia: University of Pennsylvania Press, 2002.

Stone, Laura M. *Costume in Aristophanic Comedy*. New York: Arno, 1981.

Taaffe, Lauren K. *Aristophanes and Women*. London: Routledge, 1993.

Whitman, Cedric H. *Aristophanes and the Comic Hero*. Cambridge, MA: Harvard University Press, 1964.

Middle Comedy

David, E. *Aristophanes and Athenian Society of the Early Fourth Century B.C.* Leiden: Brill, 1984.

Dobrov, Gregory W. *Beyond Aristophanes: Transition and Diversity in Greek Comedy.* Atlanta: Scholars Press, 1995.

Nesselrath, Heinz-Günther. *Die attische mittlere Komödie: Ihre Stellung in der antiken Literaturkritik und Literaturgeschichte.* Berlin: de Gruyter, 1990.

New Comedy

Goldberg, Sander M. *The Making of Menander's Comedy.* Berkeley: University of California Press, 1980.

Hunter, Richard L. *The New Comedy of Greece and Rome.* Cambridge: Cambridge University Press, 1985.

Lape, Susan. *Reproducing Athens: Menander's Comedy, Democratic Culture, and the Hellenistic City.* Princeton, NJ: Princeton University Press, 2004.

Rosivach, Vincent J. *When a Young Man Falls in Love: The Sexual Exploitation of Women in New Comedy.* London: Routledge, 1998.

Segal, Erich, ed. *Oxford Readings in Menander, Plautus, and Terence.* Oxford: Oxford University Press, 2001.

Traill, Ariana. *Women and the Comic Plot in Menander.* Cambridge: Cambridge University Press, 2008.

Walton, J. Michael, and Peter D. Arnott. *Menander and the Making of Comedy.* Westport, CT: Greenwood, 1996.

Webster, T. B. L. *An Introduction to Menander.* Manchester: Manchester University Press, 1974.

———. *Studies in Later Greek Comedy.* 2nd ed. Manchester: Manchester University Press, 1970.

Wiles, David. *The Masks of Menander: Sign and Meaning in Greek and Roman Performance.* Cambridge: Cambridge University Press, 1991.

Zagagi, Netta. *The Comedy of Menander: Convention, Variation, and Originality.* London: Duckworth, 1994.

Old Comedy: Aristophanes' *Peace*

As we have seen, the plots of Old Comedy are based on fantastic plans fulfilled against all probability. In one respect *Peace* is an exception. Jack the Reaper brings peace to Greece by rescuing the goddess Peace from her captivity in a cave on Mt. Olympos. That accomplishment is certainly a fantasy, but when *Peace* was first produced at the Greater Dionysia in March of 421 BCE, peace was not only possible but just around the corner: a peace treaty between Athens and Sparta went into effect less than two weeks after the festival.

Athens had been at war with Sparta and her allies (the Peloponnesian War) since 431 BCE. The war had brought great suffering to the city (as well as to much of the rest of Greece), but to none more so than the farmers of Attica (the region around Athens), who become Jack's primary allies in the play. Relying on their fleet and the walls that surrounded the city and connected it to the port at Piraeus, Athenian leaders decided to avoid land battles with the Spartans and to treat the city as an island. Each campaigning season the Spartans invaded Attica. Farmers and their families were forced to flee within the city walls and wait until the end of the summer while Spartan troops ravaged their farms. Compounding the suffering was a plague that ravaged the Athenian population crowded within the walls from 430 to 426 BCE.

By 421 victory had eluded both sides, and a number of events had opened the way for peace. In 425 the Athenians gained a foothold at Pylos, not far from Sparta, from where they could attack Spartan domains. In the process they captured nearly three hundred Spartan soldiers, who became an important bargaining chip in negotiations. Later, in 422, battles took the lives of both Brasidas, Sparta's greatest general, and Kleon, the most important leader of the pro-war faction in Athens. After extended negotiations the warring parties finally agreed to what became known as the Peace of Nikias in 421. The peace, alas, was not to last. After a disastrous attempt by the Athenians to conquer Sicily in 415 BCE, the Spartans and their allies renewed their attacks until, in 404 BCE, Athens was forced to surrender.

Aristophanes and his fellow Athenians, of course, could know nothing of this gloomy future. For them, the wild celebration at the end of *Peace* anticipated an actual celebration only days away.

The structure of *Peace,* as presented in Parker's scene headings, is as follows:

Verses	Section	Events
1–298	Prologue (everything before the first entrance of the chorus)	Jack flies to Olympos and learns of Peace's captivity
299–345	Parodos	Chorus enters, eager to help rescue Peace
346–427	Syzygy I (a pair of metrically equivalent songs combined with scenes)	Chorus and Jack win over Hermes

1

428–458	Scene I	Jack, chorus, and Hermes remove the rocks hiding Peace
459–519	Syzygy II	Jack, chorus, and Hermes rescue Peace from the cave
520–552	Scene II	Conversation with Peace, dismissal of chorus
553–656	Parodos II	Chorus celebrates; Hermes explains causes of war
657–728	Scene III	More conversation with Peace; Jack sets off for home with Lady Bountiful and Jamboree
729–818 (775–818 not translated)	Parabasis (address to audience)	Chorus and Aristophanes praise Aristophanes and ask for victory
819–921	Syzygy III	Jack returns, prepares to marry Lady Bountiful, and leads Jamboree to the Senate
922–1038	Syzygy IV	Jack, Xanthias, and chorus prepare for sacrifice
1039–1126	Scene IV	Jack and Xanthias drive off Holy Joe
1127–1190	Parabasis II	Chorus celebrates peace, contrasting it with war
1191–1304	Episode I	Jack drives off arms dealers and hears boys sing
1305–1317 (not translated)	Stasimon I	Jack offers food to chorus, who offer it to the audience
1318–1367	Exodos	Wedding of Jack and Lady Bountiful

ΑΡΙΣΤΟΦΑΝΟΥΣ
ΕΙΡΗΝΗ

PEACE !!!

BY
ARISTOPHANES

translated by
douglass parker

The Set

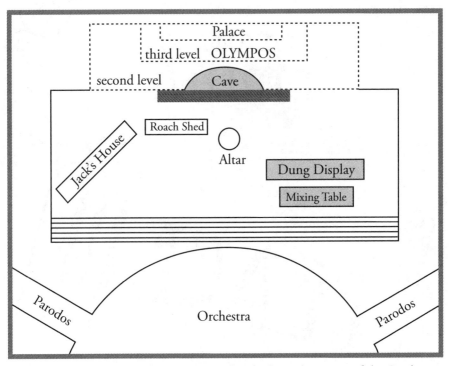

As was noted in the General Introduction, details about the nature of the Greek stage, especially in the fifth century, are uncertain. Parker's proposal of a multi-level stage is a plausible way of addressing the changes of scene in this play.

Dramatis Personae

Xanthias,	*slave to Jack the Reaper*
Sosias,	*slave to Jack the Reaper*
Jack the Reaper,[1]	*Athenian citizen, ex-farmer*
Cockroach,[2]	*a cockroach [mute]*
First Daughter of Jack	
Second Daughter of Jack	
Hermes,	*a god of sorts*
War,[3]	*a nasty god*
Humongous Din,[4]	*a minor god*
First Semichorus of Workmen	
First Koryphaios[5]	
Second Semichorus of Workmen	
Second Koryphaios	
Peace,	*a goddess [mute]*
Lady Bountiful,[6]	*a minor goddess [mute]*
Jamboree,[7]	*a more minor goddess [mute]*
Holy Joe,[8]	*a specialist in oracles*
A Sickle Seller	
A Breastplate Baron	
A Trumpet Tycoon	
A Helmet Honcho	
A Slave [mute]	
First Boy	
Second Boy	

SCENE: Athens and Olympos
TIME: an ordinary early spring morning in 421 BCE

---

1. His Greek name is Trygaios or "harvester." The title character's name thus incorporates the central theme of the play, the triumph of the peaceful rustic life over war.

2. In the Greek text this is a dung beetle.

3. His Greek name is Polemos.

4. His Greek name is Kudoimos, meaning "uproar" or "tumult."

5. The Koryphaios is the leader of all or part of the chorus.

6. Her Greek name is Opôra, meaning "harvest."

7. Her Greek name is Theôria, meaning "the watching of spectacles, especially at festivals."

8. In the Greek text he is Hierokles, a noted oracle monger in fifth-century Athens.

PEACE

Prologue [1–298]

[SOSIAS   Oh, SHIT!

XANTHIAS   How much? Be more specific.

                              Let's start:][9]

They start, Xanthias mixing various ordures and squeez-
ing the mess into patties, which Sosias loads on his platters, carries across the stage at a run, and slings over the wall into the
Enclosure, where a horrid gobbling sound is immediately heard.

SOSIAS   *Vite, vite! Pass me a pattycake for ze cockroách!*

XANTHIAS   *Voilà.*

Press. Hand over. Mix. Run. The process is repeated throughout.

        Serve eet to 'eem, zat espèce d'espèce,
    weez compliments from ze chef an' ze weesh zat 'ee
    weel nevair taste a sweetair patty zan zat!

SOSIAS   *Anozzair! Ze special!*

XANTHIAS   *Ze special? Ze donkey shit*
    al burro?
          Voilà encore.
               What 'appen to ze patty
  you take 'eem jus' now? 'Ee should 'ave gobble eet down.

SOSIAS   *Gobble? Eet eez to laugh! 'Eee reep eet away*
    from ze plattair, 'ee geeve eet a queeck pirouette or two
    on all zose toes, an' Chomp!—'ee surround zee patty!
    —Plus vite! 'Ee want beaucoup—arranged in layers!
    An' mind ze texture!

XANTHIAS

Turning to the audience and dropping the dialect entirely.

            An appeal to sanitary engineers:
    Will you PLEASE get on with your job and haul this away?
    Unless you'd prefer an unobstructed view of me
    in terminal asphyxiation.

---

9. Here and in a few other passages in *Peace* and *Money, the God*, Parker adds, for modern
performance, verses and anachronistic stage directions to Aristophanes' text. The brackets
around these additions are Parker's.

6

SOSIAS   *Anozzair! Anozzair!*
An' use ze gay shit!

XANTHIAS   *You mean ze turnovair?*

SOSIAS   *Oui.*
'Ee want ze fine grind zis time. 'Ee don' like lumps.

XANTHIAS *An ordure like zat eez hard to feel. But steel . . .*
Voilà.

    —Well, gents, I've got to admit this job
has one advantage. No one's going to accuse me
of sneaking nibbles off *this* cake.

SOSIAS   *Yeeuch! Anozzair!*
—An' steell anozzair!
                —Anozzair yet!
                            —Grind more,
an' keep zem coming—vite!

XANTHIAS   *Zut! Merde alors!*
    —I'm quitting. I can't take this shit.

SOSIAS   *Zen MOI*
weel take zees sheet!

XANTHIAS   Well, take it straight to hell,
and yourself in the bargain.
               —I don't suppose
that anyone out there knows where I can buy
a nose that isn't pre-bored?
               Worst job on the roster:
"Turd Enhancement—Cockroach, for Nourishment Of."
Your basic Hog or Dog, now, they're Plain Folks.
Shit occurs, and they're on the job. Simple,
no frills.
    But this thing here—Lord Muck—has whims:
His Majesty sulks and rants and refuses his food
unless it's blended—so I have to spend all day
mashing it up in that mortar. Straight shit, plain, 's
not enough for him—he has to have *Crap Suzette*.
—I wonder if he's *fini* with *p'tit déjeuner* —
let's see.
    Just open the door a crack and sneak
a peek.
    —Eh, bien, continuez! *Stuff on, my old!*
Pile een ze goodies unteel you croque, Monsieur!
—His manners must be under a curse:

                                    He eats
in a wrestler's crouch, all six elbows on the table,
slipping his choppers sideways, whipping his nippers
and head like a ropemaker spinning a heavy cable.
Squalid, fetid, putrid, all solid greed. . . .
This must be a plague sent down by a god—but which?
Aphrodite, maybe?
                Wrong odor . . .
                              Perhaps the Graces?

Too greasy . . .
                What God does this monster belong to?

SOSIAS   Got it!
Zeus, the God of Law and ORDURE—

XANTHIAS
                              Zeus,
the God Who Won't Be DeTURD—

SOSIAS
                        Zeus, the God
By Whom All Deeds Are DUNG—

XANTHIAS
                      His B—M—inence, Zeus—

BOTH SLAVES   The God Who's NUMBER ONE *and* NUMBER TWO!

They drop the fit as quickly as they started it. Then XAN-
THIAS turns back to the audience.

XANTHIAS   Already among you some bright self-referent youngster
is making a sign to be heard. And what's he saying?
"Decode this text and expose the roach's deep structure!"
Beside him, a deft deconstructionist, newly arrived
from across the Sea to the East, speaks up:
                            "Zat's easy:
Ze cockroach configuration prefigures ze figure of KLEON.[10]
We commence wis ze eating-codes, ze unblushing ingestion
of sheet, both solid an' runny. . . ."

SOSIAS   *Pardonnez-moi,*
I 'ave to go. Ze cockroach 'ave ze Great Sirst.

He disappears within the shed. A loud trick-
ling sound is heard [followed by a flush].

---

10. Kleon was a demagogue, the son of a tanner, and a leader of Athens' pro-war party. One
of the principal victims of Aristophanes' satire, he died in a battle in Thrace in 422 BCE,
well before the performance of *Peace*, but that did not stop the playwright from abusing him
repeatedly in this play.

XANTHIAS   And I shall pronounce the traditional statement of Plot
to enlighten our viewers, the spectrum of Male[11] Humanity—
from tots and toddlers and tads, pubescents and adolescents,
to *Men:*

      Men merely mature,

            Men eminent, dominant,
Men super-exalted, elite, our lords of creation—
it's especially these I address:

            My Boss is crazy.
No stock psychosis. It's not your S & M bent
for courtroom castration.[12] Oh, no, this twist is fresh,
unexampled, unique. He spends the whole of his days
with his eyes on Heaven, gazing and gawking and squawking
in ceaseless abuse of Zeus.

           "Goddammit, Zeus!"
he shouts, "just what are you trying to DO?

                Stop flopping
your murderous mop, or else you'll depopulate Greece!"
—But Hist and Hark!
Shut up—I think I hear him grousing now.

An exasperated wail from inside the house.

JACK   Goddammit, Zeus! What do you think you're DOING
to our people? Don't you see you're leaving the cities
pitted and gutted?

XANTHIAS   *Voilà*—the precise affliction
that I was discussing. What you are hearing now
is a sample, of course, of the fully blown psychosis.
On inception, the tic, or obsession, displayed itself
rather differently—please pay attention—thus:
Subject indulged in compulsive agonized babble—
"How can I get to Heaven the quickest way?"
Subject then took receipt on an order of light
extension ladders; extending same, he essayed
a swarming clamber upward to the sky . . . resulting
in precipitate damage to Subject's occipital ridge.
This brings us down to yesterday:

---

11. It is uncertain whether women were permitted to attend dramatic presentations in Athens. Whether or not women were present, actors consistently address the spectators as if they are all male.

12. Law courts with very large juries (sometimes several hundred men) were an important part of Athenian democracy, and Aristophanes often jokes on the litigiousness of his fellow citizens.

Shattered Subject

hared off to who-knows-where and led home on a leash
one jumbo Cyclopean cockroach, a purebred whopper.
Me he forced to fodder and groom this monster,
but curried its chitinous flanks himself, clucking
and cooing. You'd think he was calming a yearling colt:
"My pretty Pegasus,[13] *wide-winged pedigreed prancer,*
you'll break from the gate and waft me aloft to Zeus
ASAP."

So what's he up to now?
I'll just bend down and peek . . .

Trouble! Disaster!

I'll call the neighbors.

Neighbors!

Quick!

Over here!

The Boss is airborne!

Cantering off in the blue!
Horsing around between Heaven and Earth on a

COCKROACH!!!

A giant cockroach, bearing JACK, the master of the house, rises suddenly from behind the façade of the shed.[14] He tries to control it, with varying degrees of success. At start, it is bucking furiously.

JACK   *YAH MULE!*

He soothes and coaxes the roach, patting its flanks and crooning to it.

Easy does it, nice and easy.
Start off soft—no flap, no tizzy,
save your rush until the stretch.
Let those wings wave soft and lazy,
build a sweat up, warm and cozy,
make those muscles flex and reach.
SLOW, you rash, impetuous roach.

The roach comes to rest about eight feet in the air, center, and turns its head to him. He recoils, and breaks off his song momentarily.

—You appear to have a breath problem.
Look here, roach: You steed; me rider.

---

13. The mythical hero Bellerophon tried to ride the winged horse Pegasus to Olympos. Much of what follows includes parody of *Bellerophon*, a tragedy by Euripides.

14. Jack and the cockroach use a device called a *mechanê*, a crane from which actors could be lowered to or lifted from the stage. In tragedy the *mechanê* allowed for impressive entrances by divinities.

Kindly keep that awful odor
facing front. You make me nauseous.
One more burst of halitosis
means no fun-filled airborne trips,
puts you in the house for keeps.

The roach turns its head away sadly and gives a shake.

Easy, boy, you make me dizzy.

XANTHIAS   *Mighty Lord on High, you're crazy.*

The sudden voice from the ground sets the roach off again,
and JACK must cope with a new frenzy of bucking.

JACK   *Silence, down there! Shut your trap!*

XANTHIAS   *Why this airy-fairy flap?*

After a tussle, Jack calms the roach, but it is now within Xanthias' reach. The Master strikes a noble attitude in midair.

JACK   *Saving Greece I fare on air,*
                  bringing Hellenes everywhere
                  succor from my Happy Plan,
                  blessings from my Grand Design
                  won at such expense of brain. . . .

XANTHIAS   *Flying? Fruitless. Plain insane.*
                  Why this airborne uselessness?

JACK   *You'd better stick to speechlessness*
                  and stow those grumpy mumbles, boy.
                  A shout or two of pious joy
                  denoting Awe or Deep Respect
                  is all that you're allowed—except:

                  Transmit this word to the Human Race,
                  to close its mouth and shut its face
                  and plug its heads, infarct its loos,
                  brick up its privies out of use,
                  obstruct its stools hermetically,
                  and cork its assholes under key.

XANTHIAS   You have no chance of securing my silence, unless
                  you transmit to me your flight plan's destination.

JACK   I thought it was obvious. I am Zeusward bound,
                  to Heaven.

XANTHIAS   You have some reason for this, I presume?

JACK   I intend to put him a question: What does he mean
                  to do *in re* the Greeks?

XANTHIAS   Which Greeks?

JACK   All Greeks:
                  In re the Greeks *in toto.*

XANTHIAS   Suppose he refuses
                  to say, *tout court?*

JACK   He'll answer in court, *tout de suite,*
                  For anti-Hellenic subversion—betrayal of Greece
                  to the Medes,[15] the Beasts of the East!

XANTHIAS   I swear by Bacchos,
                  the *Best* of the East, you'll go over my dead body!

He grabs the roach by the halter and hangs on.

JACK

Flailing at the Slave with his crop, as the roach is unable to rise.

                  That *does* appear to be the only way. . . .

XANTHIAS

Clinging to the struggling roach.

                  O WAly WAly WOE is ME!

He calls to the house:

                          CHIL*DRENNN*!

Two little girls, JACK's Daughters, appear at the house door and gape aghast.

                  Poor Orphan Tots, your dear departing Daddy
                  is sneaking away to Heaven even now.
                  Dissuade your Dad! Beseech him, Luckless Tykes!

Jack stops flailing, the roach sinks to the ground, and the
Slave staggers off, exhausted as the Daughters approach
their father in appropriate attitudes of supplication.

DAUGHTERS   *Oh Father, dear Father, a Weather Alert*
                  has quite overcast our fair home,
                  predicting you'll ground us, take wing, and desert
                  the earth for a high-pressure dome.

---

15. The principal threat to Greek sovereignty in the fifth century was the Persian empire.
Persians and Medes, two peoples united in the Persian empire, are often equated in Greek
literature.

The forecaster's words say our Dad's for the birds
hell-bent for the heavens of blue.
Are you haze? Are you jog? Partly cloudy? Or smog?
You'll be missed, Father dear, if it's true.
Confirm or deny this
in part or in whole,
dear Dad, if you love me.

JACK   *Infer and deduce it*
you can and you may,
dear Tots, yes indeedy.
Your father, dear Daughters, is cut to the quick
to hear you cry . . .

DAUGHTERS   *. . . Bread, Pappa, Bread!*

JACK   *No cash in the house, nary smidgen or speck—*
dear Daughters are not to be fed,
But once I return in success from my quest,
I'll feed your sweet faces in haste:
A gummery bun for a feast and a fest . . .
and a fistful of knuckles to taste.

He aims a loving swipe at the nearest Daughter, but misses. She
and he segue, accompanied by a tremolo from somewhere, into
tragic parody, in this case of Euripides' play *Bellerophon*.

1ST
DAUGHTER   *What shape or passage might attain*
the terminus of this outrageous voyage,
a route's end not to be raught by bootless boat?

JACK   *On flying foal I'll fare, yes, carried shipless.*

1ST
DAUGHTER   *Whence crashed the notion in your little mind,*
O Daddy sweet, to harness up a roach
and post on insect-back t' accost the Gods?

JACK   *I chanced upon a spot in Aesop's Fables—*
Ay, there's a spot, I said: The roach, alone
of all the winged creatures, reached the Gods.[16]

1ST
DAUGHTER   *O Dad, poor Dad, your tale doth breach belief:*
Your roach is rank; it smells to Heaven—but no

---

16. One of Aesop's fables describes how a beetle, wronged by an eagle, gained vengeance by
destroying the eagle's eggs. The eagle fled to Zeus for protection and left its eggs in the god's
lap, but the beetle harassed Zeus so that he let the eggs fall, and they were broken.

such reeking beast can go there; the Gods might choke.
[Besides, it wasn't a roach; Aesop says beetle.]

JACK   [Details aren't important. Don't bug me, kid.]
*Lang syne, the ROACH did flit and float to Heav'n
in fit of pique at Zeus's bird, the EAGLE,
to drain revenge to the dregs by breaking its eggs.*

1ST
DAUGHTER   *Far better might you yoke the equine pinion
of Pegasus, horse of a feather and subject dear
t' th' tragic stage, whereat you might appear
more wretched, messy, and sad to the Blessed Gods.*

JACK

Dropping the paratragedy; his Daughter continues with it.

I'm sorry, Love, that would have doubled the outlay.
This way, I cut the provisions in half:
                            First time,
I eat them, and then, in the normal course of events,
I turn around and feed the same to *him.*

1ST
DAUGHTER   *But put the case he slip and plumb the depths
o' th' sea's abyss: How might this wingy thing
extract himself, escape the soggy deep?*

JACK   No problem.

He raises his phallus.

                My rudder's ready to hand; I'll turn
this cockroach into a frigate. At least a dinghy;
I'll bring it off.
                  He's really a capital ship.
In case of disaster, I'll lash myself to his poop.

1ST
DAUGHTER   *What harbor snug would deign to yield you haven?*

JACK   What son of a bitch can't reach a beach on a roach?

1ST
DAUGHTER   *Observe all caution, lest you totter and spill
fro' th' heights, and in your fall, a-limp and gimpy,
supply Euripides one of his humpbacked plots.*
Don't be a tragedy, Daddy.

JACK   I'm on my guard.
And so, farewell.

The Daughters wave, and return to the house. The roach rises into
the air and flies to aloft, center, where it swivels to face the audience. From its back, JACK delivers his farewell words.

To you out there, a word:
The troubles that I am about to endure are *yours*,
and I therefore request your tensest cooperation:
A THREE-DAY
                    MORATORIUM
                                        ON FARTING
                                                            AND
SHITTING.
Because, if my cockroach catches one whiff of those goodies,
be he ever so high in the sky, he'll dump me, ass
over elbow, and streak for that simple country fare.

Hoisted by the crane, the roach rises majestically to Jack's inspirational strains.

Up, my Pegasus! On, my Pegasus!
Winged steed of tale and song,
Slip the surly bonds of earth,
Gaily fling yourself among
Sun-split clouds in tumbling mirth.
Gilded trappings slap and flap
'Gainst your glist'ning ears . . .

The roach suddenly jerks and points downward.

—Oh, **crap**!
Careful, dammit! You can't mean
to aim your nose at that latrine!

The roach rights itself.

Mount with proud and easy grace
Through untrespassed tracts of space,
Leave below the multitude
Of dreary daily cares. Like food.
Straight to Zeus's halls you flit,
Head averted from . . .

The roach twists violently down, nearly throwing him.

—Oh, **shit**!

He addresses a presumed offender on the ground.

—Hey, you, down there, what was *that*?
By the whorehouse, someone **shat**!
My steed can sniff the whole damned town out . . .
The red-light district has a brownout!

—Look here, asshole, dig a trench,
Inter that turd to cut the stench,
Pile six yards of dirt on top,
Set out cuttings for a crop
Of parsley, sage, rosemary, and thyme!
This is to let you know that I'm
Very expensive property:
My fall and sure fatality
Could wipe out some poor backward nation
—Just for your one defecation!

The roach, annoyed, begins to buck.

I'm scared, I'm really scared.
                              And that's no gag.

He looks up.

You up there! Stagehand! Could I have your attention?
Inner distress is building a plussage of gas
below my navel. So keep this contraption steady,
or else I cater lunch for one fat roach.

The roach stops bucking and soars higher.

I do declare, I must be near the Gods.
And—yes, I see it now: the House of Zeus.

He glides in for a landing, dismounts, walks to the door, and knocks.

Who keeps the Gate of Zeus?

No reply. He bangs again.

                              Come on, open up!

The door opens, disclosing Hermes [donning his porter's garb and] sniffing.

HERMES   Me thought I caught a whiff of mortal . . .

He sees the roach.

                                        Man
Alive defend us! What in the world is **this** disaster?

JACK   I ride a cockhorse, and this is my Shitland pony.

HERMES   You, Sir, *offend*. You're Gross! Repugnant! Foul!
But mainly DisGUSTing—in fact, DisGUSTinger—
Ad Nauseam Summa-cum-Bloody DisGUSTingest!
But why come here, O creature, of all disgusts
the Ad Nauseam Summa-Cum-Bloody DisGUSTingest!
Well, what's your name? Speak up!
                              Give me your *name*!

JACK	Ad Nauseam Summa-Cum-Bloody DisGUSTingest.
HERMES	Land of family origin? Out with it!
JACK	Ad Nauseam Summa-Cum-Bloody DisGUSTingest.
HERMES	Hmmm. And this would make your father's name . . . ?
JACK	Ad Nauseam Summa-Cum-Bloody DisGUSTingest, Senior.
HERMES	I swear by the dirt below, your death is an absolutely foregone conclusion unless you make an accurate statement of your *name* in full!
JACK	I'm JACK, stamm' aus Athmonaia, bin gar kein Petti fogger, echt Athenisch. From Athmonaia, on Athens' far north side.[17]
HERMES	And what's the purpose of your trip?
JACK	I've brought this dish of tasty giblets. For *you*.
HERMES	

Changing tone completely and cringing.

> Oh most deserving disadvantaged needy
> type, I trust you had a pleasant trip?

JACK	Oh *cordon bleu* of beggary, what became of Ad Nauseam Summa-Cum-Bloody DisGUSTingest?

Giving Hermes the meat, he turns imperious.

> And now, get on with it, herald—summon me Zeus!

HERMES

Breaking up.

> Titter . . . snicker . . . chuckle . . . wheeze . . . GUFFAW!
> Nearer thy gods to thee is not in thy future.
> The Gods are gone!
>   Since yesterday. Moved out.

JACK	Where in the world?
HERMES	Nowhere in the world.
JACK	Well, *where?*
HERMES	Way, way away. On high. To the tippy-top of the zenith's nipple.

---

17. The Athenian state was divided into 139 territorial units called demes. Jack comes from Athmon, a deme just northeast of the city of Athens.

JACK   But if they moved out, why
did they leave you here alone?

HERMES   I'm Olympos-sitting.
There's all this divine apparatus that has to be *watched:*
Pots here, breadboards there, and empties
all over the place.

JACK   But why would the Gods move out?

HERMES   A fit of pique at you Greeks, of course. They turned
Olympos over to Polemos . . .

JACK   Polemos?

HERMES   . . . the war god, stupid . . .
To Polemos they passed the power to exploit you Greeks
precisely as he prefers, while they moved out
and up to the top of creation to quit their role
as captive audience—the endless strain on the eyes
of you Greeks in battle, the endless assault on the ears
of you Greeks at prayer.

JACK   But what did *we* do to make
the Gods do that to us?

A pause. Hermes seems embarrassed, exasperated.

                                  Don't keep it a secret; speak up.

HERMES   Because, through all their many attempts to effect
a Peace on earth, you all steadfastly preferred
to make War more and more. Example: They allotted
the Spartans a little leverage, nothing large—
and what did the Spartans do? Go home in triumph?
Nooo. The Spartans broke into vocal vengeance:
"By gum and by golly, them Attickers gonna pay!"
But suppose they did come up to you at Athens
and press for a parley on Peace—just what was your
considered knee-jerk reaction?
                                  "A Hoax, by Athenê!"
"Plus Fraud and Flim-Flam!"
                                  *"Never trust
a Spartan, by Zeus!"*
                                  *"They'll start the war again,
if we keep Pylos."*[18]
                                  "And we'll keep Pylos, for sure!"

---

18. One of Athens' greatest military successes in the years before *Peace* was produced was the capture and fortification of Pylos, in Spartan territory.

JACK   You certainly grasp Athenian verbal patterns.

HERMES   The bottom line is, I don't think you'll ever
                see Peace again.

JACK   *She's* left? But where did she go?

HERMES   Polemos pitched her deep down into a cave.

JACK   What cave?

HERMES   Down into this cave down there. You see
                that pile of stones he heaped up here on top?
                That's how he made sure you won't excavate her. Ever.

JACK   One more thing: What's he planning to do to us?

HERMES   I only know this: Last night he had them wrestle
                a mortar inside of really colossal size.

JACK   What for? Or, rather, what does the mortar impórt?

HERMES   His Grand Design is to grind your cities down.

Crashes, roars, and a dull booming from the palace.

                —I'm off. I'm pretty sure War's breaking out.
                Hear all that fuss inside?

He soars aloft and away.

JACK   What awful luck!
                I'd better make my getaway, too.

Paratragic.

                                        Methinks
                I hear the accents drear of mortar dread.

He hides behind something. Enter War, with mortar.

WAR   WOE, MORTALS!
                            MADLY, MORBIDLY MARTYRED MORTALS!
                It's such a paste in the jaw you'll get from me!

JACK   Apollo, see the size! That mortar's immense!
                And all pure evil!
                            And look at the Face of WAR!
                Can this be the very same war we speed to avoid—
                War Dread, War Dire, War Doomed to provoke a squat?

WAR

Holding up a head of lettuce.

                And here's my lettuce:

> *WOE to MILETOS!*[19] *triply,*
> *quintuply, zillionuply bruised and battered,*
> *today will be the day you're utterly wasted!*

He drops the lettuce into the mortar.

JACK

To the audience.

> That's too bad, friends, but it's really not *our* worry.
> Let's chalk that catastrophe up to the other side.

WAR

Holding up a bunch of garlic.

> And here's my garlic:
> *WOE to MEGARA!*[20] *A moment*
> *or two, and you'll be sliced and riced and diced*
> *and mashed and smashed and trashed in totissimo!*

He drops the garlic into the mortar.

JACK   Golly gee willikers sakes alive and whatever!
                  That's mighty bitter mourning he dumped on Megara!

WAR

Holding up a round of cheese.

> Now, cheese:
> *WOE to SICILY! That's all for you!*

JACK   A mighty city is shredded . . . That grates, somehow.

WAR

Holding up a vial of honey.

> For dressing, Attic Honey. On you go!

JACK   A word of advice: Use other honey, please.
                  The Attic brand is ruinously expensive.

WAR   Slave? Oh, slave? Where's Humungous Din?

---

19. Parker replaces Aristophanes' Prasiae, a town near Sparta that had been sacked by the Athenians in 430 BCE, with Miletos, a more famous city on the coast of what is now Turkey (modern Balat).

20. A city just to the west of Athens. An Athenian decree restricting trade with Megara was cited as one of the reasons for the Peloponnesian War, and the Athenians attacked Megara during the war. Garlic was one of Megara's primary exports.

**HUMUNGOUS
DIN**

Waking with a crash and standing upright, dhoti and turban askew.

                                                      Duhhh . . . You called?
                        Puh-present.

WAR   Din! Din! Din! Where the mischief have you been?
                   You will be belted and flayed.
                                            Asleep at attention? Take this!

He gives Din a clout on the nose. Din sniffs.

**HUMUNGOUS
DIN**   Dat's a pungent jab, sir. Woe and alackaday.

JACK   Strange. Do you think he seasoned his knuckles with garlic?

WAR   Get me a pestle! Double-time, quick!

**HUMUNGOUS
DIN**   Please, sir,
                   we got no pestles. We just moved in last night.

WAR   Then borrow one from Athens! And hop it, hear?

**HUMUNGOUS
DIN**   Aye, aye, sir.
                        —Or else I shall surely suffer sorely.

He lumbers off, trying to run.

JACK   Oh, wretched squibs of humanity, what can we do?
                   Observe our peril, so ineluctable, so large!
                   If that dolt can obtain a pestle and bring it back,
                   then War will employ said pestle at leisure to hassle
                   and crush the cities of Greece to smithereens!
                   Dionysos, see that he dies before he brings it!

Humungous Din ambles back, empty-handed.

WAR   Well?

**HUMUNGOUS
DIN**   Well, what?

WAR   Have you got it?

**HUMUNGOUS
DIN**   The whatchamacallit?
                   The Athenian, duh, er, pestle has passed away,
                   that leather-peddler who left Greece completely strapped.

JACK   Thanks, mighty mistress Athenê! Nothing Kleon
          ever did so became him as this precision dying,
          when Athens needed it most to avoid this worst
          of destructions, annihilation by salad dressing!

WAR   Then go and get another pestle from Sparta,
          and shake a leg!

HUMUNGOUS
DIN   Duh . . . gotcha, chief.

WAR   And this time
          HURRY BACK!

JACK   Gentlemen all, what fate
          is in store for us? We totter at destiny's hinge.

He scans the audience.

          —Pardon. Has anyone here taken holy orders?
          The mysteries down at Samothrace?[21]

Finding an adept among the spectators.

                                    —Oh, very good!
          I'd like to entreat a small prayer, sir: Please request
          that on his return he sprain both ankles. Thank you.

HUMUNGOUS
DIN   *Woe and alas and woe and another woe!*

WAR   What now? You didn't come back without it **again**?

HUMUNGOUS
DIN   The Spartan, duh, er, pestle has passed away, too.[22]

WAR   How, idiot, how?

HUMUNGOUS
DIN   They, duh, er, sent it on loan
          to someone up on the Thracian shore, and lost it.

JACK   Thanks, sons of Zeus! Oh, finely, beautifully done!
          —Courage, mortals! We might have a happy ending!

WAR   You gather up all this stuff and take it back.
          I'll hustle inside and rustle up a pestle on my own.

Exeunt War and Din into the palace. Jack steps toward the audience.

---

21. The island of Samothrace in the northern part of the Aegean Sea was known for its cult
of twin gods called Cabiri, which included secret initiation rites.

22. Brasidas, a highly successful Spartan general, was killed in 422 BCE in the same battle as
Kleon.

JACK   And now, friends, foreplay's over:
THIS IS IT!!!
That day of joy foretold by Jerkoffilos Handjob
and the Fingers Five, when he burst into timely tune
at his regular noon pop concert and laid it on the line:

> *Hello Happiness, Goodbye, Gloom*
> *Wop baba loo bop a-wop bam BOOM!*

Y'all come, too.
The time's at hand to end
affliction, suspend hostilities, simply by grabbing
Peace, the apple of every eye, and pulling
before another pestle can jam her back down.

> *Therefore, all you plowmen, yeomen,*
> *spadesmen, tradesmen, clerks, and hands,*
> *rustics, tourists, stay-at-home men,*
> *friends and foes from foreign lands . . .*
> > *Onward, all!*

> *Hoist that lever, tote that crowbar,*
> *wield that shovel, rope and noose,*
> *trenching tool and wrenching tool*
> *to work that lovely lady loose!*

And take a long and long-missed pull from the cup that cheers!

Parodos I [299–345]

Through the two parodoi enter the two Semichoruses, of Greeks of all
occupations from all over[23]—1ST SEMICHO, right parodos; 2ND SEMI-
CHO, left parodos. Each is urged on by a Koryphaios (a.k.a. Kory).

1ST KORY   Speed, goal-oriented zealots! Deliverance dead ahead!
It's now or never, if ever: United Greece to the rescue!
Break loose from close-order drill! Strip off that uniform gear!
Liberation Day is dawning—the day the generals hate!

2ND KORY   Just say the word, sir! Assign us our spot in your overall plan,
this tireless group that hereby resolves to keep on the job
until we've taken our tools in hand and forked into daylight
that mightiest, blessedest goddess who dotes on the fruits of the vine!

JACK   Silence! This noisy transport of joy at current events
could ignite the War and bring him out here in a blaze!

---

23. The 2001 performance script adds, "their identities in the following scenes will shift for
different purposes. Most consistently through the whole play, however, they are farmers."

1ST KORY   But the news is so exciting! It's so much better than hearing:
       A draft's going back to the front:
                      So muster downtown with full mess kit!

JACK   Be careful, dammit! Down there beneath the ground there sleeps
     a three-headed dog—a one-time dealer in leather goods,
     adept at bluster and barking—as you all know only too well.
     Wake Kleon up, and you'll never fork that goddess again!

2ND KORY   There's no dog dead or alive who can pry her loose if once
     I clasp these loving hands around her!
                      ZOWIE! WHURROO!

JACK   Destruction's at hand, and it's mine, and quick, if you don't shut up!
     He'll pop out of Hell and dropkick Our Plan into utter muddle.

1ST KORY   *So . . .*
     let him meddle, let him muddle,
     let him kick us into chaos,
     but we won't give up rejoicing
     at the wondrous day today is!

JACK   NOW what? Have you all gone crazy? For god's sake, gentlemen, NO!
     Don't ravage our wonderful project with choreographic madness!

2ND KORY   *I . . .*
     got no plans, I got no dance, I
     never had a lesson and I won't take none!
     Joy's my driver—nothing fancy—
     but my legs go flipping till the dance is done!

JACK   Enough for now! Enough! Please cease this weighty fantastic!

2ND KORY   *Well . . .*
     One last hip, and one last hop . . .
     Satisfied now? I've come to a stop.
                 . . . scooby do . . .
                     . . . scooby do . . .
                        . . . scooby do . . .

JACK   *Promises, promises—look at you!*
     You say you stop, but you still aren't through!

2ND KORY   *Look: this foot plants, and the other goes rover . . .*
     Let me do that, and the dance is over!

JACK   Well, one last stomp . . .

2ND KORY and 2ND SEMICHO bring their routine to a crashing conclusion.

               . . . and never, never dance again!

Relieved he turns to find 1ST KORY and 1ST SEMICHO
thumping his way in their dance.

1ST KORY   *If we can help your Grand Plan get on,*
              our dancin' days are done and gone!
                                        . . . anna one . . .
                                              . . . anna two . . .
                                                    . . . anna one two three . . .

JACK   *Your days aren't done, your days aren't gone.*
              Just look: your dance goes thundering on!

The 1ST KORY and Semichorus stop . . . but the 2ND KORY has noticed.

2ND KORY   *Just one last kick, with a couple of bends . . .*
              put the right leg out, and the dancin' ends!
                                              . . . shoop . . .
                                                    . . . shoop . . .
                                                          . . . shoop . . .

JACK   *I grant you the kick if you do it fast,*
              provided this annoyance is the absolute last.

They break the promise.

1ST KORY   *Can't stop now; it's not over yet . . .*
              I have to kick the left leg—they come as a set!
              Because . . .
                  I'm bloated with enjoyment
                  I burst to laugh and crow out.
                  A pressure's building up
                  and there's going to be a blowout.
                  Let someone else check aging
                  to be a boy again—
                  I'd rather chuck my armaments
                  and know this joy again!

Both Semichoruses explode into a noisy dance. Jack makes one last futile
attempt to stop them . . . but he is gradually overcome by the possibilities.

JACK   *Gentlemen, joy is premature—*
              Patience, please, until you're sure!
              Squelch this overhasty action
              till the Goddess's extraction:
              then's the time for celebration,
              the stepping out and the sleeping in,

Crescendo and accelerando, the dance taking over.

                  then's the time for jollification,
                  the giggle, the whoop, the delirious din,
                  then's the time for intoxication,
                  the chugalugs and the bar-top bets,

then's the time for a long vacation
to foreign climes and holy fêtes,
then's the time for fornication,
the tickle, the slap, and the grand guffaw,
then's the time for gratification
with a hip,
          and a hip,
               and a HIP HOO RAW!

Guiltily realizing that he has to set a good example, he stops.

—So keep it down, huh?

The 1ST KORY and Semichorus advance to sing and dance.

Syzygy I [346–427]

1ST KORY   *There's a happy day a-comin',*
                              and I pray that I survive,
                           since a happy day is better
                              if it comes while you're alive.

1ST SEMICHO   *—There's a painful time behind me,*
                              active duty rubbed me raw:
                           I've been a Hero, Second Class
                              and bedded rough on straw
                           —But it planed my disposition
                              and sanded down my fury
                           And now you'll find no smoother man
                              at serving on a jury.

JACK   You used to be a bastard; you're a swéet héart nów.

1ST SEMICHO   *—And when they separate me*
                              from the service and its woe
                           I'll be the nicest juvenile
                              that you could ever know.
                           —I have spent enough time dying,
                              I have made myself quite ill,
                           hefting spear and schlepping shield
                              from drill to drill to drill.

1ST KORY

Turning officiously to Jack.

                           —But good luck has elected you
                              our generalissimo.
                           How to please you? Give the order!
                           Point us, sir, and let us go!

JACK   Okay. Just how do we clear these rocks away?

Hermes zooms down.

HERMES   Disgusting? You again? What rash act are you plotting?

JACK   *Nothing atrocious*—to quote your basic traitor.

HERMES   Your luck's run out: You're *dead*!

JACK   Well, those are the breaks . . .
               and who is better at rigging the breaks than Hermes?

HERMES   You're *dead,* I tell you! *Extinct*!

JACK   Beginning when?

HERMES   Beginning this very moment!

JACK   Impossible! Sorry,
               but I haven't bought the gear I need for the trip—
               no grits, no cheese . . .

HERMES   To put it another way,
               you're *fucked*!

JACK   That's really quite an honor . . . *but*
               I do wish you'd let me know a bit in advance.

HERMES   You must know Zeus has proclaimed the penalty of death
               on anyone caught in the act of uprooting the Goddess!

JACK   I absolutely *have* to die, and there's no appeal?

HERMES   You got it, buster.

JACK   Well, then, float me a loan?
               Three drachs for a pig to pay my initiation fee
               at the Temple of Afterlife? I can't die *dirty*.[24]

HERMES

Raising his voice and addressing the sky.

               Prepare your lightning, Zeus! Here's news!

JACK   *NO, DON'T!*
               Don't tell on me, I beg you, lord, for gods' sake!

HERMES   I can't even *consider* silence!

JACK   Remember the meat
               I brought for you?
                                  I beg you, lord, for *food's* sake!

---

24. Sacrifice of a pig was part of the purification ceremony included in the Eleusinian
Mysteries, initiation into which was believed to bring the initiate a better afterlife.

HERMES   Friend, you don't understand. If I neglect
                to raise the hue and cry and proclaim the facts,
                I face complete *erasure* by Zeus's thunder!

He takes a deep breath.

JACK   Sweet Hermes, *please*! No cry! No hue! Not you!

He turns to the 2ND SEMICHO and their Koryphaios, who are standing by bemused.

                Friends, why the resounding silence? You're thunderstruck already!
                If you don't make noise, dammit, then Hermes hails high Heaven!

2ND KORY   *Never, Hermes! Master, never*
                          put our friend in such a fix!
                        Such behavior is a no-no . . .
                            no, a not—in fact, a nix!

2ND SEMICHO

Trying an improbable expedient.

                        —Try to remember
                         the pig from the embers
                         and how it tasted
                         when you ate it.
                        —It was a present
                         a present that we sent,
                         and since you ate it
                         you're obligated . . .

JACK   It's flattery, of course, but really quite sín-cére.

2ND SEMICHO   *—Oh, don't oppose us*
                    and try to hard-nose us
                    from saving the Goddess
                    who brings such pleasure . . .
                   —Be helpful and hearty,
                    and flush the war party,
                    and pleasure us
                    beyond all measure.

2ND KORY

Returning to the other tune and rhythm.[25]

                        —There's a happy day a-comin'
                         for Hermes, who's the Top:

---

25. A parenthetical note in the 2001 performance script suggests that the "other tune and rhythm" was that accompanying the words "Never, Hermes! Master, never" above.

Our sacrifices, promenades,
and songs will never stop!

They stop expectantly. Jack turns to Hermes.

JACK	Their dulcet strains deserve your compassion . . .
HERMES	. . . my *pity* . . .
JACK	The honor they show you beggars that of the past . . .
HERMES	Their inborn larceny buggers the entire *future* . . .
JACK	I hate to bring this up but I'd better tell you: a plot is afoot against the Olympian gods!
HERMES	Hey, keep on talking; you just might change my mind.
JACK	The Moon's in on it, with that son of a bitch the Sun. It's a tricky intrigue they've been working on for years: To deliver Greece into the hands of *non-Greek* nations!
HERMES	You mean . . . ?
JACK	*Barbarians*—yes.
HERMES	But why do that?
JACK	In a word, *Oblation*! We Greeks offer up to *you,* to Hermes-and-the-rest; the barbarian types, of course, to *them,* to Sun and Moon. The rest is simple: Reduce us Greeks to nil, and Sun and Moon can cut themselves a nice, fat slice of all our cults . . .
HERMES	. . . and cut *us* out! So that explains the constant trimming and nipping away at the year— a day here, a day there; it all adds up. And they call it Calendar Reform!²⁶ It's really obscene!
JACK	It is. So, Hermes, join in our task with might and main, and fling yourself into pulling Peace out. And we shall show our thanks with a little Reform of our own, assigning all holy feasts and fêtes to—wait for it—*Hermes*! Now, *Panathenaea* sounds nice, but what about *PanHERMAEA*? *Hermetic Mysteries,* maybe? *The Feste of Him Who Guards the City,* *Hermes* (*formerly Zeus*)? And then there's Adonis . . . This won't be confined to Athens, of course; oh, no!

---

26. Attempts were repeatedly made to align the Athenian lunar calendar with the solar year.

Each Greek city freed from the horrors of War
will make oblation to *Hermes, Arrester of Disaster*!
And that just scratches the surface.

He hands Hermes a very large golden bowl.

                                        In pledge and earnest
whereof, accept this useful bowl, for pouring
your very own libations!

Hermes inspects the gift.

HERMES   You've bowled me over—
it's gold! Gold *does* bring out my better self.

He grasps it lovingly, and is now on Jack's side.
Jack addresses both Semichoruses.

JACK   And now, my friends, it's over to you. Your job? Go in
              with shovels and dig out that pile of rocks, on the double!

Scene I [428–458]

1ST KORY   Precisely what we'll do. O most informed of the gods,
              could you stand by to give us your expert opinion on what
              to do? You'll find our especial talent is Taking Directions.

Hermes moves near. Members of the Chorus enter.

JACK   Hermes, we need your bowl. Hold it right there.
              We have to pray to the gods before we start.

Hermes complies. Jack fills the bowl with wine, and Hermes holds it up.

HERMES   Libation-time! Libation!
                                    Let all keep holy silence!
              The while we pour this wine, this be our prayer:

              May this day constitute a new beginning
              of superabundant blessings on every Greek!

              May every man who hauls away at a rope
              in this our endeavor never touch shield again!

JACK   . . . but let him lead his life in quiet and peace,
              petting his popsy and poking away at the fire!

HERMES   *May every man who chooses War over Peace . . .*

JACK   . . . spend every hour of every day removing
              arrows from his elbows and other hinder parts.

HERMES	*May every would-be captain who prefers advancement*
	to restoring Peace to earth spend all his battles . . .

JACK   . . . chucking his shield and ruining his career!

HERMES   *May every profiteer in shield or spear*
            who furthers War to build a bigger market . . .

JACK   . . . be snatched by pirates and fed only barely, on barley!

HERMES   *May every man who shirks our holy work*
            from lust for high command or base desertion . . .

JACK   . . . fetch up stretched out taut on the wheel and flogged!

HERMES   *And now, for the work before us, a big round hand!*

He starts to applaud, but is stopped by Jack.

JACK   We need our hands for the work. Shout "*Hail!*" instead.

HERMES   Oh, very well:
                                        Hail!
                                              And *Hail!*

He waves at Jack.

                                                    Look, Ma: no hands!

He gets down to serious Hailing, sneaking a drink with each.

                        First, *Hail to Hermes!*
                                              —Next, *Hail to the Graces!*
                                                                    —*the Seasons!*
                        —*Hail Aphrodite!*
                                              —A big fat *Hail to Desire!*

JACK   No Hails for Ares!

HERMES   None.

JACK   And none for Battle.

HERMES   None at all. He's hardly a proper god.

Syzygy II [459–519]

The rocks are gone, the ropes are fastened to the Goddess inside. Jack addresses the entire Chorus.

JACK   Attention, men! And plenty of tension, too—
              pull tight on the ropes and warp the Goddess alongside!

The Koryphaioi and Semichoruses begin their pulls, using
the "Sound Off" chant that falls a minor third.

1ST KORY   *SOUND OFF!*

1ST SEMICHO   *HEAVE! HO!*

2ND KORY   *SOUND OFF!*

2ND SEMICHO   *HEAVE! HO!*

1ST KORY   *Sound Off,*

2ND KORY   *Sound Off,*

BOTH KORY   *Sound Off,*

BOTH SEMICHO   *HO!* **HO!**

Nothing at all happens. Hermes and Jack inspect the formation.

HERMES   The pull's not even. Unequal tension.

JACK   Look, *all together*, you bunch of prima donnas!
Bloody Boiotians—you boys better look sharp![27]

The process starts again.

1ST KORY   *SOUND OFF!*

1ST SEMICHO   *HEAVE! HO!*

Exasperated, the 1ST KORY approaches Hermes and Jack.

1ST KORY   Join in, you two, and help us reel her in!

The two comply, Jack with rather defensive guilt.

JACK   I *have* been reeling in! Look: hand in place,
and pulling away,
                              and getting caught in this rope!

1ST KORY   Well, why haven't we made any headway, then?

JACK

Shooing away a wraithlike figure who has appeared in the 1ST SEMICHO.

                    Goddamn ghost! Lamachos, out of the way!
Even dead, he blocks the approach to Peace![28]

Exit the ghost of Lamachos.

---

27. The people of Boiotia, just north of Athens, were bitter enemies of the Athenians and resisted efforts at peace.

28. Lamachos was a leading Athenian general. In fact he was still alive when *Peace* was produced. The Greek text says that Lamachos' monster, perhaps the Gorgon on his shield, was blocking the progress of the pulling.

HERMES

Inspecting the 2ND SEMICHO.

These Argives here—they haven't been pulling for years!
All they do is make fun of people in pain,
and still they're drawing full rations, full pay—from both sides![29]

Exit the Argives.

JACK   But look at these Spartans pull—a virile bunch!

HERMES   Think so? The only Spartans who really want to pull
are stuck in the stocks and the locksmith keeps them from moving.[30]

Exit the Spartans.

JACK   These Megarians here are not achieving diddly.

HERMES   But watch them pull—they grit their teeth like puppies!
The effort shows on their faces!

JACK   And so it should.
They're starving to death; it's an effort to stay alive.

1ST KORY   Men, we're accomplishing nothing. Let's get it together!
Now, let's give one more pull, with a single stroke!

He starts it off.

SOUND OFF!

1ST SEMICHO   *HEAVE! HO!*

2ND KORY   *SOUND OFF!*

2ND SEMICHO   *HEAVE! HO!*

1ST KORY   We moved a little, I think.

JACK   It's really depressing.
The pull is moving one way—but this single bunch
keeps pushing the other way! You watch it, Argives!

2ND KORY   *SOUND OFF!*

2ND SEMICHO   *HEAVE! HO!*

2ND KORY   I sense sedition running through our ranks.

---

29. The city of Argos, in the eastern Peloponnese, had been neutral in the war and had benefited from both sides in the struggle.

30. Aristophanes refers to a group of Spartans who had been captured by the Athenians on the island of Sphakteria, near Pylos, in 425 BCE. Desire to get their captives back was a principal motivation in Sparta's move toward peace.

JACK   It could be worse. The men obsessed with Peace
              are hauling with gusto.

2ND KORY   And others sabotage gusto.

HERMES   —Will you measly Megarians please proceed to hell?
              The Goddess knew you of old; she remembers and hates.
              You started all this by coating her over with garlic,
              and she's been in bad odor ever since.

Exit the Megarians.

                                          —Athenians,
              please put a stop to your well-nigh endless inertia—
              You are not pulling an inch from where you started.
              You must have *something* better to do than Law!
              If you really desire to bring the Goddess out,
              take firmer footing somewhat nearer the sea.

1ST KORY   Now, men, a pull from the farmers among us, and no one else.

A pull. Progress is made.

HERMES   Congratulations, gentlemen. A very marked advance.

2ND KORY   Hear that? "A marked advance." Everyone show them how!

JACK   It's still the farmers who move it along, and nobody else.

1ST KORY   Everyone up and at it!

HERMES   That's it! Nearly there!

2ND KORY   Don't slack! Don't flag!
                            Increase the tension!

HERMES   That's really it! We're there!

1ST KORY   *SOUND OFF!*

1ST SEMICHO   *HEAVE! HO!*

2ND KORY   *SOUND OFF!*

2ND SEMICHO   *HEAVE! HO!*

1ST KORY   *Sound Off,*

2ND KORY   *Sound Off,*

BOTH KORY   *Sound Off . . .*

BOTH SEMICHO   *HO! **HO!***

Peace, accompanied by her handmaids Lady Bountiful and Jamboree, is drawn into view.[31]

Scene II [520–552]

JACK   O mistress, cheerful grantor of the grape to man,
       what words might I employ in your address,
       and where secure a megalomorphic lexeme
       of connotation vast to cry you welcome?
       (I couldn't bring one from home.)
             —Welcome to you,
       my Lady Bountiful.
           —Jamboree, joy of the day.

He moves in closer.

       Oh Jamboree, the charm of those classic features!

He sniffs.

       And such a breath—the merest whiff of myrrh,
       a *soupçon* of Exemption, a hint of Reduction in Force.

HERMES   I gather it's not the smell of the basic mess kit?

JACK   I hate the dreadful hamper with its hideous hollow,
       rank with the reek of scallions and halitosis!
       But Jamboree's aroma—bounty and plenty,
       open house and theater-party, the flute[32]
       and tragic poet, the hush of Sophoclean lyric,
       the thrush, the rush of Euripides' delicate line . . .

HERMES   You may regret that slander. She isn't inclined
       to delicate lines of cross-examination.

JACK

Still sniffing.

       . . . of wreaths and clarified wine, of bleating sheep,
       of bosoms jouncing over the open fields,
       of tiddly maids all in a row, of emptied bottles . . .
       and all sorts of good stuff like that there.

HERMES   Look down—
       you can see the nations engaged in conversation,
       and reconciliation, and happy jollification . . .

---

31. The 2001 performance script adds in brackets, "There is no reason why Bountiful and
Jamboree should come from exactly the same place as Peace—they just need to come out at
the same time."

32. I.e., aulos (see introduction).

JACK   . . . their faces bruised and contused in traumatization,
              black eyes in various stages of restoration . . .

HERMES   Well, scan the audience here. Take one good squint
              at a face in the crowd and you know its owner's trade.

JACK   Now, that's depressing.

HERMES   You see that crestmaker there?

JACK   But how can you tell?

HERMES   Easy. He's pulling his hair out.

JACK   And see? A maker of hoes just farted full
              in the face of a swordsmith.

HERMES   What a tickled maker
              of sickles . . .

JACK   . . . flipping the bird at the maker of spears!

HERMES   Well, time for the farmers to leave. You make the announcement.

JACK   Attention, please! Attention!
                                All farmers are free
              to fare off home to their countryside, accompanied
              by a full and complete complement
                                        of barnyard implements.
              No need for javelin, spear, or sword; the earth down there
              is now aflood and awash in High Old Vintage Peace.
              A hymn of praise, then all slog off to work the land!

Parodos II [553–656]

1ST KORY   *There's a happy day arrivin',*
                      and I'm glad the day is mine:
                  It's a day that just men lust for,
                  It's a day that farmers long for . . .
                      it's the day I greet the vine.
                  There's a happy day arrivin',
                      it's a great day, and it's big
                  for the shoots that once I planted,
                  for the fruits I've so long wanted . . .
                      it's the day I greet the fig.

JACK   Now, gentlemen all, we'll start with a song of thanks to the Goddess,
              who swept our landscapes clear of crests and heraldry horrors.
              Then off to the fields of home as fast as we can toddle
              with a fresh-bought ration of smelt to spice up our spring campaign!

The Chorus assembles in ranks and catches the eye of Hermes.

HERMES   Look at those ranks and files—so fine, so fair, so squared-off!
           The neatness of petits-fours!
                               The panache of smörgåsbord!

JACK   I quite agree. And see the gleam of the readied mallet!
           Behold the blinking of pitchforks against the noonday sun!
           To see them engage with the weeds in the vineyards—
                                                   what an exchange
           of cultivation! Desire rises within me to make
           my way to my blessed plot . . .
                               and break it up with my hoe!

           Please remember,   gentlemen,
           all the food we   ate back then:
           all the gifts of   fertile earth,
           spawned in plenty,   never dearth:
           figs just-picked and figs long-dried,
           myrtle-berries   on the side,
           all the products   of the vine,
           vintage drafts and   sweet new wine,
           the violets and   buzzing bees,
           lovely, long-missed olive trees . . .
           For such blessings, gather near,
           tell the Goddess,   "Thank you, Dear."

The assembled Chorus passes the Ode around.

1ST SEMICHO   *Oh, Goddess, all our welcome,*
                          and, Goddess, all our love.
                      It's a happy day you bring us
                          You're the thing we're gladdest of.
                      —My longing's been a strong one,
                          years and miles I've had to roam;
                      My longing's been a long one
                          and I'm longing to go home.
                      —Oh, Peace was all my profit,
                          and Peace is all I covet:
                      The farmer's life is made by Peace . . .
                          It's glorious! I love it!

2ND SEMICHO   *—In Peace's time, her benefits*
                          are mighty and are many.
                      They're sweet and dear and always here
                          and never cost a penny!
                      —Oh, Peace brings many benefits
                          but these are favorites:
                      the basics of the rustic life:
                          Deliverance and Grits!

> *—Oh, the vines break out in chuckles*
> *as you come across the loam,*
> *and each tender figlet smiles*
> *that you nevermore will roam,*
> *and the plant world laughs in greeting:*
> *"Welcome, Goddess! Welcome Home!"*

1ST KORY   But where was She kept away from us this great long time?
O most extremely congenial member of the gods, explain!

HERMES   O most unusually cultured cluster of rustics, attend
my pronouncement and hear, if you will, the causes of Peace's demise.
The whole mess started with art, the first step down to destruction
coming when Phidias fiddled with the gold to be used on Athenê's
statue and went into exile forthwith.[33] That statue was Perikles'
commission,[34]
and he rather feared that Phidias' guilt might rub off on him,
and earn him a share in Phidias' fate and disgrace. He knew
your vicious habits and wolfish customs only too well;
a diversion was needed: He flicked a spark—it was nothing, really—
a small blockade of our next-door neighbor Megara—and set
Athens ablaze, and blew on the embers, inflaming a conflict
whose smoke choked tears from every last Greek, on whatever side.
And once the first protesting vine went crackle and pop . . .
well, something snapped. A pot got batted, and booted another
pot in a pet, and pretty soon there was no one left
to arrest the ongoing process, and so Peace left Athens.

JACK   What original news! I never heard that from anyone else—
there wasn't a word anywhere that Phidias was linked with the Goddess!

2ND KORY   It's certainly new to me, too. The two of them are related?
Of course, that's why she's so pretty!
                                    There's lots in this world we don't know.

HERMES   Moving right along:
                        Your subject allies were soon apprised
of Athens' internal dissent, backbiting, and mutual strife,
and cooked up a plan to dissolve their fear and loathing of all
that tribute they paid you—they bribed the mightiest men in Sparta.
These Spartans, of course, were corrupt and greedy, and xenophobe
bigots:

---

33. The great sculptor Phidias was responsible for the statue of Athenê in the Parthenon.
Other sources report that enemies of the politician Perikles accused Phidias of embezzlement
and impiety, and that he was either imprisoned or went into exile.

34. Perikles was the leading statesman of Athens when the Peloponnesian War began in 431
BCE. He died of the plague in 429.

they slung Peace out of their state, and hooked their hands on War.
From this, they profited nicely . . . to the sad expense of their farmers.
Seeking revenge and reprisal, you sent out the navy from Athens
to gobble down all the figs of utterly innocent men.

JACK   No, that was perfect justice! The Spartans had razed to the ground
                  my darling fig tree—the one I planted and raised to the skies!

2ND KORY   Justice is right, sir, right! They stoned and utterly wasted
                  a mighty pipkin of mine and ruined six bushels of wheat!

HERMES   *To continue:*
                            The rustic workforce here abandoned the fields
                  and crowded inside the walls with no intimation that they
                  were being sold out in the very same way as the Spartan farmers.
                  Deprived of their daily raisins, addicted to absent figs,
                  they turned for relief to the politicians. But the politicians,
                  perceiving this new urban poor as impotent, foodless, and feckless,
                  and hence, of course, no source for any personal profit,
                  pitchforked Peace out of Athens with shouts and hoots again
                  and again on the frequent occasions when she gave in to nostalgia
                  for the land she loved and showed her face in town. They preferred
                  to fasten and batten on allies—the richest and flushest fat cats,
                  whom they could drag into court and fleece quite bare on the charge of
                  "Pro-Spartan Opinions!" And you, on the juries, would do as expected:
                  Spring on the defendant and rip him to shreds like a mongrel puppy.
                  The city's color was bad; it was terrified, stuck in dead center;
                  its diet was nothing but slander, so it doted on gorging on that.
                  Well, now, those aliens assessed the number and source of their bruises,
                  and stopped the toothy maws of their assailants with gold—
                  they enriched politicians, and, as for Greece, it could have become
                  a depeopled wasteland without your taking the slightest notice.
                  And that was the doing of the leather merchant, of . . .

Before Hermes can say "Kleon," Jack interrupts.

JACK   No! Don't say it,
                  great lord Hermes! Leave that man deep down below!
                  He-who-shall-be-nameless is ours no more; he's *yours!*
                            I grant you, when he was
                            alive and among us,
                            that man was a thug,
                            an informer, a fungus,
                            a recreant, miscreant,
                            babbler, and cur,
                            a bastard, an agent—
                            oui!—provocateur . . .
                            But don't call him those names,

> *however true:*
> *he's family, now, and they*
> *come back to you!*

Scene III [657–728]

JACK

> He addresses the Goddess.

>> My lady, tell me why you stay so still.

HERMES   The audience here; she refuses to speak to them:
She's furious, thinking of what they put her through.

JACK   Well, have her whisper some little item to you.

HERMES   What are your thoughts on that, dear? You can tell me.
Okay, O most unbellicose of women?

> He bends to the Goddess's mouth. An unheard conversation.

>> Okay, I hear you . . . That's your grievance? Gotcha.

> He turns to the crowd.

>> Now all attend the charge the Goddess brings:
>> That subsequent to the business in Pylos, she did,
>> of her own free will, convey to Athens a chest
>> quite stuffed with treaties to end the War, and was
>> three times defeated in Congress by your votes.[35]

JACK   We did . . . and we were mistaken. Excuse us, Goddess:
Our thinking was stuck in the stink of untanned leather.

HERMES   Well, listen here: She just put me this question:
Who was her greatest opponent here in Athens?
And who was most devoted to stopping the War?

JACK   Her greatest champion? Kleonymos, in a walk.[36]

HERMES   Kleonymos, eh? Well, on Peace versus War, how well
did this Kleonymos stand up?

JACK   Extremely well.
Much straighter than those who insisted on *keeping* their shields.

HERMES   Well, here's another question fresh from her lips:
When Congress meets these days, who's in the chair?

---

35. "Congress" is the *ekklesia*, an assembly at which all male Athenian citizens could vote.

36. Aristophanes repeatedly mocks the politician Kleonymos for allegedly dropping his shield and fleeing during a battle.

JACK   These days? The speaker's chair's Hyperbolos' turf.[37]

The statue of Peace averts its head.

—What's all this, Goddess? Why turn your head to the right?

HERMES   When the popular party endorses a derelict doyen,
              she can't stand to look to the left.

JACK   He's only a stopgap.

HERMES   A stopgap?

JACK   They had to have *something* to plug the loopholes.
              No worry; Hyperbolos is due for extraction soon.

HERMES   What boon—she asks—can he possibly bring to the city?

JACK   Vision.

HERMES   How vision?

JACK   Hyperbolos fabricates *lamps*.
              We used to fumble at planning in absolute darkness,
              but now we'll make it go by the glow of a lamp!

HERMES   *STEADY! WHOOPS!*
              Such searching questions she's having me have you answer!

JACK   Such as?

HERMES   So many, and most are ancient,
              from out of the dear dead days before she left.
              The first is: How is Sophokles getting along?

JACK   He's happy and healthy . . . except for that little matter
              of metempsychosis. Sometimes he's convinced that he's
              Simonides, writing choral lyrics . . .

HERMES   . . . for *cash*? How awful!

JACK   The craft he launched was much too light, the seas
              were much too heavy . . .
                                        and Sophokles took a bath.[38]

HERMES   And how's Kratinos, that masterly comic poet?

JACK   Past-masterly, now. The Spartan invasion killed him.

HERMES   An atrocity?

---

37. The demagogue Hyperbolos became especially influential after the death of Kleon.
38. Simonides was a lyric poet of the early fifth century BCE with a reputation for avarice.
The context for Aristophanes' joke about Sophokles is unknown.

JACK   Well, in a way. When the Spartans spilled
A jeroboam of wine, Kratinos expired on the spot.[39]
—And how much more of the same has the city seen!
Oh, it was hell, I tell you . . .
                      —Wherefore, Goddess,
we'll never ever let you go again!

HERMES   And those are the very conditions we seek.
                              Wherefore,
receive the Lady Bountiful here in marriage,
and keep the house with her in the carefree country,
in fecund indulgence producing a gaggle of grapes!

JACK   Oh darling, oh my darling, come and kiss me!
—Hermes, it's been quite a while. If I, at my age,
should splurge on her bounty, and splurge again, and keep on
splurging, what are the possible ill effects?

HERMES   None, if you swallow the barest hint of mint
immediately after.
                     And now for Jamboree,
the party girl. Property, once, of the Senate:[40]
Conduct her back with all precipitate speed.

JACK   Oh jaunty Senate, sublime in Jamboree!
Three days of slurping on liquid joy, three days
of licking and munching away on a high-fat diet!
—And now, oh Hermes on high, farewell and good-bye.

HERMES   Proceed in peace, oh mortal, and forget me not!

JACK   Now, homeward, roach, with all dispatch!

HERMES   Your roach was *fetched*.

JACK   Who poached my roach?

HERMES   Don't bitch.
Your roach has found its niche: It's hitched to the coach
of Zeus, and bears the lightning, each last *flatch*.

JACK   My wretched roach will starve!
                             It needs a very
special diet.

---

39. Kratinos was a rival comic poet with a reputation for drunkenness. We do not know whether Kratinos had actually died recently or if his "death" in this joke is not to be taken literally.

40. Parker's "Senate" is the *boulê*, an assembly of five hundred citizens that handled much of the city's day-to-day business.

HERMES   But Ganymede's here in Heaven.

JACK   You mean . . . ?

HERMES   Ambrosia, of course—no lumps at all.

JACK   But how do I make the Grand Descent?

HERMES   No problem;
                 don't give it a thought. Just skirt the Goddess here . . .

JACK   Step this way, girls; follow me.
                                      A mob expects you—
                 all cocked and erect, and ready, in fact, for the Act.

Exeunt Jack and the women. Exit Hermes into the Palace.

Parabasis [729–818]

Here Occurs ye Parabasis:

1ST KORY

Calling after Jack.

                 Now on your way
                 and don't lack luck!

Abandoning his stage persona, he addresses the members of the Chorus.

                 All right, all. Let's take
                 a break for Security Measures.

Voice up.

                 —Could we have the crew out here?

The stagehands appear. He turns back to the Chorus.

                 A recent outbreak of completely
                 unlicensed lurking on set
                 by very suspicious types
                 has regrettably resulted in a rash
                 of thefts. A dirty business.
                 Let's each deposit our hand props—
                 our shovel, our spade, our rope—
                 with the handiest stagehand. Please.

The stagehands collect the props. He addresses the stagehands.

                 It's a heavy responsibility, but
                 we trust you to keep these safe.

The stagehands depart. He turns back to the Chorus. He claps lightly.

Places, everyone, please! It's time
for the metatheatrical bit.

He steps forward as Author's Spokesman to address the audience.

Self-advertisement on stage—the hallmark and curse of the age!
I hold as a tenet of faith the conviction that comical playwrights
who infect and infest anapestic[41] addresses with personal plaudits
ought be drubbed from the stage with the claymores and clubs of our
    stalwart
Security Force. Egotistical claptrap deserves no slice
of your valuable time, friends!
                    However. Put the case,
O Muse, that this could be the proper place for a reasoned appraisal
of the *oeuvre* and verve of one who just happened to be the world's most
illustrious light of the comic stage, both past and present!
On that hypothesis, friends, our author/producer allows
that he'll put in for a rather large slice of just desserts.
First, he fumigated the genre:
                    Was it less than ten years ago
that the comedy others produced was hagridden with gags, with gags
about rags, and stuck in shtick, in shtick about ticks and fleas?
He shtopped that shtick and flagged those gags; now nobody does them.
He then was the first to oust those exhausted blackouts and skits—
the hero preening in an apron, the demigod diddled out of dinner—
and rousted out of the repertoire those sick subservient roles:
the slaves who [A] were always running away, or [B]
were embroiled in feckless intrigues, or [C] were constantly clubbed
and whipped to provide a hook for cracks about lacerated backs:
"Poor guy—that eczema's made you a wreck!"
                       "You haven't been beaten:
you have been graded!"
               "Your ribs have been blitzed by a full division!"
"What's the punishment policy here—scorched earth?"
                      He leveled
these sorry structures, these tawdry trash-heaps, these slapsticky wrecks,
and raised an edifice up to enshrine this new Art, broad-based
on greatness of word and thought and jokes that were funny, not vulgar.
His themes were vast. He eschewed the sitcommy plots that mocked
mediocrity—Mr. and Mrs. Average Athenian Clod—
but with Herakles' courage and rage he loaded his Chorus for

MONSTER

---

41. Anapests, or repetitions of the pattern short-short-LONG, with variations, were the
standard meter of the comic parabasis.

and marched on the mighty, assailing all manner of Gogs, Magogs, and Demagogues, traversing the stinking stench of rotten leather and sloshing across the sucking swamps of unmitigated muck. A quote:

He rips off a wig exposing a bald head, and speaks as Aristophanes.

> "*From my first performance, I dared to measure my strength*
> *with that rankest of reptiles, the Brown-Tailed, Saw-Toothed*
>
> ## *KLEONOSAURUS REX!*
>
> *Its eyes flashed fire with a whorehouse glare, while in its hair*
> *in a writhing mass, a hundred heads of lousy leeches*
> *circled and waved, and kissed its foul ass. It screamed in the voice*
> *of a roaring river in labor, and bore the stink of a seal,*
> *the greasy balls of a female troll, the rump of a camel.*
> *At such a sight, did I take fright? Ah, no, friends, no.*
> *For you I warred then; for you I war now.*
>
> *   And the allies, of course.*
> *Wherefore, you are in my debt; I present myself for payment.*
> *In me you have that rarity, an Established Modest Winner:*
> *I refused to milk my fame before by doing the circuit,*
> *cruising the gyms to come on strong to admiring boys;*
> *rather, I packed my tools and strode away, leaving a legacy:*
> *pain, little; pleasure, much; and everything fit and proper.*

He picks up the tempo.

> *And one thing more:*
> *I urge and advise*
> *the men and the boys*
> *to be on my side;*
> *additionally, I'd*
> *like to enlist*
> *the hitherto missed*
> *votes of those called*
> *the smooth, or the bald.*
> *For if I'm the winner*
> *and they go to dinner*
> *or picnic or feast,*
> *each provident host*
> *will give them the most:*
> *'Let Baldy take*
> *this last little cake!*
> *Sweetmeats of quality?*
> *Give them to Baldy!*
> *Let's extend homage*

> *to Baldy, the image*
> *of the poet whose play*
> *took First today!'"*

The 1ST SEMICHO advances to dance.[42]

[Strophe: 1ST SEMICHO]
[Antistrophe: 2ND SEMICHO]

PART TWO

Syzygy III [819–921]

Returned at length from Olympos, JACK staggers on right,
flanked by the lovely maidens LADY BOUNTIFUL and JAMBO-
REE. He is considerably the worse for wear; they are not.

JACK   *Hard is the straight and narrow to Heaven.* In fact,
                it's brutal. I wore my legs completely out.
                And off.

He peers at the audience.

                    You've grown. Up there, I could hardly see you,
                though even from Heaven your habits were really disgusting.
                Down here, up close, they're a great deal disgustinger yet.

Xanthias enters from the house and reacts with joy.

XANTHIAS   Boss! Are you really back?

JACK   That's what they tell me.

XANTHIAS   So how did it go?

JACK   With agony, utter and awful.
                My legs weren't up to that long, relentless descent.

XANTHIAS   So, out with it! Give me the lowdown! Speak!

An awkward pause.

JACK   Well, *what?*

XANTHIAS   Were you the only one? Did you see any other
                humans roaming around in the upper air?

---

42. Parker did not translate verses 775–818, a string of insults against obscure tragic
playwrights. For a prose translation of the passage, see Appendix A.

JACK	Nary a soul . . . No, check that: Two or three psyches of poets. The ones who commit dithyrambic recitals.[43]
XANTHIAS	And what were they doing?
JACK	Soaring aloft for their art: Plucking a peck of vaporous preludes, and picking a noon-nuzzling, air-faring, cloud-capped *da capo* or two.
XANTHIAS	But people say, whenever someone dies, we turn into *stars*. You mean that isn't true?
JACK	Of course it's true.
XANTHIAS	Well, Ion of Chios is dead.[44] Which star is he?
JACK	Way back, he wrote a poem on earth called *Daystar*. So when he arrived, all Heaven shelved him under his title. *Daystar* he is.
XANTHIAS	But what does that make the shooting stars, the ones that whiz along with that very distinctive flash?
JACK	They're richer stars, the loaded leading lights, rolling home from dinner across the welkin. They carry lanterns, and, in those lanterns, fire.

He fends off further questions.

Enough!

Pushing Lady Bountiful forward.

You lead this lady inside tout de suite.
Flood the bathtub—be sure the water's warm—
then spread a bridal bed for her and me.
And when you've finished, come back here again.

Pushing Jamboree forward.

And then I'll make this girl a gift to the Senate.

XANTHIAS

Suspiciously.

Where did you get these girls?

---

43. The dithyramb was a choral song sung in honor of Dionysos at some of the same festivals at which comedy and tragedy were performed. Composers of dithyrambs were known for their poetic and musical innovations, many of which were controversial.

44. Ion of Chios was a successful writer of tragedies and other works in verse and prose of the mid-fifth century BCE.

JACK   Where did I get them?
             Heaven, of course.

XANTHIAS   I wouldn't give three lousy obols[45]
             for gods that pimp. That's not divine, it's mortal!

JACK   *THE GODS DON'T PIMP!*
                                  Not all.
                                        Some do, of course.
             Even immortals have to live.

       False-hearty, he tries to get things moving.

                                                    —Okay,
                   let's go!

XANTHIAS

       About to lead Lady Bountiful and Jamboree indoors,
       he is struck by a sudden thought.

                   One question: You want I should give her something
                   to gobble down?

JACK   Nothing. She wouldn't eat it.
             What's bread or biscuit to her, who lies beside
             the Gods on high and shares ambrosia, sucks
             the sweets of Heaven?

XANTHIAS   We'll have to fix her
             a lowdown sweet or two to suck on here.

       Indicating how this might be managed, he leads the girls into
       the house. The First Semichorus advances in admiration.

1ST SEMICHO *Our feeble old-timer is getting the breaks.*
             Prosperity pushes each move that he makes—
                   at least, in our small estimation.

JACK   *Then what's the name*
             you'll call me soon—
             a sparkling stud
             on honeymoon?

1ST SEMICHO *A focus, an acme—oh elderly sir—*
             a lusty young buck who is slathered with myrrh,
                   the subject of rejuvenation!

JACK   *Then there's the fucking:*
             What name fits

---

45. The obol was the smallest Athenian coin, worth one sixth of a drachma.

> *a man who fills*
> *his fists with tits?*

1ST SEMICHO   *We'll call you more*
              exalted yet
              than ballet-boy
              en pirouette.

JACK   *It's only just,*
              it's only fair:
              I rode my saddled
              roach in air
              and rescued every
              man in Greece.
              I brought him rustic
              calm and peace
              to do the things
              he'd rather do:
              securely sleep
              and safely screw.

Xanthias enters from the house in considerable excitement, ush-
ering the demure and beautiful maiden Jamboree.

XANTHIAS   THIS GIRL IS WASHED! SHE'S CLEAN! HER BOTTOM
               GLEAMS!
           HER FRITTER'S PIPING HOT! HER BUNS ARE SHAPED
           AND SPREAD!
                         THIS GIRL HAS GOT IT ALL!
                                              —Except,
           there's one slight shortage: A lack of cock.

JACK   No matter:
           We'll finish that job by taking our sweet Jamboree
           and bestowing her joys on the Senate.

XANTHIAS   What's that you say?
           Is this girl THE Jamboree? The Jam-bor-ee
           we used to jam and bore in the Good Old Days,
           and bang all the way to Brauron when we had a buzz on?[46]

JACK   Correct. A girl not easily caught, I might add.

XANTHIAS   Well, boss, an ass like that won't come along more
           than once or twice a decade.

---

46. Brauron was a sanctuary of Artemis east of Athens, where a festival was held every four
years.

JACK

Turning to the audience.

> Okay, out there:
> I'm looking for a Man of Honor—you got any such?
> A man who can take this girl to the Senate and keep her
> intact en route?

There is no reply. Suddenly, he notices that Xanthias has extended a finger and is poking Jamboree's crotch.

> What's this? You taking notes?

XANTHIAS   Uh, no. The Great Games are coming up soon, and I want a good seat. I'm picking a box. Center, down front.

Jack pulls him away, then turns back to the audience.

JACK   I'm waiting. No takers to serve as escort and guard?

To Jamboree.

> C'mere, dear. I'll take you myself, deliver you straight
> to the heart of the Senate.

Xanthias continues to scan the audience.

XANTHIAS   I see a hand over there.

JACK   Whose hand?

XANTHIAS   Whose? It's *ARIPHRADES'* hand! He wants her brought over to him.

> His tongue's hanging out.[47]

JACK   I'll bet he's gone down on his knees. A dainty dish like this— he'd slurp all her gravy and leave her high and dry. No. We can't have that.

Turning to Jamboree, who is now at his side.

> But before we go,
> deposit these encumbrances there, on the ground.[48]

With his help, Jamboree removes her clothes. The two of them proceed towards the official guests in the first row of the audience. Xanthias follows close after. JACK stops short of the goal, and, striking a barker's attitude, makes his presentation of Jamboree to the VIPs.

---

47. In several passages Aristophanes mocks Ariphrades for his obsession with cunnilingus.

48. A note in the 2001 performance script suggests there might be a "striptease to music" here.

Senators and Members of the Board of Governors, *voici*
our sweet *JAMBOREE*! A feast for the sorest eye—
and *you* are the group upon whom I shall now bestow her.
Consider the joys that accrue to you in the next
few minutes:
                              A real *Jambalaya*—just lift her legs,
make a small deposit, and watch that clam bake!
                                                          You desire
an oven? Look no further!

He points at Jamboree's crotch, and Xanthias inspects.

XANTHIAS   Seems mighty cozy.
Some darkening, though. Before the War, the Senate
cooked all their deals in there. Talk about smoke-filled
wombs!

JACK

Turning the barker's spiel up a notch.

          But That's Not All! Tomorrow morning,
now that you have Jamboree, it's the Best In Sport!
It's WRESTLING, all in and all out, on a natural mat
where riding time counts, catch-as-catch-can, the quick
reverse with the left leg over, the flex, the drop
to the knees, and then, your muscles shiny and slick
with body-rub, slide into a full spread-eagle
and throw her the *pin*!
                              (Freestyle, no holds barred,
score with a hard cross above, a jab below.)
But That's Not All!
                              Day after tomorrow, it's RACING!
Back in the Saddle Again:
                              The frantic jockeying
nose-to-nose, the sudden upsets of sulky
on sulky as, puffing and blowing, the bangtails bang
away at each other, bunched for a flat-out thrust
in the final stretch to drive home and Win by a Head!
And the other jocks, in shock, their colors still flapping,
their steeples still chaste, lie littered around the offtrack,
losers who skidded, who stuck in the pack and Came Short.
—Well, then, Governors, please accept, by deed
of gift, JAMBOREE, and place her upon your Agenda.

Jamboree moves to the dignitaries. One of the Governors accepts the offer with alacrity and enfolds her.

Now, there's a picture.
> A practical parliamentarian:
Gives her top spot on his docket.
> > *—GO, GUV, GO!—*
But if you didn't have a piece of this action,
you'd put out a hand, entertain a move for adjournment,
take bids for a recess,
> > and let her lie on the table.

With Xanthias, he returns to center stage. The Second Semichorus advances.

2ND SEMICHO   *An excellent citizen, dogged and dear,*
a quality colleague for everyone here,
> *is one with this paragon's nature.*

JACK   > *But when you've picked*
> *the grapes of peace,*
> *it's then you'll know*
> *my qualities.*

2ND SEMICHO   *They're clear at the moment, to those who aren't blind:*
You've helped all humanity, rescued mankind—
> *a savior in state and in stature.*

JACK   > *But first the drinking:*
> *What name's mine*
> *when you've swilled a*
> *bowl of wine?*

2ND SEMICHO   > *"You're NUMBER ONE!"*
> *we'll shout till hoarse—*
> *except the Blessed*
> *Gods, of course.*

JACK   > *Your great esteem*
> *is justified:*
> *Trygaios from*
> *the Near North Side,*
> *I've lifted from*
> *a wretched hole*
> *the rustic rube,*
> *the urban prole,*
> *and now, to cheers*
> *unanimous,*
> *I flush that bum*
> *HYPERBOLOS!*

The Second Semichorus retires.

Syzygy IV [922–1038]

Jack and Xanthias confer.

XANTHIAS   Well, let's get a move on. What job's next on the list?

JACK   You have to ask? We install the Goddess, of course—
             a ceremony, by the book. That means an offering . . .
             Where do we keep the pots?

XANTHIAS   The *pots*? Look, this
             is *PEACE*! She's not some two-bit terracotta
             figure of Hermes.

JACK   You have a better suggestion?
             What do we sacrifice?

XANTHIAS   Well, it has to be *lucky*.

JACK   A white-faced steer?

XANTHIAS   *We'd* be the white-faced ones—
             a bum steer back to war.

JACK   A fatted calf?

XANTHIAS   We'd just be suckers again.

JACK   Well, how about pigs—
             a potbellied saddleback boar?

XANTHIAS   You have just described
             Theogenes—You'll make us all into utter swine.[49]

JACK   I've run out of victims. What do *you* suggest?

XANTHIAS   Me? A *tup*.

JACK   A *what*?

XANTHIAS   A *tup*. An Ionic
             isogloss for ram.[50]

JACK   You want us to sacrifice
             an Ionic isogloss?

XANTHIAS   *Tup*.

JACK   And why a *tup*?

XANTHIAS   So when we go to Assembly, and they say, "Vote
             for War!" we'll shout back, "Ewe can *Ram* it *Tup* your . . ."

---

49. Theogenes was a leading citizen mocked elsewhere for being boastful and dirty.

50. Ionic is one of several Greek dialects. Aristophanes uses the Ionic form *oî,* which can mean either "sheep" or something like, "oh no!"

JACK   Astute idea.

XANTHIAS   . . . and we'll be perfect **lambs**,
               all gentle and whiter than snow, and never fleece
               our allies . . .

JACK   You've sold me. Go get a sheep, and **hurry**.
               We need an altar to do this; I'll find one somewhere.

Xanthias hurries into the house. Jack scans the stage in consternation.

1ST SEMICHO   *The man who's on*
               A roll with God
               *   Is never at a loss.*
               Success resolves
               his every need;
               *   of Luck he is the boss.*
               His time is right,
               His place is right:
               *   God always comes across.*

Jack bumps into the altar that graces every stage.

JACK   *Your story's true:*
               God doth provide . . .
               And here's my altar
               Right outside.

1ST SEMICHO   *Then hurry, while*
               the wind is right;
               *   and catch the peaceful blast.*
               God's turned the war-wind
               right around—
               *   fair weather may not last.*
               Get blown or else
               get blown away—
               *   you'd better do it fast.*

Jack discovers a huge pile of sacrificial supplies right outside his house.

JACK   *Goodness, what have*
               I espied?
               All our wants are
               now supplied!
               Coincidence
               is running rife:
               The basket! Fillets!
               Fire! The knife!
               The holy meal—

                a handy heap!
                The only thing
                we need's a sheep.

1ST SEMICHO   *Then hustle! Rustle*
                up that sheep!
                    Before the smoke and din
                entice a flutist[51]
                on the prowl,
                    intent on sitting in.[52]
                He'll turn your service
                    into mayhem . . .
                And worse than that,
                    you'll have to pay him.

Jack swoops into the house. Xanthias, leading a sheep, and Jack, with a
basin of holy water, emerge almost immediately. Both are wreathed.

JACK   Okay, now. Take this basket and this basin
                and make the lustrational circuit around the altar.
                Left to right, and *fast*!

He turns back to the pile of sacrificial items.

XANTHIAS   Here we go.

Without moving from the spot, he spins in place, left to right.

                So what's the next direction? Circuit's done.

JACK   Let's see. I snatch a brand from the burning—*so*—
                and dip it into the water—*so*—and shake it
                over the sheep—like this—and the sheep responds
                with a shake of its head . . .

No response from the sheep.

                                and the goddamned sheep responds
                with a shake of its mangy head!

The sheep gets the idea, and shakes its head haltingly. Jack turns to Xanthias.

                              Hand me some barley
                and watch: I sprinkle it over the altar—thus—
                and just a *soupçon* on the tippy-tip-top of the sheep.
                And now I wash my hands.
                              And now I hold
                the ewer while you wash *yours*.

---

51. I.e., an aulos player (see introduction).

52. Aulos players regularly accompanied sacrifices. The Greek text refers to a particular aulos
player, Chairis, mocked elsewhere for his bad playing.

> Now take the meal
> and scatter it broadcast in driblets over the crowd.

He turns back to the pile. Xanthias does nothing at all, but speaks immediately.

XANTHIAS   Finished!

JACK   You've given the driblets already?

XANTHIAS   You bet.
> But see for yourself. There isn't a man in the place
> without his very own driblet.
>   Some quite large.

JACK   The women didn't get any.

XANTHIAS   Just wait a while.
> The men will see that each woman gets it tonight.[53]
> Dribble, dribble, dribble.

JACK   Time for the prayer.

He raises his voice to priestliness.

> Who attends this rite?
>   What men among you here
> can qualify as righteous, brave, and **pure**?

No reply. Xanthias looks at the Chorus.

XANTHIAS   Let's try this bunch. A perfect plethora of purity.

The two of them pick up basins of holy water and drench the two Semichoruses. The members flinch, but stand their ground.

JACK   Those are what you mean by *pure*?

XANTHIAS   Of course.
> They don't know enough to come in from the rain. That's *pure*.

JACK   To the prayer, and quick!

XANTHIAS   You're right. *Now let us pray.*

JACK   *Hail Peace, full of grace, blessed beyond the rest,*
> *O goddess majestic, so unthinkably exalted and all-round best,*
> *Peace our Lady, utterly august and serene*
> *regnant and regent queen,*

---

53. This passage is an excellent example of the ambiguities in our evidence for or against the presence of women in Athenian comic audiences. Does Aristophanes mean that women are in the audience but did not get driblets, or that they did not get driblets because they are not in the audience?

who hold both joyous wedding party and riotous corps de ballet
beneath your sway,
may this our sacrifice and these prayers which now youward rise
find favor in your eyes.

XANTHIAS   *May they do just that, O goddess clearly beyond all esteem, and please*
be upfront about it; don't tease.
Don't imitate those ladies in town
who are always hot to trot, but can never quite get up to getting down.
They sneak to a crack in the door and flash us a peek,
but if they catch our attention, back into the house they streak,
until we lose interest and turn away . . .
at which point they rush back for another enticing mini-display.
Please to avoid such heinous
coyness, your highness.

JACK   *Precisely, your eminence. Your lovers, which is to say We,*
herewith request full-frontal epiphany,
the better to contemplate your charms after a thirteen-year layoff
for which the payoff
will be the cessation of battles and wars and other such passé tricks,
wherefore we shall hail you as PACIFICÁTRIX.
We also beg for an utter remission
of that baroquely paranoid suspicion
which leads to the endless gabbled harangues of each other
that marks this internecine bother.
In fact, undo everything we are and have done,
return to square one
and blend us again, this time into friends,
Hellenic, not manic,
suffused with empathy's gentle precipitate.
We further supplicate
that our market be stuffed with a plenitude
of all good things, to include
Megarian garlic, pomegranates, apples, and early cucumbers
in astonishing numbers,
a line of svelte little jackets for slaves to sport,
a line of carters slaving away to import
Boiotian thrushes and ducks and pigeons and geese
and baskets of scrumptious eels from Lake Kopaïs.[54]
In short, a mass of abundantly glorious stuff
of which there is always enough . . .
until one day, as we cruise the ways
shopping cheek by jowl with all the famous gourmets

---

54. Because Lake Kopaïs was in Boiotia, enemy territory, it was inaccessible to Athenians during the war, and Aristophanes' characters often long for the eels that were caught there.

supplemented by bands
of established gourmands,
we encounter Morychos, gobbler supreme and playwright genteel,
in search of an eel,
but eels are exhausted, so after emitting a yawp of utter frustration
he turns to his only too well-known Medea for an apt quotation:
"She is lost! She is lost! My lovely is lost! She is garnished from human ken!"[55]
And with the request that this will supply a minim of joy to the men
who are standing around, at length I touch
the end of my prayer. Be generous, Goddess.

Thanks very much.

Jack and Xanthias return to the physical business of the ritual.

JACK   Here's the cleaver. Now butcher that sheep with expert
skill.

XANTHIAS   It is not meet and right to do so.

JACK   Why not, pray tell?

XANTHIAS   Peace takes no pleasure in slaughter;
her altar does not drip with gobbets of gore.

JACK   Conduct the victim inside; and do the deed
off-stage, then bring those thigh-pieces back out here . . .
and reduce the producer's expense by the cost of a sheep.

Xanthias leads the sheep into the house. Jack starts to follow, but the Second Semichorus bars his way.

2ND SEMICHO   *Hey, not so fast!*
Don't run away:
*   You have to stay out here*
and pile the altar
high with wood;
*   the rite is very near.*
Then load the rest
upon the top—
*   Get busy! Persevere!*

With astounding skill, Jack prepares the altar
fire, and puts the necessities on top.

JACK   *Right in order*
Goes the wood . . .
Skillful, no?
I thought I could.

---

55. Parker combines Morychos (listed in the Greek text along with several other alleged
gluttons), with the playwright Melanthios, whose *Medea* appears to be quoted here.

2ND SEMICHO   *I stand amazed.*
No expertise
  escapes your subtle hand.
Degrees of skill
from low to high
  are oh so deftly spanned.
The smallest twist
of thumb or fist
  responds to your command!

Jack kindles the fire on the altar. It blazes up.

JACK   *Now the faggots*
are alight,
and, what's more, they're
lighted right.
What do ritual
experts know?
I work like a
real pro!
Where's the table
that we own?
I can get it
all alone.

Off he tears, back into the house again.

2ND SEMICHO   *Who now, perceiving*
this man's might,
  would hesitate to raise
a shout of pure
approval, yea,
  of universal praise?
Your struggles made
  the city free;
your laud will last
  eternally!

Scene IV [1039–1126]

Xanthias and Jack emerge from the house, Xanthias with
the cut-up pieces of sheep, spits, trimming knife, etc., and
Jack with a table, which he places by the altar.

JACK   Well, that's taken care of. Put the thighs on the fire,
while I go get the cakes and the organ meats.

XANTHIAS   The dainty bits? My job.

*He slings the thigh-pieces on the table and races inside. A
pause. Jack, assembling the thigh-pieces, calls out.*

JACK   You're overdue!

*Xanthias tears out of the house, bearing plates of
innards and cakes. He is swallowing.*

XANTHIAS   Present and accounted for. How could you doubt
my promptness?

JACK

*Enter Holy Joe, an itinerant flogger of oracles. He is
warmly dressed in two huge sheepskins.*

Now roast these with finesse; we seem
to have a visitor, fully dressed for the occasion.

XANTHIAS   And who might that be?

JACK   Has all the marks of a humbug.

XANTHIAS   You mean he's a prophet?

JACK   No. A religious expert.
He travels in oracles . . . Yes, it's Holy Joe,
come in from the East.

XANTHIAS   What do you think he'll say?

JACK   If he holds to form, he'll find some way to disrupt
the Peace.

XANTHIAS   Oh, no. The aroma dragged him over.

JACK   Let's pretend he's invisible.

XANTHIAS   Good idea.

HOLY JOE

Descending on the two and officiously inspecting their preparations.

The name and nature of this rite, if you please,
plus proper designation of god-to-which?

JACK   Now, roast in silence . . .
Oops! Away from the rump!

HOLY JOE   Which god? Speak up!

JACK   The tail's coming along
quite well.

XANTHIAS   It is that. Thank you, goddess Peace!

HOLY JOE

Moving up close to the table.

> Commence the slicing!
>   First cut goes to me.

JACK

Finally noticing the pushy intruder.

> It's better when it's cooked.

HOLY JOE   These delicious innards
> are done already.

JACK   I don't care who you are,
> you're interloping.

Piling the spitted innards high in Xanthias' arms.

> Cut these up.

XANTHIAS

Stumbling, his vision blocked.

>   The table—
> where'd it go?

He finds it, puts the innards down, and commences carving.

JACK   Now bring the libation out!

Two goblets are brought from the house.

HOLY JOE   Remember: the tasty tongue is cut and reserved.

JACK   We know that perfectly well. Do you know what
                   you really ought to do?

HOLY JOE   Can you give me a hint?

JACK   Stop trying to start a conversation. We
                   are engaged in a sacrifice to the goddess Peace.

This is a signal for gouts of epic oracular proclamation while Jack nibbles away.

HOLY JOE   *Mortals both luckless and feckless . . .*[56]

---

56. Here Holy Joe and Jack change the meter to dactylic hexameter (6 units of LONG-short-short, with variations), the standard meter of oracles as well as of epic poetry. Parker has recreated the dactylic hexameter in English stressed verse (six units in each verse, each containing a stressed syllable followed by two unstressed syllables [e.g., *Mórtals both*], with variations).

JACK   Your epithets, sir. But add *hopeless.*

HOLY JOE   *Who, in your witlessness, reckless of all the gods' good intentions,*
            deign, though men, to contract a treaty with blazing-eyed apes, and . . .

JACK   Lovely!

HOLY JOE   You find this amusing?

JACK   I enjoyed that *blazing-eyed apes.* It's
            oxymoronic and really a startling new way to say *Spartans.*

HOLY JOE   *Bird-brained boobies entrusting your lives to the mercies of foxes,*
            foxes whose hearts and minds are deceitful, and tricky, and wily!

JACK   Oh that your lungs were just as inflamed as the ones that I'm tasting.

HOLY JOE   *Never did Nymphs bamboozle Bâkis the oracle, nor did*
            Bâkis bamboozle us mortals, nor did Nymphs bamboozle great Bâkis[57] *. . .*

JACK   May your decay be at hand, if you don't put away all this *Bâking!*

HOLY JOE   *Wherefore fate has not yet ordained the unleashing of Peace, ere*
            certain occurrences happen . . .

JACK

    Still nibbling, to Xanthias.

                                  This meat is in need of some salt, no?

HOLY JOE   *Given the blessed gods are extending no favor to quenching*
            battle cries before the wolf joins the lambkin in wedlock . . .

JACK   How in the hell could that happen—the wolf join the lambkin in
                wedlock?

HOLY JOE   *As long as the terrified stinkbug emits her foul crepitation,*
            as long as the polecat in labor emits her blind whelps on the dead run,
            so long will it ever be wrong for a Peace to be brought into being.

JACK   What were our options? Continue the war, unfinished forever?
            Maybe a casting of lots to see who cried uncle the soonest?
            This, when Peace would enable both sides to rule Hellas in tandem?

HOLY JOE   *Never will scuttling crab be made to proceed in a straight line.*

JACK   Never again will you be fed at the city's expense, or
            publish a prophecy forecasting happenings after they're over.

HOLY JOE   *Never will porcupine's spiky back be planed into smoothness.*

JACK   When will our Athens attain some relief from your endless deception?

HOLY JOE   *Cite the oracular text that permitted the cooking of thighs here!*

---

57. Bâkis was a famous oracle of an earlier generation.

JACK   Homer, of course. I'm amazed you don't know it. It's one of his best:[58]
            Thus they rejected the loathsome miasma of wars and of battles,
            chose for themselves bright Peace, with a sacrifice set up her worship.
            And, when the thighs were consumed and when they had eaten the innards,
            poured they libation in goblets; 'twas I led the others in drinking . . .
            but to oracular expert no glistening cup did they proffer.

HOLY JOE   I'm not included in Homer. It would have to be said by the Sibyl.[59]

JACK   Homer's a wise one, however, with many a pertinent passage:[60]
            Cast out from family, homeless and heartless, an outlaw is he who
            lusts to embrace the hideous horror of communes in conflict.

HOLY JOE   *Warning! Beware lest the swooping vulture beguile your perception,*
            snatching away . . .

JACK   Now, there is an oracle worth looking out for:
            Clear and present distress forecast for these delicate innards.
            Pour a libation, and bring me a comfortable serving of organs.

HOLY JOE   Well, then, if nobody minds, I might as well be my own waiter.

Jack and Xanthias call to the house.

JACK   Libation!

XANTHIAS   Libation!

Their cups are refilled.

HOLY JOE   Pour out another for me. And hand me a share of those innards.

JACK   *Nay, for the blessed gods are extending no favor to you, ere*
            certain occurrences happen . . . to wit, our drinking, your slinking.
            —Peace, our Lady, attend us as long as our lives shall continue.

HOLY JOE   Pass me the tongue.

JACK   Remove *your* tongue, or lose it completely.

HOLY JOE   Libation!

JACK

Dumping the castoff trimmings on Holy Joe's head.

                        Here, catch! The libation demands a selection of munchies.

HOLY JOE   Will nobody grant me my portion of organs?

---

58. Jack combines various bits of actual Homeric verse with his own compositions.

59. Sibyl was the name for a number of prophetesses found throughout the Mediterranean world.

60. This is a direct quotation of *Iliad* 9.63–64.

JACK   Impossible; sorry.
      Never to happen until the wolf joins the lambkin in wedlock.

HOLY JOE

  Going to his knees in supplication.

            Innards, I beg you!

JACK   In vain is this sobbing appeal, fellow . . .
      Till that you plane the porcupine's spiky back into smoothness.

  He addresses the audience.

            —Spectators, join us for supper—which features in mighty profusion
            innards for everyone!

HOLY JOE   Me in the bargain?

JACK   You suck on your Sibyl.

HOLY JOE   *Never, by Earth beneath, will the two of you gobble these sweetmeats
            all by yourselves! I'll spirit them off—they're there for the taking!*

  He swoops at the table. Xanthias picks up a club and beats him away.

JACK   Batter that Bâkis black and blue!

HOLY JOE   I'll sue!
            Witnesses—get this down!

JACK   It's etched in my mind
            that you are a charlatan, sir, with a huge appetite.
            Lay on with the quarterstaff, Xanthias! Thwack the quack!

XANTHIAS

  Handing the club to Jack.

            You try for a while. I'm all for stripping the body:
            That set of skins he's wearing must be the fruit
            of deception.
                        —All right, prophet, unship the sheepskins!

  Jack waggles the club at Holy Joe.

JACK   You heard the man!

  Holy Joe drops his coverings and runs off the way he came in.

                        A one-man plague of ravens
            out of the East.

  He calls after the departing Holy Joe.

                    Fly home, and bedevil Euboia!

  Taking as much of their paraphernalia as they can, Jack and
  Xanthias enter the house. The Chorus advances.

Parabasis II [1127–1190]

Here Occurs ye Lesser Parabasis

1ST SEMICHO

Stuffed with gusto	*laced with zest*
by deliverance	*I am blest:*
No more sticky	*helmets now;*
I've been freed from	*army chow.*
Now's the time for	*happiness:*
Battles, No—but	*Bottles, Yes.*
Battles leave me	*sad and dashed;*
what I love is	*getting smashed*
when at fireside	*we recline,*
me and that old	*gang of mine,*
as the seasoned	*twigs and stumps*
flare aloft in	*blazing jumps,*
and the chickpeas	*brown and toast,*
and the acorns	*crack and roast . . .*
with the maid to	*kiss and rub*
while my wife is	*in the tub.*

1ST KORY   No greater gusto exists than that moment at planting's end
when mist filters down from heaven and neighbors stop by for advice:
"So what do we do NOW, Fezziwig?"
                              Expert at revels, I answer:
"My pleasure of choice, when God has done us his best, is Getting
Plastered. Hey, wife, make munchies! First parch three quarts of beans,
then stir in kernels of wheat. And bring out some of those figs.
AND have the girl run out and call Rastus in from the field:
No point whatever today in stripping those dripping vine-leaves
or taking a hoe to the mud when the ground's as squishy as this."

A neighbor chips in:
                              "Someone go to my place and fetch us
that thrush and the brace of finches. And, yes, we had some beestings,
sweet and thick, and rabbit meat, four helpings—unless,
of course, the cat got in last night and ripped them off.
Something was certainly in there, rattling and raising a ruckus.
Anyway, bring us three plates of the rabbit, boy, but save
the fourth as a present for Dear Old Dad. And don't forget
to drop by Aischinades' place and borrow some myrtle, the kind
with berries. And on the way, give Kharínades a holler:
                              God's blessing our fields
                              and upping their yields.
                              He needs to be thanked:
                              Drop by and get tanked."

2ND SEMICHO

When the locust —*sweetes' thang!*—
trills his hymn of *chirp and twang,*
zest and gusto *make me purr,*
rapt inspector, *glad voyeur*
of the early *ripening signs*
on my loaded *Lemnian vines,*
watching tender *figlets swell,*
go from small to *big as hell,*
till they're bidding *fair to pop,*
when I eat and *never stop,*
celebrating *all the day*—
Season's Greetings' *what I say*—
mixing toddies *topped with thyme,*
chomping, swilling, *knowing I'm*
back in my own *habitat,*
spending summer *getting fat . . .*

2ND KORY

. . . a distinct improvement on watching some blot of an infantry
    captain
decked out in three-way crests and a cloak of blinding scarlet,
a hue he declares is imported from Sardis—*Regimental Red.*
But should he be compelled to wear that Red into battle,
he turns a lowdown, homemade shade—*Excremental Brown*—
and leads his troops in retreat, a yellowing figurehead monster
with crests aflap. I stand there aghast, observe him agape.
—Back home from the war, such types don't clean up their act, but
    do us
down and dirty with draft-list juggles, enlisting some
and erasing others all higgledy-piggledy, two-three times:
THE FOLLOWING NAMES
                WILL MUSTER FOR ACTIVE
                        DUTY TOMORROW!
And lo, a draftee who hasn't stocked his mess kit. He wasn't
informed he was due to campaign till a moment ago, when he chanced
to scan the list tacked up in Statuary Row,[61] and, oh,
what a snit, as he races and hurtles around with a curdled face.
And that's how they treat us Rubes. The Townies fare a bit better
at the hands of these commanders, renowned in heaven and earth
as dastards who litter the field of honor with castoff shields.
Please god, their day of accounting is nigh, and I'll get even.
            They've been quite obnoxious,
            *these lions-*cum-*foxes:*

---

61. Public notices were regularly posted among a set of statues on the western side of the
Athenian agora.

At home, they're all roar;
but they skulk in the war.

The Chorus retreats.

Episode I [1191–1304]

Jack, resplendent in the trappings of wealth, emerges from the house.
He gazes off and sees a crowd of tradesmen approaching.

JACK Jiminy!
 Gee willikers!
 Look at those crowds!
I'd say our wedding banquet's about to be *mobbed*.
Take this inside and use it to give the tables
a last-minute swab. That's all it's good for now.
After you've cleaned them, set them: we'll want the sponge cakes,
and piles of thrushes, and rabbit—a mess of rabbit—
not to forget the buns.

SICKLEMAKER Where's JACK?
I say, where's JACK?

JACK He's here. He's boiling
the thrush *potage*. He's me.

SICKLEMAKER O Benefactor Jack!
Our friend in need and indeed, how can I reckon
the blessings and boons that your achievement of Peace
has conferred on us? To be candid, before Today
the sickle trade was simply *sick*. You couldn't
make sickles sell at rock-bottom giveaway prices;
top-of-the-line wouldn't move at two obols the gross.
But now my cut is fifty drachmas *apiece*,
and my colleague here nets three drachs each
on his cheapest line of utility jars for the farm.
Wherefore, Benefactor Jack, accept at your pleasure
this fine assortment of first-class sickles and pots . . .
no charge, of course.
 Plus all the rest of this stuff:
These spades and plowshares, winnowing fans and hoes,
in fond outpouring—the implements of Peace!
These wedding contributions are funded, of course,
from our truly outrageous blizzard of windfall profits.

JACK I'll take the gifts in tow; deposit them here.
And you are invited inside, for the wedding feast—
no waiting. Let's hurry it up, in fact, because

> I spy another guest on the way—a fine buck
> military-industrial profiteer,
> who's mad as hell and moving in this direction.

The Sicklemaker enters the house. A gaggle of disconsolate businessmen advances, each with his own complaint.

**BREASTPLATE
BARON**   *OOOGODDAMNOUCH!*

                    I have been ruint, Reaper!
            Uprooted and left to rot, and it's all your fault!

JACK   Poor chap, what's your complaint? You don't look well,
            with that ugly eruption of lunatic fringe on your head.

**BREASTPLATE
BARON**   My complaint, you raider, is YOU! You sent my business
            up the spout and my lifestyle down the drain!
            You ruint ME,
                    and this trumpet[62] tycoon,
                                    and this big
            bazoo in the javelin game.

JACK   I'll start with you:
            What's the going rate for this brace of crests?

**BREASTPLATE
BARON**   You first. Let's hear your bid.

JACK   My bid? I blush
            to tell you.
                    Still, it's very labor-intensive,
            what with this grommeted flange to steady the hairs . . .
            For the pair, I guess I could go as high as a peck
            of sun-dried figs.

**BREASTPLATE
BARON**   I'll take it. Go get your figs.

To the Trumpet Tycoon beside him.

            —Well, chum, I figure that figs are better than zilch.

Jack inspects the crests and throws them back.

JACK   No! Take, oh, take these crests away, to hell
            and beyond! Such dreck, I wouldn't give it houseroom!
            They're shedding out of season—we're talking **shoddy**.
            For crests gone bald, a *single* fig's too much.

---

62. The Greeks used the salpinx, a long trumpet-like instrument with no valves, almost entirely for military signals.

BREASTPLATE BARON	I'm desperate; please take advantage of me! Look: such beautiful lines, a guaranteed perfect fit. . . .
JACK	What is it?
BREASTPLATE BARON	That, my friend, is a genuine Cuirass!
JACK	Queerest one I ever saw.
BREASTPLATE BARON	To you, a breastplate. Materials, labor alone—a thousand drachmas.
JACK	That's cheap enough; you should break even on this one. I'll take it—provided, of course, you sell it at cost. My, what a practical shitpot. A most convenient convenience. For one who has to Make Do.
BREASTPLATE BARON	*STOP!* No more muckraking. I won't let you smear my stock!
JACK	Observe: Add three smooth stones at the side, for personal daintiness . . . Voilà! The crapper supreme! Smart, no?
BREASTPLATE BARON	Of all the idiots . . . How do you wipe yourself?
JACK	Remember, the way to the asshole is through the armhole. So, first the right . . . and then the left.
BREASTPLATE BARON	Both hands at once?
JACK	I'm ambidextrous. Besides, I wouldn't care to be charged with leaving an unplugged loophole.
BREASTPLATE BARON	You are about to employ a thousand-drachma breastplate to sit on and *SHIT*?
JACK	I certainly am. My ass, on the open market, should surely bring in considerably more than a measly thousand drachmas.
BREASTPLATE BARON	The deal is sealed; go get the money.

JACK   No way.
I just fell through, my friend; so did the deal.
Observing my rule of trade—*No Skin Off My Ass*—
I void our contract. No Sale; back to the factory.

The Baron retreats in consternation. The Trumpet Tycoon advances.

TRUMPET
TYCOON   Well, how can I convert this trumpet to peacetime
use? It cost me sixty drachmas, back
when a drach was a drach!

JACK   Absurdly simple.
Invert the trumpet, and fill the Orifice A—
the bell—with molten lead.
                              —You follow me?

TRUMPET
TYCOON   I think so . . .

JACK   Fine. Next, after it cools, invert
the trumpet again and insert, in the Orifice B—
the mouthpipe—a long, thin rod.
                              —You see?

TRUMPET
TYCOON   I guess . . .

JACK   Perfect. Then secure two disks, of equal
diameter, pierced in the middle with equal holes.
Fit one down low, on the bell of the trumpet; the other
is balanced atop the end of the long, thin rod.
—You're getting this all?

TRUMPET
TYCOON   Oh, yes!

JACK   Then carefully take
the whole damned mess and jam it up your ass.

TRUMPET
TYCOON   I will not be made fun of!

JACK   Well, then, try this:
The trumpet, loaded with lead, will make a convenient
weight for a scale in weighing out figs and the like.

The Trumpet Tycoon stalks off in rather depressed dud-
geon. The Helmet Honcho advances.

HELMET HONCHO

Clutching a pair of huge helmets.

> O curse abiding, who will not go away!
> I once put down *my* drachma to purchase this pair,
> and now they're worthless. Who's going to bail me out?

JACK   The Egyptians might. They have a thing about bowels,
and one of these should hold a dose of cathartic.

BREASTPLATE BARON

To the Helmet Honcho.

> *I* sympathize, friend. Disaster has struck us both.

JACK   I don't see why you say that; he's all right.

**BREASTPLATE
BARON**   *All right?* With the shape the helmet market's in?

JACK   That's just the point. He only needs to add handles—
using his very own ears for models—and bingo!
he makes a real killing and corners cups!

BREASTPLATE BARON

To the only businessman left.

> Spearmaker, let's get out of here.

JACK   Oh, no,
not him. I'll put down good hard cash for his spears.

**BREASTPLATE
BARON**   How much good hard cash?

JACK   Saw them in half—
good vine-props. I can go as high as, oh,
a drachma a gross.

**BREASTPLATE
BARON**   Gross is the word—gross insult!

To the Spearmaker.

> All right, friend, let's split.

They leave. Jack watches them go.

JACK   A good idea.
The guests' little kids are already coming out
to take a pee—or rather sound an A
and practice the songs they're going to sing for the party.

Two little boys have come out of Jack's house. He beckons to the first one.

> Stand right here, son, and strike up the opening bars
> of the song you intend to sing to regale us all.

1ST BOY   *Now begin we our song of Warriors, younger in . . .*

JACK   Stop
> singing a song about warriors, wholly abominable infant,
> now that the country's at Peace. What an utterly stupid delinquent!

1ST BOY   *Now when at last they confronted each other in closest of quarters,*
> *clashing together their bucklers and shields with studs at the navel . . .*

JACK   Shields? I don't like shields. Please cut the shields from your song.

1ST BOY   *Now there arose ululations of agony, howls of triumph . . .*

JACK   Agony? Howls? By Bacchos, watch out, or I'll ululate *you*, kid!
> Bawling in agony, doubtless because of the studs in your navel.

1ST BOY   Tell me a song, and I'll sing it. Are there *any* subjects you like?

JACK   *Thus did they banquet hearty on ox-flesh.* Or else try this one:
> *Breakfast was laid out before them, a positive feast for the taste.*

1ST BOY   *Thus did they banquet hearty on ox-flesh, and freed from yoking*
> *the glistening necks of their horses, for that they were sated with battle.*

JACK   *Sated* is good. They were *sated* with battle, and next had dinner.
> That's the song you should sing: First sating, then eating. Go on:

1ST BOY   *Then did they load themselves . . .*

JACK   I'll *bet* they did . . .

1ST BOY   *. . . with their armor,*
> *and flooded out over the walls, and the war cry wailed in its triumph . . .*

JACK   You are the most embattled kid I have ever encountered.
> Can't you sing about anything else? So who's your daddy?

1ST BOY   Mine?

JACK   That's who I mean.

1ST BOY   Lamachos, general of the army.

JACK   Yecch.
> Yea did I wonder, anon that I heard you, whether you might be
> brat of some bellicose booby who misses being in battle.
> Scat, and sing to an infantry company somewhere.

The 1st Little Boy re-enters the house.

> And now, could I have Kleonymos' offspring up here?

The 2nd Little Boy advances.

> Sing me a song before you go back inside.
> Whatever song you want; it doesn't matter.
> I know that it won't be a song about danger, given
> the rather cautious nature your Daddy has.

2ND BOY *Some Saian soldier now takes his joy in my blameless shield.*
I left it in all its beauty behind a bush. Not that I wanted to . . .[63]

JACK You're singing an excerpt, I gather, from Daddy's biography—no?

2ND BOY *But I saved my life . . .*

JACK   Thereby preserving the family shame . . .
> Let's go inside.
>   You'll certainly never forget
> the Song of the Shield. Not with the Daddy you've got.

The 2nd Little Boy goes into the house. Jack turns to the Chorus.

Stasimon I [1305–1317]

> [Herewith a small lacuna.][64]

Exodos [1318–1367]

JACK

Forming the head of a wedding procession with Lady Bountiful.

> Silence, all!
>   Escort the bride out to greet her husband!
> Fetch torches! Let throng rejoice and cheer us on!
> Move all our belongings out of the city, back to the country!
> But first the dance, and then the libation, and then the ejection
> of Hyperbolos out of the city, just to be thoroughly certain,
>   and then the prayer to the gods:
>   grant the Greeks prosperity,
>   the planting and harvest
>   of barley in loads
>   and wine in plenty
>   and figs to finish the meal,
>   and wives who bear us children,

---

63. The boy quotes the opening of a poem by the seventh-century poet Archilochos (fragment 5).

64. Parker left untranslated verses 1305–1317, in which Jack offers food left on stage to the chorus, and they offer the same food to the audience. For a prose translation of the passage, see Appendix A.

and full restoration in gathering
all we have lost and putting
it back together.
And let the shiny steel rust.

To Lady Bountiful.

The way lies clear to the country.
Lie by my side in beauty.

1ST SEMICHO	*Hail, Hymen Hymenaios!*[65]
2ND SEMICHO	*Hail, Hymen Hymenaios!*
1ST KORY	*Happy and more than happy,* *To have the blessings you deserve!*
1ST SEMICHO	*Hail, Hymen Hymenaios!*
2ND SEMICHO	*Hail, Hymen Hymenaios!*
1ST KORY	

Turning to Lady Bountiful.

What do we do with the bride?

2ND KORY	*What do we do with the bride?*
1ST SEMICHO	*We reap her harvest!*
2ND SEMICHO	*We reap her harvest!*

They raise Lady Bountiful on their shoulders.

1ST KORY	*All you who stand in the front rank,* *exalt the groom on high!*

They raise Jack on their shoulders.

1ST SEMICHO	*Hail, Hymen Hymenaios!*
2ND SEMICHO	*Hail, Hymen Hymenaios!*
2ND KORY	*Your lives will be happy and joyous,* *empty of trouble* *and full of figs.*
1ST SEMICHO	*Hail, Hymen Hymenaios!*
2ND SEMICHO	*Hail, Hymen Hymenaios!*
1ST KORY	*His fig is big and thick!*
2ND KORY	*Her fig is lush and sweet!*

---

65. This is a traditional wedding chant invoking Hymen, the god of weddings.

JACK   *The sort of remark that gets made*
                when you're full of food
                and fuller still of wine.

1ST SEMICHO   *Hail, Hymen Hymenaios!*

2ND SEMICHO   *Hail, Hymen Hymenaios!*

JACK   Audience, hail and farewell!
                Follow me on off-stage,
                and receive a meal
                of pattycakes . . .
                                Zey are delicious!

Exeunt omnes, singing and dancing.

Middle Comedy: Aristophanes' *Money, the God*

Money, the God, first presented in 388 BCE, is the last Aristophanic comedy that survives. The play is far less conspicuously concerned with contemporary public life than is *Peace;* nevertheless, recent events in Athens and elsewhere may have helped inspire the play's fantasy of a miraculous redistribution of wealth.

As we have seen, Athens lost the Peloponnesian War in 404 BCE. With that defeat came the loss of Athens' empire and the tribute the empire brought. In the 390s Athens renewed her wars against Sparta, further depleting the public coffers. After decades of war, many other Greek city-states were similarly strapped. It is thus no coincidence that at the end of the play Money is reinstalled next to the Parthenon, the location of Athens' public treasury. Our information on the private resources of Athenian citizens is less secure, but in this respect the play appears to respond to the perpetual differences between rich and poor rather than to any specific economic downturn.

The most conspicuous difference between *Money, the God* and Aristophanes' earlier plays is that the play's text preserves no words for any long song of the chorus except the parodos. Instead, the songs are merely indicated in the manuscripts of the play with the word *chorou* ([song] of the chorus) or, in one case, *kommation chorou* (little song of the chorus). To some extent this absence of words may reflect a lack of interest in the chorus on the part of scribes and readers rather than of producers and audience members: significant words of the chorus may have simply not been preserved as Aristophanes' script was copied. Most likely, however, the dearth of choral songs in the text, especially the fact that the play has no parabasis, suggests that by 388, in a significant move away from the norms of Old Comedy, the chorus had become more decorative and less central to the play's plot.

The structure of *Money, the God,* as presented in Parker's scene headings, is as follows:

Verses	Section	Events
1–252	Prologue (everything before the first entrance of the chorus)	Khremylos and Karion capture Money, and Khremylos plans to have Money's blindness cured
253–321	Parodos	Karion leads on the Chorus and explains about Money; they dance and exchange insults
CHOROU	Choral dance	No words preserved
322–486	Proagon	Khremylos explains the situation to Blepsidemos; Poverty enters and challenges them
487-626	Agon	Poverty and Khremylos argue and Poverty is expelled; Khremylos and others take Money to the shrine of Asklepios
CHOROU	Choral dance	No words preserved

627–770	Episode I	Karion tells Khremylos' wife about the healing of Wealth
KOMMATION CHOROU	Choral Dance	No words preserved
771–801	Episode II	Wealth returns
CHOROU	Choral dance	No words preserved
802–958	Episode III	Karion welcomes the Righteous Man, and they eject the Informer
CHOROU	Choral dance	No words preserved
959–1096	Episode IV	Kremylos oversees a debate between the Decayed Gentlewoman and the Young Stud
CHOROU	Choral dance	No words preserved
1097–1209	Exodos	Karion takes in Hermes; Kremylos takes in a Priest; procession leading Money to the Parthenon

ΑΡΙΣΤΟΦΑΝΟΥΣ
ΠΛΟΥΤΟΣ

BY
ARISTOPHANES

translated by
douglass parker

The Set

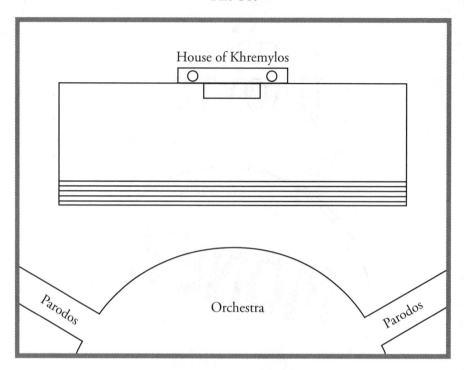

House of Khremylos

Parodos

Orchestra

Parodos

SCENE: The outskirts of Athens,[1] ca. 389/388 BCE. The *orchestra*—the Chorus's dancing ground—may as well stand for a public plaza; the platform stage represents a near-country road, on which we discern the farmhouse of Khremylos, probably center.[2] At the play's beginning, this house is a basic poverty-line hovel; suddenly, after the return of MONEY from Asklepios' temple, it will blossom into a dwelling of real opulence and ostentation. (The accomplishment of this transformation, on a stage without curtain during a performance without break, should be a real challenge to the designer, and I should perhaps stress that it is nowhere *demanded* by the original text—or, indeed, by the translation.)

There are two basic Outside ports to and from the stage. *Entrance/Exit Stage Right,* whether by wing-exit or parodos or any other liminal device, connects with parts out of town, foreign or rural: the farm, Epidauros, and Delphi, if need be. *Entrance/Exit Stage Left* is the link to the rest of Athens. It is suggested that, if possible, the three-man procession at the play's beginning should not enter from an entrance on the stage itself. Ideally, they would enter by the parodos which debouches in front of far stage right and proceed to wander around the *orchestra* for a while. But, in the event that a Greek theater is not among a given company's

---

1. In another typescript Parker sets the play on a city street in Athens.

2. Or maybe not. The location of Khremylos' house stage left or right would certainly leave more playing room on a shallow stage, and there's something to be said for that [Parker's note].

capital assets, the trio might well enter at the back of the auditorium and proceed to make nuisances of themselves while the audience is quieting down, bumping into things and people and arriving, eventually, at the proscenium stage. Consideration of such an expedient is also advised for the Chorus, which, in default of two parodoi, might enter in their two semichoruses and proceed down the principal aisles.

There need be no other buildings on stage; if designers are confronted with the necessity of using three fixed doors, there are two obvious candidates for the position of householder: Khremylos' neighbor Blepsidemos, longtime owner of the *Cottage,* stage right, and the Decayed Gentlewoman, mistress of the imposing *Manse,* stage left.

Dramatis Personae

KÁRION,	*a slave*
KHRÉMYLOS,	*his master, an aged Athenian*
MONEY,	*the God*
FIRST KORYPHAIOS	
SECOND KORYPHAIOS	
CHORUS OF AGED FARMERS	
BLEPSIDÉMOS,	*another aged Athenian*
POVERTY,	*the Goddess*
KHRÉMYLOS' WIFE	
A RIGHTEOUS MAN	
HIS SMALL SLAVE [MUTE]	
AN INFORMER	
HIS WITNESS [MUTE]	
A DECAYED GENTLEWOMAN	
HER MAID [MUTE]	
A YOUNG STUD	
HERMES,	*the God*
A PRIEST OF ZEUS	
ASSORTED ATHENIANS	

Money, The God

Prologue [1–252]

At the start, the stage is empty. Enter a strange procession of three: [1] a
blind old man, with cane, who advances erratically with a trembling stum-
ble, or possibly a stumbling tremble; [2] the aged farmer KHREMYLOS,
whose clothes proclaim him a citizen, albeit a poor one, and who dogs the
tracks of [1] without getting too close: and [3] the slave KARION, reluctantly tagging after [2], his master, and quite puzzled about the whole pro-
cedure—as well he might be, since [1]'s trail is anything but direct: The
company wanders over the stage's surface, now here, now there, making circles and figure eights that lead to no destination in particular.

KARION

To the heavens.

>   Hello, up there!
>   Hey, Zeus?
>   The rest of you gods?
> I didn't think the job would be easy, but this
> is just too much: I'm slave to a master whose mind
> has popped a hinge.
>   Now, look, I know the rules:
> As wise as a Service Person's advice might be,
> should his owner refuse it, said Service Person
> is still on the hook: The Nature of Things assigns him
> full shares in his master's disasters, since Fate or Destiny
> firmly denies to the Bought One the least control
> of his very own flesh, and gives those rights to the Buyer.
> And that's the way it is.
>   But just this once,
> I have, I believe, a justified bitch to bring
> against Apollo, the God of Spin and Skew,
> who sits on his gilded tripod and drools the future.
> Know what he's done?
>   That Sayer of Sooth (or so
> they say), that mighty divine MD, that heavenly
> whiz has made hash of my Master's metabolism
> and turned him into a brooder, a chartered compulsive,
> a follower after the lead of a stone-blind guide—
> thus reversing logical, proper behavior.
> Do I have to point out that seeing people, like us,

are the ones who *lead* the blind? But not my man.
He *follows,* and makes ME follow, on pain of . . . pain.
What's worse, any questions I have on this curious action,
he refuses to grace with the merest grumble or grunt.
[Hell, I'd be happy to hear some heavy breathing.]

He catches up with Khremylos.

Look here, respected Owner: I'm not a mute.
I canNOT guarantee silence unless you supply me
the why and wherefore: Why are we wobbling along
in that fellow's wake?
                                        You'd better answer!
                                                    I warn you:
I hereby pledge myself as a source of trouble.
You have no power to stop me; I kept my wreath
from the shrine at Delphi.
                            And now I'm putting it on . . .

He puts the wreath on his head.

You have to play by the rules: You cannot beat
or dismember a man who wears a wreath. Remember?

KHREMYLOS   That's true. But if you persist in causing annoyance
from under the shield of a wreath, I'll remove it, *thus,*

He takes the wreath from Karion's head.

and batter you blue and bloody, *thus,*

He begins to beat Karion.

                                        until
your complaints of pain acquire a bit more substance.

KARION

Dodging the blows quite skillfully.

DRIVEL!
POPPYCOCK!
                        AND LOUSY AIM!
I intend to persist in this course of questions and curses
until you inform me, *nicely,* just who the hell
HE is, inasmuch as I,

Striking a pose of obvious sincerity.

                        pursuant to my role
of Dedicated Slave, have only, in making this query,
my Master's Best Interests at Heart.

KHREMYLOS

Missing with a final blow.

                                        Oh, hell. Very well,
            I'll disclose my secret to you,

Striking a pose of obvious sincerity.

                              inasmuch as I
            regard you, of all my slaves, as the Most Devoted
            to Lightening Me of Life's Burdens—
                                        and everything else
            that's not nailed down.

Changing the pose.

                        Behold me: What do you see?

Karion starts to answer, but Khremylos hurries on.

            I know what you're going to say:
                                A Man of Marvel,
            in Piety, Peerless; in Justice, a Giant. . .
                                        but One
            Whose Virtues have Earned him Failure,
                                        Cashlessness.

KARION   I'm with you there.

KHREMYLOS   . . . while who, might I ask, got MONEY?
            The robbers of churches, the jobbers of summonses, fobbers
            of writs—in a word (to sum up the tenor of these
            remarks), the BASE!

KARION   All right. I can handle that.

KHREMYLOS

In full flood.

            The pilgrimage, then, to Delphi, for consultation
            with Prophet Apollo, I undertook not for myself—
            the wretch you see before you, quiver depleted,
            life's bow feebly bent to shoot its last bolt.
            Ah, no. I went for my Son, my One, my Only—
            as things are now, the last I'm likely to have.
            My queries were aimed at his welfare:
                                        Should this slip
            of a lad completely transform his lifestyle? Become
            a rogue, a yegg, a gem of injustice—in sum,
            a nogoodnick par excellence? Was that the way,
            the only way—as I feared and believed—for him
            to attain some worldly success before he died?

KARION

Paratragic pose.

> *What spake Apollo out from under his wreaths?*

KHREMYLOS   What I am about to tell you.

He shrugs, and strikes a paratragic pose of his own.

> *Apollo spake me*
> *Sooth.*
> *Yea, clearly.*
> *Thus.*

He drops the pose and goes ahead in plain language.

> He gave me an order
> To collar the first man I met when I left the temple
> and hang on tight until I persuaded that man
> to come on home with me.

KARION   I think I see.
> And that first man you met when you left the temple,
> Who might he have been, pray tell?

KHREMYLOS

Pointing at the Blind Man.

> *Behold the Man!*

KARION   You have just run away with First Place in the Dumbness Derby.
> How could you miss the God's meaning? It's perfectly clear:
> Follow your Culture Pattern. Make him BASE!

KHREMYLOS   How did you reach a conclusion like that?

KARION   Because
> it's simple, so simple a BLIND MAN can see it plain:
> To ensure your son's success in present-day Athens,
> the only Healthy way to raise him to manhood
> is positively Diseased:
>   To be RIGHT, be WRONG.

KHREMYLOS   Impossible!
>   No!
>   No oracle sinks so low.
> The Scales of Fate have something higher in mind,
> and this guy here is the key. If I can compel him,
> whoever he is, to tell us whoever he is,
> and WHY, whereFOR, and whereTO he made this trip
> with the two of us, we might just find out WHAT
> our oracle means.

KARION

Grabbing roughly at the Blind Man, who is, as it happens, the god MONEY.

> Okay, bud. Here's your choice:
> Your name—the truth—or else

Waggling a fist.

> I send you straight
> to the consequences.
> Quick, now; what's your answer?

MONEY

Slashing viciously but inaccurately with his cane.

> My answer to you is ***VAMOOSE***!

KARION   Never heard of the fellow.
> No Greek, that's sure.

To Khremylos.

> Does VAMOOSE strike a chord with you?

KHREMYLOS   That reply was addressed to you, not me. I fear
> your interrogation is lacking in skill and finesse.

He approaches MONEY as one gentleman to another.

> Your taste appears to run, Sir, to the Man of Manners
> whose word is as good as his bond. Make answer to Me, please.

MONEY

With another vicious and inaccurate slash.

> My answer to you is *GET STUFFED*!

KARION   Well, there's your man,
> and there's Apollo's meaning. Take *his* advice.

KHREMYLOS

Grabbing MONEY roughly by one arm.

> You have my word that your future contains no Joy.
> Your name—or I will waste you the worst way, so help me!

MONEY

Deflated and discouraged.

> Gentlemen, please go away and leave me alone?

KARION

Grabbing MONEY by the other arm.

> Why, sure.
>> —Hey, boss, take my advice on this.
> I know the best way to waste him the worst way, so let me.
> I'll set him up
>> on the edge of a cliff
>>> and then
> in cold blood—get this—
>> *I'll walk away and leave him!*
> And down he falls,
>> and snaps his neck!
>>> Please, boss?

KHREMYLOS

Thinking it over, but not for long.

> Adequate, adequate.
>> Quick, now . . . *UPSY-DAISY!*

He and Karion hoist the feebly struggling MONEY into the air.

MONEY   *NO! NO!*
> *DON'T DO IT!*

KHREMYLOS

As they set MONEY down with jarring suddenness.

> All right, then, **TALK**!

MONEY   If I do, and you learn
> my name, you'll do something PERfectly AWful. I'll never
> get loose.

KHREMYLOS   Of course you will.

Pledging with his free hand.

>   Word of Zeus:
> If loose you want, it's loose you're going to get.

MONEY   Then would you take your hands off, *please*?

The two (Karion quite reluctantly) unhand him.

KHREMYLOS   So there
> you are, as ordered. Hands off.

MONEY   Please pay attention.
> I'd planned to keep it a secret, but now I guess

I'll have to tell you:

I AM

The Great God

MONEY.

A shocked pause. Then both grab him again, very quickly and very tightly.

KHREMYLOS *O ROOT OF ALL EVIL!*

A secret like that, and you wouldn't

tell us?

O DIRTY MONEY!

KARION

Dubious, but keeping a tight hold nevertheless.

I don't believe you.

Call yourself MONEY—look at you: MONEY's not *needy.*

KHREMYLOS

In a transport, to the sky.

Hear that, Apollo? And all you other Gods?
And apprentice Gods?

Hey. Zeus, get a load of THIS!

—You know what you're saying? You really mean you're MONEY?

MONEY The very same.

KHREMYLOS The veriest same?

MONEY None samer.

KHREMYLOS

Backing off and assessing MONEY's scrubby appearance.

I've heard of filthy lucre, but you're disgusting.
Why so cruddy?

MONEY You'd be just as cruddy.

Pointing at a member of the audience.

I just twisted out of the fist of Patrokles[3] there;
he hasn't taken a bath since the day he was born.

KHREMYLOS But, friend, this horrid handicap—how did it happen?
Come on, now, you can tell *me.*

MONEY It was Zeus. He did it.
He can't stand humans having the least advantage.

---

3. A wealthy miser.

But I had ideals when I was a kid, and I shot off
my mouth, and I swore that I, that MONEY, would go
only to men who were Decent, and Just, and Wise.
That did it, Zeus made me blind; He didn't want me
to figure out which ones they were.

                                But that's
His way: Pathologically jealous of men who are Good.

KHREMYLOS I can't believe it! Who worships Zeus *except*
the men who are Good?

                    And the Just, of course.

MONEY

  Shrugging.

                                        I agree.

KHREMYLOS Well, let's see, now: If your sight were restored again,
as sharp as it used to be, you would, I take it,
shun the way of the Wicked?

MONEY   I would indeed.

KHREMYLOS You'd make your way to the Just?

MONEY   I certainly would.
I haven't caught sight of the Just since I don't know when.

KARION

  Scanning the audience.

         Big deal. I haven't either, and *I* can see.

MONEY   All right, then, let me loose.

  Firm non-compliance from the two.

                      On the subject of Me,
you've got the facts you wanted—
                        LET GO!

KHREMYLOS   In the name of Zeus,
I refuse. We're not going to let *you* go. Oh, no.

MONEY Didn't I tell you you'd make trouble for me?
My very words.

KHREMYLOS   Come on, now, MONEY honey,
Trust Me. Stay by my side. The wide world over,
you'll never find a better man than me.

KARION That's true, because there isn't one.

                        Except me.

MONEY   That's what they all say. But when they enter in
           to possession of me, become real Men of MONEY,
           they plumb new heights of utter depravity.

KHREMYLOS   Right,
           they do. Still, not everybody's bad.

MONEY   That's true.
           Every-BLOODY-body is bad.

KARION   *GET STUFFED!*

KHREMYLOS

Improvising desperately as MONEY strains to get away.

           But what about the BENEFITS if you stick with us?

A take from MONEY, who has a certain natural cupidity.

           And the PROFIT, too—
                              unless you'd rather not hear . . .

MONEY   What profit?

KHREMYLOS   Yours. Care to hear about it?

MONEY   I do.

KHREMYLOS Then pay attention.

MONEY   I'm *paying* attention.

KHREMYLOS   Because
           I intend . . .

MONEY   Yes? Yes?

KHREMYLOS   . . . I intend as God is my witness . . .

MONEY   Yes? Yes? Yes?

KHREMYLOS   . . . I firmly, and justly, and truly
           intend . . .

MONEY

Out of breath, and more than a little annoyed.

                     To *WHAT*?

KHREMYLOS

Triumphantly lighting on an idea at the last moment.

                              To reverse your Ophthalmic Dysfunction!

MONEY   To *WHAT*?

KHREMYLOS *TO MAKE YOU **SEE** AGAIN, STUPID!*

MONEY

His eager greed changing to abject terror.

NO! DON'T!

Not that! I never want to see again!

KARION   This guy is by nature your basic masochist, no?

MONEY

To the audience.

How do I deal with these loonies? If Z-Zeus finds out
their idiot plan, I know He'll grind me to bits!

KHREMYLOS   He does a good job of it now. Pure *laissez-faire:*
You bang into things, become less, and He thinks that's fair.

MONEY   All I know is, He makes me shake all over.

KHREMYLOS   Of all the timid divinities. You can't mean that.
Do you really believe all Zeus' illegal might,
with lightning thrown in, will fetch three obols at auction,
if you, for only a moment, can see again?

MONEY   Oh, *SHHHHH*! You're **NAUGHTY**! Don't *SAY* that! *PLEASE*!

KHREMYLOS   Shut up.

Observe my demonstration. I shall establish
that your puissance is a far more powerful force
than Zeus's rough presumption.

MONEY   *MINE* is? Than *HIS*?

KHREMYLOS   As Zeu—as Heaven is my judge, you are the greatest.

Unhanding Money, who is too amazed to run away, Khremylos and Karion go into their scam.

For starters: Zeus rules the Gods. What makes this happen?

KARION   It's CASH that does it. Zeus has the most CASH.

KHREMYLOS   All right,

who is it, now, that gives Him this CASH?

KARION

Jerking a thumb at Money.

This guy.

KHREMYLOS   Do men make offerings, now, to Zeus?

KARION   They do.

KHREMYLOS   On whose account?

KARION   On *his* account.

KHREMYLOS   These men:
They pray?

KARION   They do.

KHREMYLOS   And *how* do they pray?

KARION   "Oh Zeus,"
they say, "we pray on account of We Want *MONEY*!"

KHREMYLOS

With a wave at MONEY.

I rest my case. Behold the Ultimate Source.

Casually.

Of course, he could easily bring this state of affairs
to a halt, if he wished . . .

MONEY   Whazzat? I could?
                                        Halt *what?*

KHREMYLOS   The Offerings: No more cattle from men to Zeus.
And no more goodies. In fact, friend, no more Nuthin'.
If that's what you really want. . . .

MONEY   But how?

KHREMYLOS   But *HOW?*
But HOW can a man buy a gift to offer if you
aren't there to give him the CASH? Do you know HOW?

MONEY   No; how?

KHREMYLOS   ***NOHOW!***
                          Which means: If Zeus gives you
the slightest flak, you'll lay His authority low,
all by yourself.

MONEY   You mean men make sacrifices
to Zeus on MY account?

KHREMYLOS   That's just what I mean.
But wait, there's more. In the case of *Humans,* now:
    All things bright and beautiful,
        All things sweet and fine—
    They come about on one account,
        And that account is THINE!

MONEY   *MINE?*

KHREMYLOS   Everything bows the neck and bends the knee
              to MONEY!

KARION   Especially me. In my case, now:
                        My life was bright and beautiful,
                          My life was flush and free—
                        Until, in Court, I came up short,
                          Enslaved on account of THEE!

MONEY   *ME?*

KHREMYLOS   *In Korinth[4] town, the daughters of joy*
                        (I tell the tale that's told)
                Treat cashless fellows in their bordellos
                        To nothing but shoulder, cold.

                But when the Rich Man enters in,
                        The Korinth girls, en masse.
                Heat up their honey for the Man of MONEY,
                        And load him with pieces of ass.

KARION   *The smooth-cheeked boys act just the same*
                        When push comes down to shove:
                A deft maneuver—they bend right over
                        And do it for MONEY, not love.

KHREMYLOS

    Breaking off the doggerel.

              Now, wait. Not Good Little Boys. The Bad Little Boys,
              I agree. But Good Little Boys don't do it for CASH.

KARION   Why *do* they do it?

KHREMYLOS   For *Kind,* for a gentleman's *Kind.*
              A jumper, perhaps. Or a brace of pointers. Or setters.

KARION   *They turn their backs, they close their eyes,*
                        They try to mask their shame
                By calling it barter to make it better . . .
                        But they DO IT all the same.

KHREMYLOS   In fact, to put it generally. . . .
                        All human arts and industries,
                          All things that people DO,
                        Without a doubt, they come about
                        Through One Sole Cause: That's YOU!

---

4. The city of Korinth was famous for its prostitutes, including temple prostitutes for
Aphrodite.

MONEY   *ME?*

KHREMYLOS   *You're the Reason the tinker tinks,*
                          The cobbler's shoes get soled,
                          The fuller fulls, the hauler pulls . . .

KARION   *The goldsmith smiths YOUR gold.*

KHREMYLOS   *You're the Reason the launderer launds,*
                          The potter pots his jugs,
                          The harper harps, the carpenter carps . . .

KARION   *For you, the mugger mugs.*

KHREMYLOS   *You're the Reason the tanner tans,*
                          The grocer spurns his day off . . .

KARION   *When the old roué is caught in the hay,*
                          Through you he makes his payoff.

MONEY   My goodness, I don't see how I never noticed . . .

Khremylos and Karion turn to address the audience . . .

KHREMYLOS   *He's the Reason the King of Persia*
                          Is hoity and haughty and proud.

KARION   *He's the Reason a salaried session*
                          Of Congress draws a crowd.[5]

. . . and then turn back to MONEY.

KHREMYLOS   *Who fits the Navy's dreadnoughts out*
                          With officers and crew?

KARION   *The Foreign Legion's a living legend*[6]—
                          Who keeps it breathing? YOU!

KHREMYLOS   *Sham Pamphilos*[7] *embezzles, though*
                          His expectations are dim . . .

KARION   *His partner cooks the company books,*
                          But they're both doomed. Why? HIM!

KHREMYLOS   *Through HIM, Agyrrhios*[8] *lets his farts . . .*

---

5. The first citizens to arrive at a meeting of Athens' assembly (the *ekklesia*) were paid a small fee.

6. The Athenians had recently used a mercenary force with remarkable success in a battle against the Spartans.

7. An Athenian politician and general.

8. A leading politician.

KARION	*Philepsios[9] jokes on the dais . . .*
KHREMYLOS	*Our Egyptian pact is now a fact[10] . . .*
KARION	*Philonides screws Lais.[11]*
KHREMYLOS	*Timotheos raised a tower up[12] . . .*
KARION	*So it could squash YOU flat.*
KHREMYLOS	*All business' source is YOU, of course,* *And that, my friend, is THAT.*

> *You're the Cause of Everything,*
> *You're Origin Number One*
> *Of Bad, and Good, and Shouldn't, and Should.*
> *You're the Reason it's done.*

Again to the audience.

> *There's never a war he doesn't decide*
> *Almost before it begins.*
> *He simply piles himself in the scales:*
> *The side he sits on wins.*

MONEY	I'm only one God. Can I really do all that?
KHREMYLOS	*But that was merely starters. Now* *Get set for SUBSTANTIAL stuff,* *Since you're an itch, my good sir, which* *No man can scratch enough.*

> *Look: Every man can get Too Much*
> *Of all the things there are:*
> *POSITION!*

KARION	*—and biscuits—*
KHREMYLOS	*PASSION!*
KARION	*—and briskets—*
KHREMYLOS	*CULTURE!*
KARION	*—and caviar.*
KHREMYLOS	*COURAGE!*
KARION	*—and porridge—*

---

9. Another politician.

10. In seeking allies against Sparta, Athens had recently made an alliance with the leader of Egypt, which was in rebellion against the Persian empire.

11. Lais was a famous courtesan, Philonides a wealthy but ugly man.

12. Timotheos was a wealthy Athenian who built a large mansion.

KHREMYLOS	*HONOR!*
KARION	*—and onions—*
KHREMYLOS	*AMBITIOUSNESS!*
KARION	*—lamb stew—*

**KHREMYLOS
& KARION**

Into the smash ending . . .

*BUT SINCE THE WORLD BEGAN, NO MAN
HAS HAD ENOUGH OF **YOU**!*

Tableau. A pause. MONEY seems unconvinced.

KHREMYLOS You wish an example? Let's give a man thirteen talents:
*Now thirteen talents is quite a lot,
Or seems like a lot until it's got,
But then it turns out that it's not—
    So he wants SIXTEEN.
                Okay.
Now sixteen talents is quite a lot,
Or seems like a lot until it's got.
But then it turns out that it's not—
    So he wants FORTY.
                Well.
Now forty talents is a helluva lot,
But until he's got it his life is rot,
And after he's got it, it's not so hot . . .
    You see?*

MONEY You're certainly both—just my opinion, of course—
effective speakers. Very. There's just one thing
I'm afraid of . . .

KHREMYLOS   You might as well be specific. Speak up.

MONEY Well, it's this *power* you say that I've got. I don't see
how I can handle that; I'm afraid to try.

KHREMYLOS Behold a living Currency Panic—Deflation!
MONEY, you're chicken!

MONEY   Am not! It's totally false,
a deliberate slander spread by a frustrated burglar.
Encountering no resistance, he effected entrance
to my place of residence, but nicked me for nothing at all
when he discovered each and every valuable

safely secured under lock and key. My prudent
caution he libeled with the name of CHICKEN.

KHREMYLOS   Relax.
Don't worry. Just give me your full-hearted participation
in the matter I have in mind, and I'll spring you
on a waiting world with sight that's sharper than any
epic crow's-nest lookout you care to name.

MONEY   How can you bring that about? You're merely a mortal.

KHREMYLOS   With excellent prospects. Something that Phoibos[13] said
when he waggled his laurel and gave his prophetic address.

MONEY   Is Phoibos in on this?

KHREMYLOS   He certainly is.

MONEY   You'd better be careful.

KHREMYLOS   Now look, my excellent friend,
please get this straight. Your job is, Not to Worry:
MY job—a job which may entail my death—
is to carry this business through to the end.

KARION   Mine, too . . .
if you really insist.

KHREMYLOS   And that's not all. We have allies:
Heaps of fair-minded men without a grain . . .

MONEY   Of sense?

KHREMYLOS   Of grain.

MONEY   *Great* allies. Last resorts,
if you ask me.

KHREMYLOS   Not if they start from Square One again,
as Men of MONEY.

To Karion.

                          Okay, now, get on the stick . . .

KARION   And whatwhatwhat?

KHREMYLOS   Go fetch my friends of the fields,
my fellow farmers. You'll find them toiling in the toolies;
don't miss a one. I want them here at my side
to divvy up equal dibs in this windfall here.

---

13. Apollo.

KARION   Observe: I'm on my way.

Starting off, he suddenly stops, and hands Khremylos the package he's been carrying.

                        I copped this meat
            from the temple. Please have someone take it inside.

KHREMYLOS

Accepting the package with a swoop.

            I'll give it my personal care.

Karion runs off stage right. Khremylos turns to Money.

            And you, oh Mighty Money, Top of the Gods,
            please to grace my humble abode with your presence.
            This is the house which you, today, shall stuff
            with cash—
                        one way or another—
                                    or possibly both.

MONEY

Suddenly hanging back.

            Criminetlies, I don't know. This going inside
            a stranger's house—I come over all depressed.
            It's never been in my interest to do that, ever.
            Sometimes it's my luck to visit a miser's house:
            No sooner get in the door than he wads me tight
            and pinches me, grubs me, buries me deep in the ground.
            When a friend drops by, a trustworthy type, and asks
            for the loan of a couple of coins, mine host the stinge
            swears up and down he's never seen me, ever.
            With a change of luck, I visit a high-roller's house:
            No sooner inside than I'm frittered and thrown around,
            squandered on whores and dice. Before you know it,
            I'm flung out of doors, stripped, absolutely exhausted.

KHREMYLOS It's never been your luck to meet a man
            of moderation. As it happens, such is the mode
            of existence that I myself consistently follow:
            For joy in scrimping, I find a match in no man;
            for joy in spending, my achievement's equally great,
            as occasion demands.
                        Come on, let's go inside.
            I want you to meet the wife, and my only son,
            the thing I love best in this world.
                                    After you, of course.

MONEY   Now, *that* I believe.

KHREMYLOS   Sure. No one lies to MONEY.

Exeunt into Khremylos's house.

Parodos [253–321]

A pause, and then Karion moves on briskly, returned from the country. Looking ahead, he seems to believe that he is being followed rather closely
by a group, a group he proceeds to exhort without turning around.

KARION   My master's messmates, lunchers and munchers on slops and straw!
Friends, yeomen, countrymen, lovers of soil and toil,
***FORWARD*!**

Hearing no response, he looks around and sees that he is alone. He stops.

                              Quick March!

Puzzled, he squints into the distance.

                              En avant?

Nada.

                              Come *on*, guys, show some dash!

Still nada, but a shuffling can be heard.

          We have an emergency here, and emergency doesn't mean mosey!
This crisis is on us, your aid is requested, so hurry and ***BE THERE*!**

Led by their leaders, the two Koryphaioi, the two Semichoruses plod on—
cane-supported, gnarled rustics, all alike in their extreme age and slowness.
They are painful to watch, and not completely convinced of Karion. The First
Koryphaios (a.k.a. KORY) is weary and earnest; the Second is weary and nasty.

1ST KORY   A simple inspection will show you we're plodding as fast as we can,
attaining the speed prescribed for your basic decrepit male.

2ND KORY   You couldn't possibly mean to suggest that I ought to RUN?
Not till you tell me the facts behind your master's summons.

KARION   You know them; I already told you. Deliberately deaf, that's you.
My master invites you, each and every, to change your lifestyle.
Abandon your shivers and bitching, embark upon gusto and bliss!

2ND KORY   That's a mighty sweeping proposal. I presume your master has reasons?

KARION   (Bother, just bother.)
                    The Boss did not return from Delphi
empty-handed; AH NO! He imported a LITTLE OLD MAN!

> Crinkled and Hairless!
>> Crumpled and Toothless!
>>> Crippled and Bathless!
> —Plus which, this model comes with Foreskin Completely Removed.

1ST KORY What golden tidings strike mine ear? Repeat them, please!
No doubt this person is loaded with cash? prosperity? plenty?

KARION Well, actually, no. Senility, though, there's plenty of *that*.

2ND KORY You actually think you can perpetrate such a shameless rip-off
and escape without serious bruises? You can't con a man with a cane!

He aims a slash at Karion, who coolly avoids it.

KARION Am I to conclude that you see in me a consistent clown,
quite unable to speak any sober, serious sense?

1ST KORY What an unflappable felon!

2ND KORY   He must be a masochist, too.
His shins are lusting for bondage. I hear them shouting OOOH,
OOOOH!

KARION Generations of Jurors, assigned to the Court of Last Resort,
go judge in the grave!
>> Well, GIT! Your pay-packet's waiting in Hell.

2ND KORY Go split right down the middle, you jumped-up highfalutin lowlife!
You take us over the jumps and still refuse to explain!

1ST KORY We're worn to the nub; we don't have the time.
>> And think of the lovely
slops and straw we passed on the way here and left untasted!

KARION Very well, the mask is off: The Boss brought home the God
of MONEY, and MONEY, gents, is about to make you RICH!

1ST KORY Really and truly? You mean that we can all be WEALTHY?

KARION I take a solemn oath: It's EVERY MAN A MIDAS!

Aside.

After all, Midas had donkey's ears—and you can, too.

1ST KORY O Joy! O Bliss! O Delight! I am moved to express my pleasure
in song and dance . . .

2ND KORY   . . . provided, of course, you're telling the truth.

*The Chorus members doff their cloaks, symbols of age, and prepare for
a wild dance, quite out of their character as superannuated farmers.*

KARION   [And now, with a backward bow to the noted poet from Leukas,
Philoxenos, author of the popular dithyramb **CYCLOPS!**, we give you
a tragical-comical-epical-pastoral interlude, which
has only the vaguest connection with anything else in the play—
and in this translation, less yet.

                                   Still, what are interludes for?]14

Cyclops

Vamp.

KARION

Engaging with the 1ST Semichorus, he takes the part of the
Cyclops in the ensuing calypso—small "c"—rout. Vamp

With a HEYnonny-NONny and an OHtotoTOI,
I PLAY that DANcin' CYclops BOY,
SHAkin' my SHANKS, so YOU can SEE
That BRAVE viBRAtion EACH way FREE.

Vamp.

UP the airy MOUNtain, DOWN the rushy GLEN,
FOLlow me, BOYS, 'cause you're SHEEP, not MEN.
TRILL that BAA and WARble that BLEAT,
And I'LL fix YOU somethin' SWEET to EAT.

Vamp.

Tag.

**TOTAL
CHORUS**   Cyclops, oh Cyclops!
You gon' need eyedrops!
MAN who EAT MEN
NEVer never WINK at SHEEPies aGAIN!

Vamp.

1ST KORY   With a HEY nonny-NONny twit TWIT jug JUG,
We SNEAK up on the CYclops SWIGgin' a SLUG.
We TRILL our BAA and we WARble our BLEAT,
Till he DRINKS too MUCH and TUMbles off his FEET.

---

14. This bracketed section is complete invention, its object the explanation of one of the
weirder divagations from context in this play. [Parker's note. Much of what follows is a
parody of a dithyramb on the Cyclops by the poet Philoxenos. Aristophanes also draws
from the Cyclops story in Book 9 of the *Odyssey*. In what follows, "vamp" and "tag"
refer to repetitive introductory motifs Parker envisions being played by the instrumental
accompaniment.]

Vamp.

1ST SEMICHO   Now, WHEN ol' CYclops FALLS aSLEEP,
We STAND up STRAIGHT, 'cause we're MEN, not SHEEP.
While he SNUFfles and SNORES and ISn't on his GUARD,
We LOOK for a STAKE that is LONG, sharp, and HARD.

Vamp.

2ND SEMICHO   We FIND that STAKE, and we SET it aFLAME,
We HEFT that STAKE, and we TAKE careful AIM,
We LIFT that STAKE, and we HOLD it up HIGH,
And we BRING it down SMACK in the CYclops' EYE!

No Vamp.

Tag.

**TOTAL
CHORUS**   Cyclops, oh Cyclops!
You gon' need eyedrops!
MAN who EAT MEN
NEVer never WINK at SHEEPies aGAIN!

Circe

Vamp.

KARION   I'll PLAY the part of CIRce, that SORceress of OLD,[15]
Who SPEcialized in SUBstances that COULDn't be conTROLLED.
A HIT from her STASH could inDUCE mental FOG,
And MAKE the reCIPient beliEVE he was a HOG.

Vamp.

2ND SEMICHO   She TOOK her stuff to KORinth a LITtle while BACK.
PhiLONides SAMpled it, and WADdled off the TRACK:
She SERVED him a patÉ that she'd LOVingly prePARED.
He THOUGHT he'd eaten FOIS gras; inSTEAD, it was MERDE.

No Vamp.

Tag.

**TOTAL
CHORUS**   CIRRRce, oh CIRce
WE show no MERcy.

---

15. Karion mixes Circe of the *Odyssey,* who turned Odysseus' men into pigs, and Philonides'
lover, the courtesan Lais.

> GAL who DRUG MEN
> NEVer never PUSH her PRODuct aGAIN!

Vamp.

2ND KORY   We're GLAD you're playing CIRce, that WIZardess of BLENDS,
And USing her preSCRIPtions to aMAZE your FRIENDS
By DAUBing them all OVer with her PORcine SLUSH,
Since THAT makes you a PERson we'd just LOVE to CRUSH.

Vamp.

CHORUS[16]   O-DYSSeus is OUR part. We'll GRAB you by the BALLS,
And SWING you up to HEAVen, and BOUNCE you off the WALLS,
And HANG you up like BUTCHer's meat, so EVeryone can SEE it,
And THEN proceed to STUFF your nostrils CHOCK-ful of SHEE-it.

[No Vamp.]

Tag.

**TOTAL
CHORUS**   CIRRRce, oh CIRce
WE show no MERcy.
GAL who DRUG MEN
NEVer never PUSH her PRODuct aGAIN!

Geezers

The Chorus starts to retire from the field. Karion addresses such as are left.

Vamp. Slower . . .

KARION   You've GOT a lot of VIGor, but you PLAY too ROUGH:
Of BRUIses and conTUSions, I got MORE than eNOUGH.
I expected to PAS-de-deux[17] and PIRouette aROUND
But I'm RAMMED and JAMMED and HAMMered in the GROUND.

Vamp.

I'm LEAVing, GENTS, but I'll HURry right BACK
I GOTta go FIND me a FORtifying SNACK.
If I DON'T reCOVer my VERVE and my DRIVE
I WON'T get OUT of this PLAY aLIVE.

No Vamp.

GEEEEzers, Oh GEEzers!
PAINS-in-your-KNEEzers!

---

16. The typescript does not say whether Parker envisions this as the whole chorus or one of the semichoruses.

17. PAH-de-doo [Parker's note].

GUYS of YOUR AGE
NEVer never GO the DIStance on STAGE.

He exits into Khremylos' house. The disappointed Chorus performs a **CHORAL DANCE** which is bound, under the circum-
stances, to be somewhat anticlimactic. The Dance done, they
put on their cloaks and resume their roles of aged rustics.

Proagon [322–486]

Khremylos, dressed neatly if not richly, enters
from his house to greet the chorus.

KHREMYLOS *WELCOME!*
But *Welcome*'s a weary, worn-out, rotten word
to use on friends and neighbors such as you.
Your dash, and rush, and verve in getting here
deserve the grace of open-armed *Embrace*.

Embracing the Koryphaioi and, if blocking and
time permit, the Chorus members.

Felicitations.
Salutations.
Greetings.
Bonjour.
Ciao.

He gives it up.

Friends, stand firm. Reinforce my efforts here
and furnish our blessed God with true salvation.

1ST KORY   No problem at all.

He strikes a heroic pose, which is hardly convincing.

One look at me, you'll declare
that I'm the spitting image of War Himself.
I mean, I put the Assembly under siege
when all I get is three measly obols per day;
I'm not about to turn non-aggressionist now,
and let the real MONEY slip out of my clutches.

KHREMYLOS

Looking off stage left.

But what do I see? Here comes old Blepsidemos.
He obviously must have heard some gossip about
our business; he's bustling along at a pretty fair clip.

The Chorus retires to the periphery as Blepsidemos enters left. He does not immediately see Khremylos.

BLEPSIDEMOS Mighty peculiar business, if you ask me. Hah!
Khremylos rich in two shakes? Can't happen. No way.
I absolutely refuse to believe such twaddle . . .
Except, that all the boys at the barber shop,
well, damned if they didn't swear that he
had changed in a flash to Khremylos, Man of MONEY.
But that's not all that's odd. They say he's invited
his friends and neighbors over to share in his profits.
He can't have. Pure altruism in Athens? An act
like that—outlandish. NOT the Athenian Way.

KHREMYLOS

In a paratragic aside.

> *On my bright cheek let no concealment feed.*
—Ah, Blepsidemos. My fortunes have improved
since yesterday. Which means, you get your share,
since any friend of mine . . .

BLEPSIDEMOS   It's really true?
What everyone says—that you're a Man of MONEY?

KHREMYLOS I expect to be, in a very short time . . . if the God
so wills, of course. The affair contains, let's say,
contains an Element of Risk.

BLEPSIDEMOS   What kind of Risk?

KHREMYLOS Let's put it this way. . . .

An awkward pause.

BLEPSIDEMOS   Let's put it *which* way, please?

KHREMYLOS Well, IF—on the one hand—we *win,* a rich existence
is ours forever. But IF—on the other hand—
we *lose,* our reward is radical rack and ruin.

BLEPSIDEMOS This looks to me like a very dirty business,
and I don't like it at all. This messy blend
of instant millions and paranoia—that is the mark
of a man who's accomplished something extremely *sick.*

KHREMYLOS And what do you mean by *sick*?

BLEPSIDEMOS   Oh, put the case
that you sneaked back from Delphi with stolen silver,
or gold you filched from the God, and it's weighing down
your conscience.

KHREMYLOS   Apollo save me, by Zeus! I never!

BLEPSIDEMOS   No need to bluster at me, friend. I know What's What.

KHREMYLOS   I will *not* have you suspect me of something like that!

BLEPSIDEMOS   It's sad but true: This world's not a healthy place.
Love of profit brings the best of us down;
we're sadly out of the way; we're *sick, sick, sick.*

KHREMYLOS   Sweet Mother of Earth, but you're not *well, well, well.*

BLEPSIDEMOS

The sorrowful commentator on his friend, to the audience.

I knew him When, friends. You wouldn't believe the change.

KHREMYLOS   As heaven's my witness, you're utterly out of your mind!

BLEPSIDEMOS   And that shifty gaze. Can't look me straight in the eye.
Criminal type—I can spot them every time.

KHREMYLOS   I see the point of this squawking. You have the idea
that I stole something or other, and you want your cut!

BLEPSIDEMOS   My cut? What cut?
                                   Or rather, a cut of what?

KHREMYLOS   It's not like that at all. It's completely different.

BLEPSIDEMOS   You *didn't* steal?

KHREMYLOS   I didn't.

BLEPSIDEMOS   I see. You *robbed,*
intent on procuring Grievous Bodily Harm?

KHREMYLOS   Where do you get these disgusting ideas?

BLEPSIDEMOS   There's only
one thing left: You *embezzled* somebody's savings,
committed an act of Compound Defalcation,
and left the poor guy in arrears?

KHREMYLOS   *I DIDN'T DEFALCATE
ANYONE'S ARREARS!*

BLEPSIDEMOS   What now? All avenues closed.
How deal with a man who refuses to tell the truth,
squalid though it may be?

KHREMYLOS   You're indicting me
before you've heard the facts.

BLEPSIDEMOS

Conspiratorially.

>   You wouldn't want
> the City to learn your dirty little secret,
> now would you? It's cover-up time, and I'll arrange it
> at nominal cost: A few handfuls of change
> to stuff the prosecutors' mouths. What are friends for?

KHREMYLOS   Friends, I guess, are for skimming seventy-five
percent off the top while performing that little service.

BLEPSIDEMOS   I see a probable future:
>   An Old Man (nameless,
> of course) on trial for his life, feebly beating
> the air with an olive branch, his tearful wife
> and children huddle around his shivering shins . . .
> Pathetic. It rather reminds me of Pamphilos' picture
> of Herakles' wretched offspring, down in the Stoa.[18]
> You might check out its really *palpable* agony.

KHREMYLOS   I refuse to be any party to bribes. From now on,
the only men I intend to enrich with MONEY
are the Decent, the Just, and the Wise.

BLEPSIDEMOS   I can't believe it.
You got away with that much loot?

KHREMYLOS   You'll be
the death of me.

BLEPSIDEMOS   You'll be the death of yourself,
if you want my opinion.

KHREMYLOS   I don't, you disgusting person.
I will not be my death . . .

Striking the paratragic pose.

>   *for I have MONEY!*

BLEPSIDEMOS   MONEY, my eye! What MONEY?

KHREMYLOS   MONEY, the God!

BLEPSIDEMOS   Where is this God?

---

18. There are two men named Pamphilos to whom these verses might allude. One was a famous painter who painted a scene from a myth in which Herakles' family supplicates the Athenians for help when they are pursued by Herakles' enemy Eurystheus after the hero's death. The other was a general who may have been accused of a crime and produced his family in supplication before the jurors shortly before the play was produced.

KHREMYLOS   Inside.

BLEPSIDEMOS   Inside of WHAT?

KHREMYLOS   Inside the house.

BLEPSIDEMOS   Inside *your* house?

KHREMYLOS   That's right.

BLEPSIDEMOS   The hell you say!
                                    —MONEY's inside your house?

KHREMYLOS   As the Gods are my judges.

BLEPSIDEMOS   You're telling the truth?

KHREMYLOS   I swear it.

BLEPSIDEMOS   Swear it in the name of Hestia?

KHREMYLOS   Yes, by Poseidon!

BLEPSIDEMOS   You mean the God of the Sea?

KHREMYLOS   You know any others?
                   I'll swear by every Poseidon you can find.

A pause while Blepsidemos regroups.

BLEPSIDEMOS   Well, where's your sense of friendship? Why not send
                   this MONEY over to my place, and, as it were, share
                   the wealth?

KHREMYLOS   Not yet, I'm afraid. The scenario hasn't
                   quite reached that stage.

BLEPSIDEMOS   It hasn't quite reached *what* stage?
                   The sharing stage?

KHREMYLOS   Dear, no. Before we share . . .

BLEPSIDEMOS   Well, what?

KHREMYLOS   Well, you and I have a job to do.

BLEPSIDEMOS   What job? What? What?

KHREMYLOS   He has to regain his sight . . .

BLEPSIDEMOS   Who has to regain whose sight? Who? Who?

KHREMYLOS   MONEY,
                   the God. And that's our job. Any way we can.

BLEPSIDEMOS   You mean he's *really* blind?

KHREMYLOS   I swear he is.

BLEPSIDEMOS   No wonder he never came to my place before.

KHREMYLOS But now he will. If the Gods agree, of course.

BLEPSIDEMOS Shouldn't we get a doctor to make a house call?

KHREMYLOS Where can you find a doctor in Athens these days?
The fees dropped off to nothing, and so did the practice.

BLEPSIDEMOS Let's take a look . . .

They scan the audience.

KHREMYLOS   No doctor in the house.

BLEPSIDEMOS   Not one.

KHREMYLOS Too bad.
Our best recourse is the Plan to which
I've given a lot of thought. We take MONEY over
to Asklepios' temple and deposit him there for the night.[19]

BLEPSIDEMOS A first-class plan; I'll take my oath on that.

Suddenly galvanized into action.

—Well, don't dillydally! Hustle! Let's get things done!

He pushes Khremylos toward Khremylos' house.

KHREMYLOS I'm on my way.

BLEPSIDEMOS   So *HURRY!*

KHREMYLOS   Just what I'm doing!

They run pell-mell toward Khremylos' house, but their rush is interrupted, in fact stopped dead, by the sudden entrance of the Goddess
of POVERTY to block their way. Dressed in rags, she is a very formi-
dable fright. [A fair equivalent would be Margaret Hamilton's portrayal
of the Wicked Witch of the West in the 1939 film *The Wizard of Oz*.]

POVERTY   Presumptuous puppets!
                    Rash, injudicious midgets!
Misguided transgressors who rush away to commission
of Gross Enormity—
                    WHERE DO YOU THINK YOU'RE GOING?

With a horrified look, the men begin backing away.

What are you running away from?
                    STOP RIGHT THERE!

---

19. The most important temple of the healing god Asklepios, where the ill slept overnight in
order to be healed, was in the town of Epidauros, but two sanctuaries of Asklepios had been
established in Athens itself during Aristophanes' lifetime.

BLEPSIDEMOS

As the two huddle before POVERTY's relentless advance.

      Herakles help us!

POVERTY   Oh, he can't help you, my pretties.
I shall now proceed to expunge you by means most foul,
and let the extinguishment suit the crime, inasmuch
as the deed you dare is not to be endured,
an atrocity yet untried by man or God.
In sum, let's say that you have been Demolished.

KHREMYLOS Who are you—behind that simply revolting complexion?

BLEPSIDEMOS I know: She's a FURY, a cast-off from a tragic cast.
She has that taint of weirdness: the Vision of Tragedy.

KHREMYLOS No Fury. She doesn't have torches.

BLEPSIDEMOS   She'll wish she did!

He makes a valiant rush at POVERTY, but she waggles a claw at
him and sends him scuttling back to hide behind Khremylos.

POVERTY   And who do you think I might be?

KHREMYLOS

Breaking completely from the representa-
tion of fear, he thinks the problem over.

                      You could be a *Waitress;*
the voice is perfect. But the temper, the sense of wrong
when we haven't hurt you a bit . . .
                    Got it! You're in
Retail Sales! I guess you're in soup . . .

POVERTY   *NO, YOU ARE!*

At her roar, Khremylos drops back into fright.

      You haven't hurt me a bit? When now, at this moment,
you're plotting to root me out of every last nook
and cranny in Athens?

KHREMYLOS   But Granny, have you forgotten
the City Dump? It's yours; go wear it in health.
—Quick, now, let us know your name. And species.

POVERTY

Majestically, in measured tones.

      I . . . AM . . . SHE . . . WHO . . .

BLEPSIDEMOS   That's one of those foreign gods.

POVERTY   I . . . AM . . . SHE . . .WHO . . . TODAY . . . WILL . . . VISIT . . .
                PUNISH-

A slight pause.

                MENT . . . ON . . . YOU . . . WHO . . . DO . . .

BLEPSIDEMOS   Another foreign god.

POVERTY   I . . . AM . . . SHE . . . WHO . . . TODAY . . .WILL . . . VISIT . . .
                PUNISH-
                MENT . . . ON . . . YOU . . . WHO . . . DO . . . CONSPIRE . . .
                TO . . . BANISH . . .
                ME!

BLEPSIDEMOS   I'm wrong. It's the barmaid from down the block,
                the one who does the vanishing trick on my cash
                with false-bottomed mugs.

POVERTY   I . . . AM . . . YOUR . . . NEIGHBOR . . .
                FOR . . . LO . . . THESE . . . MANY . . . YEARS . . .
                                I . . . AM . . . THE . . . GODDESS . . .

POVERTY!

Tableau of Terror. Then Blepsidemos' nerve breaks.

BLEPSIDEMOS Apollo and all the rest of you, show me a hole!

He starts off, but is caught on the run by Khremylos.

KHREMYLOS What are you doing, you coward? Be a man
             and stand your ground!

BLEPSIDEMOS   Never in all this world.

KHREMYLOS Stay put!
                    One woman, two men . . . We'll take her, easy.

BLEPSIDEMOS Don't be so criminally stupid. This is POVERTY!
             The deadliest life form known in the universe!

KHREMYLOS Please stay? As a personal favor to me?

BLEPSIDEMOS   I won't,
             I simply won't.

KHREMYLOS   You'd prefer to have us descend
             to the depths of debasement? Defect and desert our deity?
             Abandon our godhead, footless and reft, while we
             run off to Nowhere Special, refusing to lift a hand
             in divine defense?

BLEPSIDEMOS	Well, yes.

When we lift that hand,
what can we find to hide behind? There isn't
the shabbiest shield, the dentedest breastplate. That goddamned
goddess has hocked them all!

KHREMYLOS *Coraggio,* chum.
I assure you, our god's the only god going who's got
power sufficient to grinding POVERTY down.

POVERTY What's this? *Mutters,* you double helping of scum,
you dainty duo entrapped in gigantic *flagrante?*

KHREMYLOS I think that's rather unfair, you creature for whom
no death, however disgusting, can ever suffice.
Why call us names? We never did you any wrong.

POVERTY *NO WRONG!*
Is Olympos listening?
You try to restore
the sight of MONEY and still persist in believing
that I'm not *WRONGED?*

KHREMYLOS But how are we wronging you
when we only aim to produce, for the human race,
a *Boon?*

POVERTY You're mooting a Boon, that it? WHAT BOON?

KHREMYLOS What Boon? Well, first we'll kick you the hell out of Hellas . . .

POVERTY Kick ME the hell out? But that's no *Boon;* it's a *Bane.*
What greater *Bane* could you make for the human race?

KHREMYLOS That's easy: NOT kicking you out. Now, *there's a Bane.*

POVERTY You've raised the very point on which I'm prepared
to debate you, pro and con, beginning Now.
And if I prove that I, that Honest POVERTY
am the single fount and source of all your *Boon,*
that your very existence comes through ME . . . *well, then.*

She cackles and pauses ominously.

If I lose the debate, of course, you're perfectly free
to do whatever you want.

KHREMYLOS You nymph of nausea,
how can you have the gall to make that suggestion?

POVERTY It's my little way. You listen, and be improved.
I can't conceive of an easier task than showing
that you're off track, out of line in enriching the righteous.

KHREMYLOS O Rod and Rack!
                          O Stakes and Stocks!
                                          Assist us!

POVERTY You really shouldn't grumble without the facts.

KHREMYLOS A proposal like yours provokes a heartfelt YECCCH
from any man . . .

POVERTY   Unless that man has a brain.

KHREMYLOS And if you lose your case, what penalty should I
exact?

POVERTY   It's up to you.

KHREMYLOS   An apt proposal.

POVERTY Provided, of course, you suffer the same if *you* lose.

KHREMYLOS

Conferring with Blepsidemos.

                You think that twenty deaths will do her in?

BLEPSIDEMOS Should . . . but remember, *we* only need one each.

POVERTY And quick you'll be in receiving that petty correction,
since Justice is on my side. Rebuttal is futile.

The prospective contestants arrange themselves for the debate.

Agon [487–626]

Arrangement for the debate: Stage left, Khremylos and Blepsidemos, supported by the entire Chorus. Stage right, POVERTY, by herself.

1ST KORY

To the two men.

                The time is at hand, complainants, to argue with craft and cunning.
                Marshal your stiff, stout masculine words and refute this harpy!

Khremylos advances to the center of the stage.

KHREMYLOS I commence with an axiom, given, established, agreed on by all:
Justice occurs when righteous humanity prospers and thrives,
and base, unbelieving humanity fares, conversely, vice versa.
It is with this goal in view, expending considerable labor,
that my colleague and I have devised an Enabling Design, or Flowchart,
distinguished by probity, virtue, and all-round application
for any and all situations.

Our scenario runs as follows:
If MONEY regains his eyesight, now, *today,* and ceases
his blind and aimless peregrinations, I know for a fact
that he'll turn his steps to the homes of the *Good,* humanity's nobles,
and stay there unswerving, ever abiding in those abodes,
the while he eschews the Vicious and shuns the hearths of the Godless.
Result? He will render mankind *in toto* not only Good,
but *Rich* as well.

And, incidentally, *Pious.*

—Well? Who
can devise a more beneficent *Boon* for the human race?

He has directed the question at POVERTY, but his colleague cuts in hurriedly.

BLEPSIDEMOS   Nobody, dammit. You have my word.

And keep it rhetorical.
Don't go asking the bitch here.

KHREMYLOS   And WHO . . .

BLEPSIDEMOS   Oh, shit.

KHREMYLOS   And WHO
can cast a glance at the present state of our feckless existence
and avoid the conclusion that this is Utter Madness—unless,
of course, he opts for Demonic Possession?

It's painfully clear:
The *Bad* and *Depraved* and *Gross,* for the most part, comprise the *Rich,*
on MONEY amassed in ways that are simply Unfair. Conversely,
the Utterly *Good,* for the most part, comprise the *Poor,* possessing
a wretched lifestyle, starvation, and YOU as their constant companion.

The question, this time, is directed at Blepsidemos.

Hence my proposal: If MONEY gets eyes and ejects this Gorgon,
what better route can he go to furnish humanity *Boons?*

Blepsidemos starts to answer, but Poverty is too quick for him.

POVERTY   *OH WHATTA PAIR!*
You twain of twits, you self-starting set
of psychic sickos, you ancients of daze, you meshuggeneh misfits,
you charter fanatics who flip and flap on the lunatic fringe!
Take note of my forecast:

If you acquire your gross desire,
the profit you'll net will be *Zilch.* Say MONEY regains his vision
and disburses himself all round in equal shares—that's Down
the Tubes with Science and Industry, called for lack of interest!
And in the resultant void, what happens to old *Motivation?*

> *Who'll want to be the maker, then,*
> *of products for you folks—*
> *of schooners, shoes, and overcoats,*
> *of pots and pans and spokes,*
> *of bricks and racks and bric-a-brac . . .*
> *and who will clean your cloaks?*
> *And who will cleave the glebe and wrest her fruits from Earth*
> when all you have to do is relax and forget such trifles?

KHREMYLOS

As will happen several times, he is flummoxed by Poverty's argument and blusters.

> *NONSENSE! TOMMYROT! DRIVEL!*

Collecting himself.

>   The bothersome details you list
> will be performed by the *Servants*, Of Course.

POVERTY   My goodness! The *Servants*!
> And where will you get these *Servants*?

KHREMYLOS   We'll *buy* them, Of Course,
> for good, hard coin of the realm.

POVERTY   And who will the *Seller* be?
> Who needs the slave trade when HE has good, hard coin of the realm?

She has Khremylos there, and he knows it.

KHREMYLOS   The . . . Profit Motive! Some free-market entrepreneur, Of Course,
down from Thessaly, land of compulsive slavers.

POVERTY   A moment:
> There won't be a single slaver left in the whole wide world,
> as you so aptly put it, *Of Course*.
>   When everyone's *Rich*,
> who'll be inclined to risk his neck on a capital crime?
> *You'll* be the compulsive, compelled to dig and to delve
> and to lead a much more wretched existence than you do now.

KHREMYLOS   *THE SAME TO YOU!*

POVERTY   You won't be able to sleep in a bed:
> *No More Beds.*
>   And no more nipping a kip on the carpet:
> *The Rich toil not, nor do they weave.*
>   *No More Perfume*
> to anoint the bride in dribbles and drops when you lead her groomward,

and as for iridescent vestments, dyed at startling expense
to drape your dewy-eyed darling just *so:*

                                                    No More Trousseaux.
Overall, when every one of these items is Out of Stock,
where's the advantage in having MONEY?

                                                    But POVERTY, now:
MY inventory is loaded; whatever you want, it's *here.*
Management, that's my business. I utilize *Need* and *Lack*
and *Worry about the Next Meal* to keep the small producer
up on his toes.

KHREMYLOS   And Oh, the Boons that accrue from YOU!
A Cluster of *Blisters* (raised by the stove in the public baths),
a Cry of *Brats* (half-starved), a Gabble of *Little Old Ladies.*
I can't reckon up the staggering total of insect life,
the *Lice* and *Gnats* and *Fleas* that launch attacks at our heads,
buzzing their reveille message:

                            "TIME TO GET UP AND STARVE!"
But that's not all:

                            Instead of a cloak, we have one big *Patch;*
instead of a bed, a bug-ridden bagful of mushy *Rushes*
designed to wake the sleeper; instead of a carpet to lie on,
a rotted-out *Doormat;* instead of a pillow to cuddle the head,
a good substantial *Rock.*

                            And dinner? Instead of bread,
there's *Rhubarb Shoots,* with *Dried Radish Tops* for dessert.
The *Top* of a *Keg,* broken off, for sitting, instead of a chair.
A *Slat* from a *Vat,* broken up, for kneading, instead of a trough.
And thus I display the bountiful *Boons* of POVERTY, blessings
you cast on humanity broadcast.

                            Or is there something I missed?

POVERTY   Your *aim.*

                    You didn't refute *my* lifestyle. Not with that page
from the Beggars' Opera.

KHREMYLOS   I stick by our local expressions, Of Course:
"Beggary's POVERTY's sister."

POVERTY   The same involuted logic
you use to equate the Savior of Athens with Sicily's Despot.[20]
But that's not the past or present state of *my* lifestyle, *nor—*
as Zeus is my judge—is that its future!

---

20. A few years before the first production of this play, Athens had tried to win over
Dionysios I, tyrant of Syracuse, as an ally against Sparta. The attempt was unsuccessful, and
Dionysios was now very unpopular in Athens.

What you describe
is the life of a *Beggar,* mere existence with nothing in hand.
My gift is the blissful life of a *Pauper,* a spare existence
devoted to Honest Toil, where Nothing Occurs in Excess,
but Nothing Needed is Lacking.

KHREMYLOS   Demeter, what a way with words!
That's really *La Dolce Vita:*
                    Nothing at all, in abundance.
A lifetime of scrimping and straining that can't buy a burial plot!

POVERTY   And the effort you spend on cheap cracks, like a worn-out *comic* plot!
I do wish you could be serious. Can't you really see
that I produce better men, yes, better in body and mind,
than MONEY ever does?
                    The Men of MONEY are gouty,
their bellies are potty, their thighs are frotty,[21] they are immorally
FAT!
     But POVERTY's Princes, *my* boys, are slim and trim,
nipped in at the waist, and their patience is thin with those who
     oppose them.

KHREMYLOS   Wasp waists, with navel to backbone—produced by a diet of Famine.

POVERTY   I shall now proceed to treat of Moral Health, and furnish
a clear demonstration that Decency ever dwells with ME,
while MONEY plays host to Wanton License!

KHREMYLOS   Such Decency, too:
Petty Theft and Breaking & Entering—how's that Decent?

BLEPSIDEMOS

Merely trying to be helpful.

          Simple enough. Just don't get caught. That makes it Decent.

He shrivels in Khremylos' glare.

POVERTY   Observe our City politicos: As long as they remain Paupers,
you'll find them Just and Honest in dealings with people and state.
But once they've come into public MONEY, these quick-change artists
are Instant Subversives: They plot at the back of the popular front
and make war against the people.

---

21. Because of the rhyme, I have assumed that this is a nonsense word created by Parker (or
found someplace in his enormously wide reading), but it may be a typo for "frothy."

KHREMYLOS

Reluctantly applauding.

And not a single lie there,
nasty bitch though you be. But don't congratulate yourself.
This won't abate one whit of your sad and sorry fate.
You're trying to make us believe the one unspeakable lie:
That POVERTY's better than MONEY!

POVERTY

You certainly aren't the man
to refute that point, not with the garbage you gabble, flapping
your arms in the hope you'll fly.

KHREMYLOS

YOU certainly aren't the focus
of people's love. They all run away when they see you—Why?

POVERTY *Because I make them Better.*

Compare the standard standoff
of child and parent. The youngsters avoid their father, whose only
concern is what's best for their children. It's *such* a difficult job
to distinguish Right from Wrong.

KHREMYLOS

You don't really mean to assert
that ZEUS can't make that distinction, can't decide what's Best?
Of Course he can! And Zeus chose MONEY!

BLEPSIDEMOS

Indicating Poverty to Khremylos.

And look what Zeus
laid off on *us.*

POVERTY

The styes in your inner eyes must date
from the Old Stone Age.

Look: Zeus is *Poor,* Of Course, as I now
shall prove so clearly that even you can see it.

Ready?
If Zeus had MONEY, if Zeus were *Rich,* please tell me WHY
that selfsame Zeus, long ago when he founded the games at Olympos,
the games where he gathers all Greece together every four years,
WHY would Zeus have declared the winners by draping their brows
with measly wreaths of leaves from the Non-Domesticated Olive?
If Zeus had MONEY, it ne-ces-sar-i-ly follows that Zeus
would have used *Gold Crowns!*

KHREMYLOS

Au contraire. It's an obvious case,
Of Course, of a God who honors his MONEY, the natural act
of a scrimper who seeks to avoid excessive—or *any*—expense:
Zeus trims the winners with trash and keeps his MONEY at home.

POVERTY   I only said he was *Poor*. But you, what a shabby garland
            you're settling on Zeus—a MONEYed God who's a cheapjack miser?

KHREMYLOS   I pray Him to drape your brow with a measly wreath of leaves
            from the Non-Domesticated Olive and drive you right into the ground!

POVERTY   The nerve! How can you continue to argue that POVERTY's not
            the wellspring and taproot of all your *Boons*?

KHREMYLOS

Producing a scroll from somewhere.

                                              To decide the question,
            "What's better, *Rich* or *Poor*?" I have here a sworn deposition
            from a certain *Hekatê*. Occupation: Goddess. She states (and I quote):
            *"Each month, the Moneyed Class delivers me dinner, alfresco . . .
            and the Poor Class pigs it down before I can get it inside."*[22]

About to make his point, he stops.

            But why am I doing this?

Advancing threateningly on Poverty.

                                    —*TAKE A WALK!*
            VAMOOSE! You've croaked your final croak.
            I won't be persuaded to share your views,
            so, even if You Win,
                        YOU LOSE!

POVERTY

Shocked, she slides straight into tragedy, complete with gestures.

            Give ear, O City of Argos, to his mouthings!

KHREMYLOS   Appeal to the Panhandler's Guild. It's a local call.

POVERTY   *O cursèd sprite, what woes betide me now?*

KHREMYLOS   Considered prison? You're certainly *fit* to be tied.

POVERTY   *Me wretched, whither shall I fare away?*

KHREMYLOS   Well, Hell seems *Fair*. But anywhere *Away*.
            Push along, now, please. Don't jostle. Keep it moving.
            Stand Not upon the Order of Your Going.

POVERTY   *At your behest one day, I shall return!*

---

22. It was standard practice to place offerings of food at shrines of the goddess Hekatê on the
last day of each month.

KHREMYLOS

Picking up a stick and advancing on her.

> No doubt. But not today. For now, *VAMOOSE*!
>> *So things turn out for the best, you see:*
>> *It's MONEY for me, and a stick for thee*
>> *with assorted bruises and battery!*

BLEPSIDEMOS

Joining the hunt.

>> *That looks like fun, so baby makes three!*
>> *It's MONEY for me and my family!*
>> *I'll wash the past off carefully*
>> *and fart in the face of Industry*
>> *with a far fatter fart for POVERTY!*

He presents his backside to POVERTY and aims. Overcome, she
exits in disarray. All business, Khremylos turns to Blepsidemos.

KHREMYLOS   And that is that. The recreant miscreant's gone.
But now the two of us have a job to do
without any delay. We've got to deposit that God,
on a cot, in the court of Asklepios' temple.

BLEPSIDEMOS   Right.
No time to waste. Another one might drop by
and stick a spoke in our spadework. Let's get done!

Khremylos moves to the door of the house and calls.

KHREMYLOS   Hey, Karion! This is an order. Bring out the blankets!
Withdraw our MONEY and lead him forth—and see
you do it right; this is a Divine Procession.
Everything's ready. Be sure you bring it all!

The laden Karion enters from the house, leading the blind god. Khremylos and Blepsidemos fall in, and the small parade exits, stage right, on its
way to the temple of Asklepios. The Chorus performs a **CHORAL DANCE**

They then regroup in their Semichoruses and wait.

Episode I [627–770][23]

Karion, triumphant, enters stage right and moves to the Chorus.

KARION   Venerable Gents and Longtime Breadline Veterans
                whose reward thus far from a grateful City has been
                a yearly sop of soup with the barest crust . . .
                O LUCKY YOU!
                                    YOUR SHIP'S COME IN!
                                              YOU'RE LOADED!
                (Likewise, of course, all other men who share
                your deserving habits.)

1ST KORY   O Best and Finest Example
                of your really rather disgusting class . . .
                                    What's Up?
                (This inasmuch as you have the look of a spokesman
                of useful news.)

KARION   The Boss has hit it big,
                and MONEY's hit bigger than big! Once eyeless and gazeless,
                now gleams the living lightning from his lids,
                made glorious shimmer by the son of Phoibos,
                the hale Asklepios, happy God of Cure.

The Chorus is galvanized into hubbub.

1ST SEMICHO   *You're talking JOYS!*

---

23. In a production of *Money, the God* at the University of Texas in April 2000, this scene
was preceded by an "epiphany," in which Money was healed at Asklepios' shrine (Yana Zarifi-
Sistovari, personal correspondence, July 8, 2013). In a note to Yana Zarifi-Sistovari written
shortly after that production (April 17, 2000), Parker wrote that he had been "fiddling with
the epiphany music" and proposed the following lyrics:

> Hail MONEY our Lord
> Omnipotent Pelf,
> Our virtues reward
> With gi-ift of yourself.
> Your affluence send us,
> Our opulence puff,
> Restore us and mend us
> With cornucopic stuff.

The lyrics were to be sung to the tune of the hymn "O Worship the Lord," which Parker
transcribed as follows:

2ND SEMICHO   *You're talking NOISE!*

**TOTAL
CHORUS**   *We praise with Joyful Noise*
                  Asklepios and his boys.
                  He sheds his blazing light
                  to set our species right.

Khremylos' Wife enters from the house in happy anticipation.

WIFE   What's all the shouting for? Can it possibly be
                  Glad Tidings? I've been sitting inside for ages,
                  pining away for word and holding my breath
                  in suspense for the happy herald . . .
                                                    and here he is!

KARION

Into the thirsty messenger shtick.

                  Oh quick—
                            a drink—
                                      not water!
                                      —Let's move it, ma'am!
                  Have one yourself (why change your habits now?)
                  and take delivery on this bulk consignment
                  of Boons!

WIFE   *Boons?* I don't see any Boons.

KARION   They're right
                  on the tip of my tongue. You'll find out shortly; no waiting.

WIFE   Well, get to the meat of the matter; don't stand there dawdling.

Realizing that plain speech is counterproductive, she sighs and translates
this into a Middle High Tragic formula for urging recalcitrant messengers.

                  Wherefore perfect with all dispatch thy speech.

KARION   *Wherefore perpend, the while I thee unveil . . .*

WIFE   You watch it, Buster!

KARION   *. . . the while I thee unveil*
                  my blessed budget's body from tip to toe.

WIFE   I'll watch your budget; you flush that body business.

KARION

Starting out as the Compleat Tragick Messenger.

                  So soon as we arrived before the God,
                  conducting in our train that erstwhile wretch

> *who now, mayhap, all happy chaps surpasses,*
> *we first conveyed him to the lapsing sea*
> *and sluiced him off.*

WIFE   That made him happy, I'll bet.
There's nothing like a frigid salt-water douche
for a little old man.

KARION   *And thereupon we bent*
our steps within the Healer's hallowed purlieus,
oblation made and wafer offered to altar,
the sacred sop poured forth to Hephaistos[24] sizzle.

Shifting to plain language.

Then we deposited MONEY, bedded him down
in the manner prescribed, and set about scrounging ourselves
some sleeping bags.

WIFE   Was anyone else at the temple
in search of Asklepios' help?

KARION   There certainly was:
Neokleides—blind as a bat, but with better aim
at a scam than any sighted thief in the City.[25]
And a crowd of others, displaying all the approved
diseases.
                        The temple sexton put out the lamps
and told us to go to sleep, adding the order:
"If you hear any noise, *stay still!*" And so, by the rules,
we all lay down.
                            I couldn't sleep, not me.
Slightly northwest of the head of a little old lady
a potful of mush was positioned, driving me crazy
with a total compulsion—divinely inspired, of course—
to slink upon it. I raise my eyes and, lo,
the priest is snaffling the figs and sacking the cakes
from the holy table. That job completed, he made
the circuit of all the altars, just to be sure
there weren't any wafers left. The ones he found
were sacramentally bagged. Struck by this utterly
sacred sanction for my intended act,
I rose to make a rush on the potful of mush.

WIFE   O rash and foolish! Weren't you afraid of the God?

---

24. The god of fire.

25. Neokleides was a contemporary politician, known to us only through insulting references
here and in Aristophanes' other plays.

KARION   You're goddamned right I was. I was worried sick
the God might zip in, banners flying, and beat me
to the pot. To judge from the priest's behavior, he would.
Anyway:
        The little old lady heard me coming
and stretched out a cautious hand for her mush.
                        I hissssed
and fastened my teeth on that cautious hand like a puff snake.
She snatched it back in a very considerable hurry,
wrapped herself tight in her rags, and lay quite still,
emitting a constant stream of farts that would make
a polecat choke. I seized that opportune moment
to gnash away at the mush. Until I was full.
When I stopped.

WIFE   But didn't the God approach you?

KARION   Not yet, but later. And then I pulled a good one.
As the God drew nigh, I cut a *tremendous* fart.
It was all that mush. My belly had really ballooned.

WIFE   That must have put you in terrible odor with him.

KARION   Nope. It shook the rest of the holy procession—
you know, his daughters: *Iaso,* Goddess of Curing
Internal Upsets, blushed;
                Panacea, Goddess
of Curing Everything Else,[26] squeezed hard at her nose
and swiveled her head away—the perfect cure:
I don't fart frankincense.

WIFE   But what did the God do?

KARION   Nothing at all. It didn't bother *Him.*

WIFE   He sounds like a tasteless God, with no cultivation.

KARION   Oh, no. He's a diagnostician: he tastes excretions.

WIFE   Disgusting!

KARION   That scared me. I buried myself underneath
my cloak. The God proceeded to make his rounds,
examining each and every disease with rigor
and TLC. A slave stood by at the ready
with granite mortar and pestle and medicine bag.

WIFE   All stone?

---

26. Iaso means "the one who heals"; Panacea means "a universal remedy."

KARION   Well, not the bag. That's taking too much
                  for granite.

WIFE   What you deserve is disaster. You said
                  you buried yourself; how could you see all that?

KARION

  Holding up his ragged cloak and peering through the holes.

                  I saw through my see-through cloak, my angling outfit—
                  it's full of fissures.
                                  —The God began his practice
                  with Neokleides. He set to preparing eye-balm
                  according to this prescription:
                                  RX: Three cloves
                  of hypercaustic garlic; grind to a pulp.
                  Add juice from a ripe jalapeño, to which has been added
                  a generous pinch of hot sea-pepper. Suffuse
                  the mess in Old Corrosive *vinegar, brut.*
                  Apply directly to the eyelids' inner surface
                  for maximum agony.
                                  Followed it out to the letter.
                  Poor Neokleides broke out in howls and screams,
                  shot up to a standing position and made for the exit.
                  But the God just laughed and said,
                                  "You've had the salve.
                  Sit down! Stay put! And that completes the treatment:
                  Congress is cured of your constant Points of Order."

WIFE   That's very shrewd, for a God. Patriotic, too.

KARION   The next of his patients was MONEY. He sat beside him
                and began the cure with a general cranial palpation,
                then applied a sterile linen compress to his lids
                and wiped them clean. The fair Panacea proceeded
                to isolate his head and face with a purple sheet.
                Asklepios gave a sharp chirp, and *Bang!*—two snakes
                of really unparalleled size raced out of the temple.

WIFE   The Gods preserve us!

KARION   These serpents slid under the sheet
                and licked away at his eyelids, for all I could tell.
                And then, before *you* could chug-a-lug six quarts
                of wine—which is to say, in a blinding flash—
                MONEY, ma'am, our MONEY rose up and *SAW!*
                Well, I was so happy at that, I clapped, which woke
                the Boss, which put Asklepios into eclipse:

The God and the serpents vanished inside the temple.
I leave to your imagination the fond embraces
bestowed by those who were bedded down near MONEY;
they stayed awake all night till the bright sun shone.
I passed the time in deep-felt praise of the God
who, in one instant, made blind MONEY see,
and blind Neokleides blinder than ever he was.

WIFE

Quite piously, possibly looking off stage right to, ultimately, Asklepios' temple.

And Thine is the Power and Glory, Lord!
                              Amen.
—But tell me, where's MONEY now?

KARION   He's on His way.
He had a really stupendous mob around him.
First came the Just, the Best and the Rightest, Have-Nots,
Have-Littles, all clustering round and clasping him close,
tugging at his hand in joy. But all the Rich,
with piles amassed by methods less than honest,
their brows a soured tangle of squints and frowns,
grumbled and stumbled away to cheerless homes.
The rest surged on after MONEY, their faces wreathed
in garlands, laughing and shouting in happy triumph.
            And forth there rang along the road
            The Geezer's Beat, the high-souled tread
            Of thin-soled clog's impassioned plod.

To the Chorus.

And so, it's over to you. All together, now:
Shiver and shimmy and prance and dance and do
whatever Choruses do. And keep it *happy*.
No more do you face the sour announcement of shortage:
No more of "*Wheat's Depleted*"
                        or "*Barley? Barely*"—
not any more!

WIFE   By Hekatê, that's Good News!
I want to reward the messenger, wrap you around
with a chain of pan-fried crullers.

KARION   Then hurry it up.
The madding throng is nearly banging at the door.

WIFE   It's just like buying a slave—you shower the new
arrival with cookies and nuts. I'll fix a batch,
a shower of goodies to welcome two roving eyes!

KARION   Myself, I'll go to meet those new arrivals.

Exeunt, Wife into the house, Karion off stage right. The Semichoruses group and engage, as directed, in a happy **CHORAL DANCE**

Episode II [771–801]

Enter MONEY and Khremylos stage right, in conversation at the head
of a mob of well-wishers and spongers, most of whom may be implied
rather than shown. Khremylos, holding them at bay, is not keeping up
his end of the conversation, but this bothers MONEY not at all.

MONEY   . . . and that's not all:

Striking a pious attitude, he looks upward.

I first prostrate myself
before the glorious Sun.

He flings himself down into an attitude of orien-
tal obeisance, then rises and looks around.

And next before
majestic Pallas's far-famed plain.

He flings himself down again, then rises. He is struck by a sudden thought.

Without
forgetting the whole expanse of Kekrops' land
that took me in.[27]

Down again. He rises rather wearily this time, with a tendency towards gloom.

My sad disasters load me
with shame. Such company kept—and all unknowing!
Such paragons, worth my constant friendship, shunned—
I never knew! I qualified then as Wretch
and Villain and Sinner, in act and omission!
Oh, dear.

By an effort of will, he pulls himself from these depths
of dejection and raises his chin to the world.

—That's all behind me, now. From this day forward,
I change direction, and demonstrate to the human race
that my stay in the hands of the base was no willing choice.

The followers become unruly. One breaks from the pack and starts
for MONEY, but Khremylos catches him and pushes him back.

---

27. Kekrops was a mythical king of Athens.

KHREMYLOS *GIT! Go to Hell!*

Order restored, he turns to MONEY.

> It's a strain to be the target
> of instant fair-weather friends. The price of success:
> Everyone wants to impress you with his very own special
> goodwill gesture—collision, contusion, concussion.
> Just look at me, will you? Nobody spared me a hearty
> Hello. No random gaggle of more than a couple
> old-timers passed up the chance to converge on my person—
> I'm a bloody *hub.*

Bearing a basket of goodies, Khremylos' Wife bursts from the
house. She greets her husband first, then MONEY.

WIFE   Darling, you're home! HelLO!
> —And a hearty Hello to you, too, Sir. It's time
> for me to perform the traditional Shower and lavish
> these goodies upon you.

She flings a fig or two, but stops when MONEY puts up a restraining hand.

MONEY   No, please. It's out of the question.
> Decorum decrees that a newly sighted God,
> effecting Initial Entrance at Deserving Homes,
> should appear as *Donor,* not *Donee.*

WIFE   Oh, darn.
> You mean you won't accept my Shower of goodies?

MONEY Oh, but I will—the traditional way, inside
> next to the hearth. That way, we also avoid
> a vulgar low-comedy shtick, since Decorum deters
> a comic poet from showering a stolid audience
> with figs and munchies, or eliciting laughs on the basis
> of *quid pro quo.*

WIFE   That's so—and you couldn't be righter:

Pointing to a member of the audience down front.

> Look! Dexinikos is home from the wars—and up
> on his feet already, stealing a march on those figs.

Exeunt Wife, Khremylos, and MONEY into the house. The Chorus
indulges in a **CHORAL DANCE,** during which Khremylos' house, now
graced by the favoring presence of a seeing God of MONEY, is suddenly transformed into a shining, palatial mansion, decked out with
all the trappings of extreme wealth. The Chorus marvels, as . . .

Episode III [802–958]

Karion, coughing and joyous, enters from the metamorphosed house. From
various nooks and crannies of his costume there protrude a wild variety of
filched goodies and utensils, prominent among which is a silver salver, a
mackerel platter, which he handles like a shield. He addresses the Chorus.

KARION   How sweet it is to live the Affluent Life—
                especially when this involves no personal outlay.
                Mountains of Boons have tottered and crashed on our house
                without our committing a single criminal act!
                On such conditions, my friends, how sweet a thing
                it is to have MONEY.
                                        The trough is stuffed with flour,
                the Finest White;
                                    the magnums flooded with wine,
                the Headiest Red;
                                    and every domestic vessel
                bloated with bullion, swollen with gold and silver
                past point of belief.
                                        The cistern brims with oil,
                the oil bottles groan with the most expensive perfumes,
                the attic loft is packed chockablock with figs.
                Each cruet and crock and pot and pitcher and plate
                is changed from clay to bronze.
                                        The grungy wooden
                mackerel platters shine with silver's clean gleam.
                Our lantern flashed, and now it's all over ivory!
                No penny-ante gambling among the help—
                we match gold staters now.
                                        For wiping asses,
                stones are *out,* we employ the freshest tender
                shoots of garlic, and throw them away after use.
                Now, *that* is Class.
                                        At this very moment, inside,
                the Boss, decked out in a wreath, is setting a record
                for Offerings, Burnt:
                                        Bellwether, buck, and bull.
                That's what drove me out here. I couldn't stay
                and stand all the smoke. It bites me right in the eyes.

Enter, stage left, a Righteous Man, well dressed and prosperous. He is followed by an extremely small slave, who staggers under the weight of
his load—a very ratty smock and a worn-out pair of cheap clogs.

RIGHTEOUS   Boy! I say, Boy! You try to keep up! We're on
                our way to the God.

KARION   And who is this approaching?

RIGHTEOUS   A man once ruined and wretched, now lucky and rich.

KARION   Clearly a man from the tribe of the Good, to judge
            by appearances.

RIGHTEOUS   Yep. You got it.

KARION   But if you're Good,
            what more can you possibly need?

RIGHTEOUS   I'm a pilgrim en route
            to the God. He's the cause of my present volume
            of Boons.
                      It all began when my Daddy died:
            He left me fixed with a very solid estate.
            I used it to furnish my needy friends with aid
            and assistance. I thought that was right, the real cachet
            of a virtuous life.

KARION   And because of the real cachet,
            you very soon found yourself cashless?

RIGHTEOUS   You betcher boots.

KARION   And, shortly thereafter, wretched?

RIGHTEOUS   You betcher boots.
            And all those needy types I'd aided—I thought
            that if *I* became a needy case, they'd be
            my firm and unswerving friends.
                                 They swerved, and developed
            a curious blindness whenever I came on the scene, and . . .

KARION   Don't tell me: They razzed your disaster?

RIGHTEOUS   You betcher boots.
            The drought in my kitchen withered me down to a lifeless
            husk. But not anymore, not now.
                              And that's
            the reason I made this journey, to thank the God
            in righteous fashion.

KARION   But what's the point of the smock
            that your tiny attendant's got here?

He lifts the offending article—stained, threadbare, full of holes—very gingerly.

                                 Just look at that thing!
            I trust there's a reason?

RIGHTEOUS   The best: I made a vow
            to dedicate this to the God.

KARION   Er—sentimental value?
         You wore it when you were confirmed in the Mighty Rites?[28]

RIGHTEOUS   When I was congealed in thirteen years of cold nights.

Karion returns the smock to the Slave and holds up the clogs.

KARION   These ramshackle clogs?

RIGHTEOUS   They shored me up throughout
         the winters of my discontent.

KARION   And these you intend
         to dedicate also?

RIGHTEOUS   Zeus knows that's why I brought them.

KARION

Returning the clogs to the Slave and shaking his head.

         You're gracing the God with a brace of dandy gifts.

A loud and sudden offstage clamor, and on there stalks, stage left,
an Informer,[29] caught in an unattractive paroxysm of mingled anger
and grief. His clothes are worn and torn, but by no means a match,
in sheer rattiness, for the Righteous Man's smock and clogs. He is followed by an extremely small and timid Witness, whose function,
should he ever exercise it, will be to attest to the commission of some
enormity. [To that end, he might carry something to write on.]

INFORMER   *WOE and MISFORTUNE!*
                         Catastrophe, Breakup, and Smash!
         O THRICE UNLUCKY ME!
                         FOUR TIMES UNLUCKY!
         Who'll bid Five?
                 Or Twelve?
                     A MILLION?
                             (Sob!)
         My edge is blunted by a God's distemper!

KARION   Apollo Protector and all like-minded Gods,
         what in hell can have happened to this hysteric?

INFORMER   Misery, that's what happened—it's happening now!
         It's Misery—no?—when I lose every last possession

---

28. The Eleusinian Mysteries, where it was customary for initiates to dedicate to the goddess
Demeter the clothes they wore when they were initiated.

29. The informer is a *sykophantês*, who brought accusations of wrongdoing before the courts
or the assembly. As Athens did not have a public prosecutor, private citizens brought charges,
and they won a part of the fines charged if the accused was convicted. The profession of the
sykophantês was therefore both potentially lucrative and despised.

> my household holds, at the hands of a God who'll shortly
> be blind again unless the action-at-law
> has lost its force in Greece?

KARION I think I begin
to see what the problem is. This man approaching
appears to be in some trouble.
His character's bad:
Just before they made him, they broke the mold.

INFORMER Where's that God with the promises?
Lead me to him!
"Just let me regain my original sight," he said,
*"and I'll make you Moneyed Men on the spot, without
exception."*
Exceptions there were in plenty, and those
he demolished!

KARION Whomever might he have demolished?

INFORMER *ME,*
right here!

KARION You must represent the Base and the Burglars.

INFORMER I *DONT!*
It's YOU!
You all are *sick, sick, sick!*
What's more, you stole my property, *mine, mine, mine!*

KARION My goodness gracious me, we're taking receipt
on one berserk *Informer,* gnashing his teeth.
Obvious bulimiac psychotic—all the symptoms.

The Informer zeroes in on Karion.

INFORMER You, there! Down to the center of town, on the double!
You have a date to be cracked on the wheel, and raise
your voice in confession of *Jiggery-Pokery!*

KARION

Brandishing the silver mackerel platter.

The voice
that's raised will be yours. In pain.

RIGHTEOUS Zeus save me,
this God MONEY is a blessing beyond all price
to every thinking Greek, if he can solve
the informer problem and lay those ravagers waste.

The Informer, who has retreated from Karion, turns on the Righteous Man.

INFORMER   It's too damned much! You, too—you swell the ranks
of the mockers?

He swaggers up to the Righteous Man like an inspecting officer.

All right, buddy—where did you get
this handsome cloak? I saw you yesterday wearing
a real bundle of rags. Looks mighty suspicious.

RIGHTEOUS   I could care less about you. I'm wearing protection—
this prophylactic ring from Eudemos the Ring King. Cost me
a drachma.

KARION   But that's for *snakes,* not *informers.* He doesn't
sell rings for *sneak-bite.*

INFORMER   *That* is the absolute limit!
You make your little jokes, but I notice you keep
quite mum on the motives behind this unlawful assembly.
Whatever they are, I know you're up to no good.

KARION   As Zeus is my judge, it's not *your* good we're up to.

INFORMER   As Zeus is my judge, you're plotting to *eat my dinner*!

RIGHTEOUS   If that's the case, may you and your witness split
on a line at the waist . . .

KARION   . . . distended by nothing but *Nothing*!

INFORMER   *That* constitutes a Denial, unprincipled scum?
Inside that house over there is a perfect hilt
of broiled fish fillets and basted roasts!

Moving toward the house, the Informer scents like a hound.

SuhNIFF! SuhNIFF!
SuhNIFF! SuhNIFF!
SuhNIFF!

KARION   Do you smell something, Loser?

RIGHTEOUS   He may have a cold.
That cloak he's wearing doesn't give much protection.

INFORMER   I tell you, Zeus and the rest, I will not stand it—
this utter lack of respect from bums like these!
For Shame! Such treatment meted out to myself,
a Paragon Patriot!

RIGHTEOUS   Paragon Patriot? *You?*

INFORMER   I, sir, am one of a kind.

RIGHTEOUS   That's true enough.
—All right, we'll have a quiz. I ask; you answer.

INFORMER   Shoot.

RIGHTEOUS   Are you a Farmer?

INFORMER   I'm not that crazy.

RIGHTEOUS   A Business Man, then?

INFORMER   Ye-es, I pretend to be one
when I get the chance.

RIGHTEOUS   I don't believe I follow.
Did you ever learn any trade or profession?

INFORMER   God, no.

RIGHTEOUS   But if there's nothing you *Do,* just how, and on what,
have you stayed alive?

INFORMER   I'm a Middle Manager, see?
Whatever goes on in the City, public or private,
well, I'm in the middle, managing.

RIGHTEOUS   But why do you do it?

INFORMER   It's my Concern.

RIGHTEOUS   You're an obvious Burglar, but claim
a Paragon's virtue—How? Your only vocation
is pestilent poking and prying, concerning yourself
with things that don't Concern you.

INFORMER   *That don't Concern me,*
you featherbrained klutz? My City's Welfare, on which
I work myself till I'm weak—well, what about *that*?

RIGHTEOUS   By Welfare, I take it, you mean Buttinsky Meddling.

INFORMER   I mean, Preserving the Duly Enacted Statutes
and Not Permitting the Least Infraction of Same
to Go Unpunished.

RIGHTEOUS   I thought the City chose Judges
for just that specific function.

INFORMER   And who's the *Accuser*?
Who, by Athenian law, *prosecutes* the case?

RIGHTEOUS

Shrugging at the obvious.

Whomever It May Concern.

INFORMER   That's *ME*! I'm *HIM*!—
Concerned! And all the City's business makes
its way to *ME*!

RIGHTEOUS   And what a defective defender
it finds, by Zeus. But why not be Concerned
with a peaceful rural existence?

INFORMER   You mean give up
the pursuit of my chosen calling and live like a *sheep*?

RIGHTEOUS   You couldn't take up something else?

INFORMER   Not for the God
of MONEY in person. Not for all the Spice
in Kyrenê.[30] I won't be bought!

Karion, who has been watching all this with mounting impatience,
has now had enough. He intervenes, confronting the Informer.

KARION   That's it. Take off
your cloak and be quick about it.

RIGHTEOUS

To the Informer, who appears not to have heard.

                                        He's talking to *you*.

KARION   *And* out of those shoes.

Elaborate unconcern from the Informer.

RIGHTEOUS   This is all directed at *you*.

INFORMER

Deciding to make a stand, he addresses both of them.

Come and get me! I fling a challenge toward
Whomever It May Concern.

KARION   That's *ME*! I'm *HIM*!

He catches the Informer by the cloak and rips it off. The naked
Informer scuttles away from him in a posture resembling "Sep-
tember Morn." The Witness, bemused, exits stage left.

INFORMER   It's too damned much! Denuded in open daylight!

KARION   And that's what you get for making your living by meddling
in others' business.

---

30. Kyrenê in what is now Libya was famous for its abundant silphium, a plant whose resin
was highly valued as medicine and as a spice.

He runs the Informer down and grabs him.

INFORMER   *WITNESS!* You see what he's doing?
                    WITNESS! Get this down!

KARION

Holding the Informer fast while he strips off his shoes.

                              The Witness you towed here
                    must have slipped his cable. He's long gone now.

At long last, the Informer realizes the full enormity of his situation.

INFORMER   Trapped like a rat—and a lonely rat, at that!
                    CRY WOE!

KARION   A scream? I've barely begun.

He tightens his hold.

INFORMER   Once more,
                    with feeling:
                              CRY WOE!

Still holding him, Karion turns to the Righteous Man.

KARION   Hand me your ragbag smock.
                    It's just the thing to wrap around this Informer.

RIGHTEOUS   I'm sorry, but that's a pledged *ex voto*. I vowed it
                    to MONEY long since.

KARION   But where's your sense of Decorum?
                    Where can this trash be better offered than on
                    the back and sides of a bum and burglar like this?
                    And MONEY should be invested in formal dress.

The Righteous Man secures the smock and clogs from the little Slave [and,
incidentally, at some time during the shuffle gives him the Informer's cloak
and shoes in exchange]. Karion takes the tacky smock and forces the
Informer inside it, while the Righteous Man looks ruefully at the clogs.

RIGHTEOUS   I hope that you can tell me some use for these clogs.

KARION   No problem. I'll quickly nail them up on his forehead:
                    It resembles the trunk of the Non-Domestic Olive.

Producing a hammer from somewhere, he performs this task,
then frees the bedraggled Informer and steps back to sur-
vey his work. The Informer pulls himself together.

INFORMER   I'm leaving. I realize I'm no match at all
             for the two of you. But let me find a sidekick,
             corrupt and rotten to the core, to serve as Witness,
             and before tomorrow I'll see your muscle-bound MONEY
             convicted of Treason.
                              He's clearly Guilty, of course:
             One lone individual bringing Democracy down,
             with arrant contempt for Due Process, refusing to ask
             the Senate or Congress for either advice or consent!

He stalks grotesquely to and through the stage left exit.
As he goes, the Righteous Man calls after him.

RIGHTEOUS   And now, as you slog through the Winter, clad in my armor,
              a word of advice:
                              Make all speed to the bathhouse.
              Station yourself at the head of the line, by the stove,
              and try to get warm. If you can.
                                   An important post—
              I held it once myself, not long ago.

KARION   The bathhouse manager won't let him stay. He'll grip him
              tight by the balls and drag him outside. One look
              will make him certain that this is a man debased,
              that just before they made him, they broke the mold.
              —Inside with us, to pray and praise the God.

Exeunt, into the house, Karion, the Righteous Man, and the latter's little Slave. The Chorus advances and does a **CHORAL DANCE**

Episode IV [959–1096]

Enter, stage left, a Decayed Gentlewoman, ancient and rich, her great bulk
covered by good clothes, which are, frankly, a great deal too young for her,
and provide a strange counterpoint to her face, which is strikingly unattractive, a hideous ruin. She affects a coquettish manner of speech that
ill befits her years and voice. Her appetites have not waned with the passage of time; she is one of those who, for some things, Have Always
Depended on the Kindness of Strangers. [In this translation, the cadences
of her speech are Southern American; I have eschewed outright dialect,
which may be supplied or not, according to choice.] She is attended by
a small female slave who carries a large dish filled with pastry and covered with a cloth. She is also lost, and appeals to the Chorus for aid.

DECAYED   Oooh, such cuddly Senior Citizens! Might you
              kindly inform me where I am? Have we really
              arrived at the house of that brand-new God, or did we
              go completely astray and lose our way?

The 1ST Koryphaios is caught up in the mode.

1ST KORY   Why, bless you, child, your journey's over. You're standing
right at the door, you sweet little thang with such
a maidenly manner of asking your elders directions.

DECAYED   My goodness! I guess I'll send in a call for someone.

Before she can do this, the door opens and Khremylos appears. He is smartly dressed and all business.

KHREMYLOS   No need; I've come on my own. There is one fixed
matter of business: State the Purpose of your Visit.

DECAYED   I have been wronged, kind Sir, most foully and lawlessly
WRONGED! The moment this God-come-lately regained
his eyesight, he rendered my life absolutely unfit
for decent living!

KHREMYLOS   You must have committed some crime.
Let's see:
                    Did you possibly serve the distaff half
as Informess—I mean, Informette?

DECAYED   The very idea!

KHREMYLOS   Contempt of Court? You argued before the Bar
completely loaded?

DECAYED   You're funnin' little old me,
and I'm to be *pitied*. Why, I have been deeply scored
and scratched by circumstance!

KHREMYLOS   Be more specific. Where—
no, *HOW* did this scratching take place?

DECAYED   It's a sorry tale:
I had me a fancy young gigolo—poor, of course,
but oh what a face, good family, well bred, and *worthy*.
Whatever my heart desired, my every wish—
and I do mean *every*—that boy fulfilled to the hilt
and beyond.
                    In the most respectable manner, of course.
Which is not to say that I didn't hold up my end
in this relationship. Every request that he made,
I supplied in full.

KHREMYLOS   Again, please be specific.
What sort of requests did he make on these occasions?

DECAYED   Oh, piddly things. He held me enskied and sainted
in a way that's quite *recherché*. Let's see, what was there?
He'd ask for twenty drachmas to buy a cloak,
and maybe another eight for a pair of shoes.
And then, for his sisters, the price of a sweet little dress.
Sometimes, for his mother, the price of a sweet little smock.
And now and then he'd need four pecks of wheat.

KHREMYLOS   Quite modest. Piddly indeed. To judge by that list,
it's abundantly clear that he held you enskied and sainted.

DECAYED   Don't think for a moment he made those demands out of *Greed*!
I have his *word*! It was purely purest *Love*.
He used to say that wearing a cloak I'd bought him
would keep me fresh in his mind.

KHREMYLOS   Now, *that's* a consuming
passion. *Recherché* is scarcely the word.

DECAYED   But that's all over now. His affections have waned:
he's utterly changed his mind and himself. The bastard.
Looky here.

Grabbing the dish from her Slave, she whips off the cloth and displays an impressive collection of dessert pastries.

                    I sent him late this cake and all
the cute little *petits fours* on this plate as pledges
of Love, appending a note that allowed as how
I'd drop by his place at sundown . . .

She breaks down in sobs.

KHREMYLOS   So what did he do?

DECAYED   He sent it all back, and topped it off with *this*—
a three-layer cream *gâteau*—for me to eat
on condition I never came to see him again!
But that's not all—he sent a message with it:
The hoary glory of yore is Gone with the Wind!

KHREMYLOS

Tasting a fingerful of cream from the gâteau.

                    To judge from his actions, he certainly doesn't seem vicious.
It's merely a matter of diet. In POVERTY's day,
he had to subsist on whatever scraps he could scrounge.
Then MONEY came his way, and he logically lost
his taste for warmed-over dabs of diluted gruel.

DECAYED

Nodding; sarcasm is wasted on her.

> Back then, I swear that there wasn't a day went by
> without he'd come and take up his post by my door.

KHREMYLOS To join your cortège?

DECAYED   No, silly. He was mad
> for the sound of my voice.

KHREMYLOS   And madder for the clink of your coin.

The format for the next sequence is now set; the Decayed Gentlewoman will feed her grief with fond reminiscences of her lost love;
Khremylos will undercut each recollection with a nasty aside.

DECAYED Whenever he'd see that I was upset or poorly,
he'd call me pet names—*Ducky* and *Turtle-Dove.*

KHREMYLOS *And inveigle a love-struck Loon into buying him shoes.*

DECAYED I rode in my carriage down to the Greater Mysteries
at Eleusis once, when some fellow gave me the eye:
For that, he hammered me black and blue all day.
I tell you, my young man was a jealous lover!

KHREMYLOS *No great mystery—why share his place at the trough?*

DECAYED He'd praise the unblemished beauty of my tiny hands.

KHREMYLOS *Whenever they held huge twenty-drachma handouts.*

DECAYED He claimed my skin's bouquet smelled sweeter than sweet.

KHREMYLOS *You swill that Thasian wine. It soaks through your pores.*

DECAYED He raved about my soft and enchanting gaze.

KHREMYLOS *Well,* he *saw sharp; no fathead* he. *He knew
the way to his stomach lay through your horny heart.*

DECAYED And there's my case, good Sir. Your God's a Four-Flusher.
He's simply not living up to His promise of aid
to the innocent injured.

KHREMYLOS   So what do you want Him to do?
Put your request in words, and it's already granted.

DECAYED I have to be paid, by Zeus, and I want Compulsion.
It's only just that a person I've . . . Treated Nice
should be, well, *forced* to Treat *me* Nice in return.
Or doesn't it strike you as fair for me to receive
the measliest Boon?

KHREMYLOS   Correct me if wrong, but hasn't
               your boyfriend paid already in nightly installments?

DECAYED   But he swore he'd never leave me while I was alive!

KHREMYLOS   Correct. On available data, he deduces you're dead.

DECAYED   But mental and physical anguish—I've wasted away!

KHREMYLOS   To judge from a brief inspection, you've *rotted* away.

DECAYED

  Displaying her girth with a gloomy satisfaction.

               Look at that waist. You could slip me right through a *ring*.

KHREMYLOS   Easy. The hard part's getting the ring off the barrel.

DECAYED

  Looking off stage right.

               Well, I declare! Here comes my gigolo now,
               the very boy I've spent all this time accusing!

  Enter, stage right, a smart Young Stud, expensively dressed, wreaths
  on his head and shoulders, a lighted torch in his hand. He is very
  drunk, and in the feisty mood of the Newly Independent.

               He looks like he's fixing to go to a party.

KHREMYLOS   Seems so.
               At least, he's coming this way with wreaths and a torch.

YOUNG STUD

  To the Decayed Gentlewoman.

               Hail to thee . . .

DECAYED   Wozzat?

YOUNG STUD   . . . Outdated Sweetheart!

  He peers at her hair.

               What? Silver threads among the grey already?

DECAYED   I can't endure this—insult added to injury!

KHREMYLOS   Don't fret. You know he hasn't seen you for ages.

DECAYED   Ages, hell—he was over to see me last night!
               I will not stand this!

KHREMYLOS   A metabolic upset, that's all.
               Some people are strange. They take an excess of wine—
               as he clearly has—and it makes their vision *keener*.

DECAYED   Oh, no! It's his little way: He's always been
an undisciplined punk.

YOUNG STUD   Poseidon, God who Soaks
in the Sea! Ye Gods of the Elder Time! I dare you
to count the wrinkles and ruts that riddle this face.

Peering more closely at her, he neglects to be careful of his lighted torch.

DECAYED   *HALP! FIRE!*
You keep that torch away from me, you hear?

KHREMYLOS

A half-aside, to the audience.

                    Sound, sage advice. The least insignificant spark
on that withered hulk would ignite her; she'd blaze up faster
than a festival wreath left over from last fall's harvest.

YOUNG STUD

Coyly, to the Decayed Gentlewoman.

                    You wanna play me a game in a little bit?

DECAYED

To the Stud, more coyly, and—were it possible—blushing.

                    You naughty boy! But where?

YOUNG STUD   Right here—where else?

Handing Khremylos a handful of nuts.

                    Here, have some nuts.

KHREMYLOS   But what sort of game are we playing?

YOUNG STUD A guessing game. Guess how many teeth she's got.

KHREMYLOS I know the answer, it's *Three*!
                    Or maybe Four?

YOUNG STUD You lose—so pay me!

He snatches back the nuts.

                    Only one lonely molar!

DECAYED   You must be the scummiest man alive, and crazy
to boot. No sane and healthy man would use me
like this, to wash his dirty linen in public—

With a wave that embraces the audience.

                    and such a public—all men.[31] Respect must be paid:
I am not one of your laundry tubs!

---

31. The Greek text reads literally, "among so many men."

YOUNG STUD   You're right;
cut "laundry."
                         A wash job would do you good.

KHREMYLOS   I doubt it.

Moving to the Decayed Gentlewoman and pointing a finger at her face.

    Look at her. All tailed up for the retail market.
    But wash this paint away, dissolve this plaster,
    and expose to public gaze a face of shreds
    and patches, slowly flapping in the wind.

DECAYED

Feeling doubly betrayed; however illogically, she had
come to look on Khremylos as her ally.

                                       You are
             a Dirty Old Man. What's more, you're as crazy as he is!

YOUNG STUD   Aha, there! I spy *Hanky-Panky!*
                                  The Moving Finger
             Massages the Tit—and he doesn't think I notice!

The Decayed Gentlewoman and Khremylos, not really all that close
together and by no means engaged in any such activity, covert or
otherwise, leap guiltily apart and reply to the accusation.

DECAYED   Not me, by Our Lady of Heaven!
                              You are *disgusting*!

KHREMYLOS   Not me, by the Hag of Hell!
                              I'd have to be *mad*.
             —Come on, young man. This confrontational orgy
             simply must stop. I can't allow you to hate
             this sweet young thing.

YOUNG STUD   Me hate her? I love her. Insanely.

KHREMYLOS   Regardless, she has accused you.

YOUNG STUD   Accused me of what?

KHREMYLOS   Of insolence, outrage, and slander. Of sending the message,
             The hoary glory of yore is Gone with the Wind.

YOUNG STUD   All right, then, let's be serious.
                              Reverend Sir,
             I will not fight you over this woman.

KHREMYLOS   Why not?

YOUNG STUD I respect your age too much. And so . . .

I wouldn't

do this for anyone else in the world; I couldn't
stand to think of another man . . .

But no. Each thing

in its season . . .

He has maneuvered Khremylos into position beside the Decayed
Gentlewoman. With sudden deftness, he joins their hands.

Be kind to my little girl.

He backs slowly toward the stage right exit.

Take her,

she's yours.

Still backing.

Go on your way rejoicing . . .

Khremylos breaks free of the spell, dashes to him, and grabs his arm.

KHREMYLOS   ***HOLD IT!***

You don't fool me in the least. You've decided to cut
your losses—such as they are—and give this lady
the slip.

DECAYED

Grabbing the Young Stud by the other arm. He is
now framed between the aged pair.

And who could stand to think of that?

YOUNG STUD I really have nothing to say to this clunker, serviced
and junked by every one of the thirteen thousand
men out there.

This with a wave at the audience. He has shrugged free of
the pair's hands, but they are keeping him in range.

KHREMYLOS   Regardless, you thought the wine
was good enough to drink, and now you've got
to swig the residue, dregs and all.

Bottoms Up!

The Young Stud turns to him in distress.

YOUNG STUD Those dregs are past their peak!

And moldy, too.

KHREMYLOS   Well, use a filter. Be selective. It'll work out.

> Pushing the Young Stud backward toward the door of the house.

Now into the house with you.

YOUNG STUD

> Moving backward in joyful surprise, and not see-
> ing the Decayed Gentlewoman.

That's just what I want!
I have these garlands here to vow to the God . . .

> He turns around and finds her at the door.

DECAYED   And *I* have a little something to say to him, too.

YOUNG STUD   And *I* have something else to do.

> He turns to break away, but is redirected by the officious Khremylos.

KHREMYLOS   Courage!
Why so paranoid? She isn't going to rape you.

YOUNG STUD   Well, that's a happy relief. I did some hard time
caulking that leaky hull in the recent past.

DECAYED

> Moving in behind him as, preceded by her Slave, they start for the door.

All right, dinghy, here's dry dock. Warp right in;
I'll tend your stern.

> The little procession disappears into the house as Khremylos watches.

KHREMYLOS   O Zeus our Heavenly King,
what zip for a worn-out ship of the line! Formation
flush to the taffrail; no barnacle holds it closer.

> He follows them into the house. The Chorus engages in a **CHORAL DANCE**

Exodos [1097–1209]

> A pause, and then the machine whirs, letting down from above, in fact from
> Heaven, the God Hermes, celestial Pooh-Bah and archetypal con man, now
> somewhat bedraggled. This is a silent epiphany, even furtive, heralded and
> hailed by no one. Hermes slips cautiously off the rig, then looks up and
> waves; the crane hauls it up. He surveys the house, runs on tiptoe to the
> door and bangs furiously on it for an instant—then, chuckling, sprints away
> and hides, in view of the audience. (It is important that this action is seen for
> the child's trick it is, the equivalent of, say, Halloween doorbell ringing.)

KARION

From inside.

> Who's that knocking at my door?

Hermes chuckles. Karion emerges from the door and looks around, puzzled.

> > Well, what's all this?
> It looks like nobody's out here.

This delights Hermes, who is hard put to stifle his chuckling.

> > Stupid door
> and its pointless noise. I'll give it a reason to howl.

He gives it a vicious kick—which Hermes finds delicious—and starts inside. Hermes comes out of hiding and speaks low, in the tones of the tout.

HERMES   Hey, bud!

Karion stops and turns.

> Yeah, you. Karion. Wait up.

KARION

Moving truculently to the newcomer.

> > Say, bo,
> are you the one who was banging away on the door?

HERMES

All injured innocence.

> Why, no. Not me.

Karion is not convinced.

> > I really meant to, of course,
> but you opened it first.

Karion, still suspicious, has moved downstage to Hermes.

> You've got a quick hand on a door.

Karion relaxes, and Hermes shoots full-speed into his scam.

> *ALL RIGHT, LET'S GO, GET A MOVE ON!*
> > Call your Boss!

Galvanized into frenzy, Karion rushes for the door.

> There's more!

Karion races back to Hermes.

> Call his wife and children, too!

Karion nods and races for the door.

There's more!

Karion back to Hermes again.

Call the servants!

Nod, and to door.

More yet!

Back again.

The dog!

Nod, and to door.

There's more!

Karion, by now quite tired, runs back.

Call yourself!

Karion, puzzled but caught up in the rhythm, nods, shrugs, starts for door.

One more!

Karion back, nettled and worn.

The pig!

That does it. Karion, exasperated, plants his feet.

KARION   *NOW JUST A GODDAMNED MINUTE! WHAT **IS** ALL THIS?*

Spoiling for a fight, he stalks toward Hermes, but
Hermes turns his godhead up to full.

HERMES   This, O base malefactor, is *the Will of Zeus*!

This deflates Karion, who stands bewildered, wondering whether to be frightened or not.

> He means to mash you all in His mighty mortar
> and void the resultant mess of revolting remains
> in the City Dump!

KARION

Not really frightened, but, to be on the safe side, speaking in an aside.

> *The bearer of news like that*
> *should receive, as reward, a full glossectomy, free.*

His cool recovered, he addresses Hermes.

> That's quite comprehensive. I trust that Zeus has reasons
> for treating us all that way?

HERMES	*Reasons!* The best

in the world, for that your deeds are the worst in the world!
Know This:
                    Upon that very instant when MONEY
commenced to see, all sacred sacrifice ceased.
Donations, Immolations, Oblations, from Cupcakes to Cattle,
the tiniest leaf of laurel or sniff of incense—
all gone. No offerings come to us gods any more.

KARION   Nor will they ever. Consider the wretched bollix
you used to make out of looking after *us*.

HERMES

Shifting out of the austere divine attitude.

        Oh, I'm not your bleeding heart half-god. The rest of Heaven
can go to Hell, for all I care. *My Ass* is
what matters, Hermes the Late, now dead and demolished.

KARION

One con artist to another.

        I can identify with that.

HERMES   *The Good Old Days!*
I had *carte blanche* with every barmaid in town
from the moment they opened for business. Endless goodies.
Honey and figs, and *baba au vin* . . .
                            I'd work through the dainties
deemed fit for a Hermes to eat.
                    The Bad New Days. . . .
Inactive.
        Downgraded.
                Retired.
                    And No Free Lunch.

KARION   Seems fair enough. From those bars, you were on the take,
took plenty, promised protection—and didn't deliver.

HERMES   Woe and alas! To think of that special cheesecake
they baked for my birthday—
                    I had twelve birthdays a year!

KARION

Quoting from a tragedy now, providentially, lost.

    In pain thou crav'st the lost and call'st in vain.

The two shift into a mode we have already seen: Hermes
in an orgy of nostalgia, Karion undercutting.

HERMES   Heigh-ho! Lackaday for the cutlets I gobbled up!

KARION   *Up, up, and away, my godlet—you're due for the chop.*

HERMES   Bereft of the giblets and chitlins I nibbled with vim!

KARION   *Get stuffed, O Great One—the Wurst is yet to come.*

HERMES   Oy vey, the lush bouquet of the votive wine!

KARION   *A good bush needs no wine—try some of mine.*

He lets a tremendous fart, which staggers Hermes out of his nostalgia.

HERMES   Canst thou not minister to a friend abused?

KARION   A modest proposal might not be refused.

The antiphonal mode is dropped.

HERMES   That food you're offering up in the house—do you think
you could possibly sneak me out a fresh-baked loaf
(I can taste it now) and maybe a big, strapping hunk
of beef?

KARION   I'm sorry. Those items don't circulate.

He turns to go.

HERMES   Wait!
You owe me one. On those all-too-frequent occasions
when you were filching the odd domestic utensil,
I was the one who arranged that the Boss didn't notice.

KARION   Provided you got your cut, you compulsive crook.
On those occasions, you levied a fresh-baked cheesecake.

HERMES   So what? As I recall, you ate it yourself.

KARION   As *I* recall, you didn't put in for a cut
of the beatings and bruisings and such that fell to my lot
when one of my scams went wrong and I got caught.

HERMES   Enough of injustice collecting. You've won the world
for fifty miles around, so Amnesty, please!

Struck by a brilliant idea.

          By the Gods!
                    And *from* the Gods, in fact.
                                        I herewith
          apply to you here for Permanent Resident Status.

KARION   You mean you want to *defect*? Leave Heaven for *here*?

HERMES   Opportunities, lifestyle—you offer the Better Deal.

KARION   But *desertion*—that's not much proof of Civic Feeling.

HERMES   *Breathes there a man with soul so dead,*
          Who never to himself hath said,
          "Where'er my profit doth expand,
          THAT is my own, my native land!"?

KARION   But us? What's in it for *US* if we let you in?

HERMES   Well, look. I'm loaded with attributes—no god more so.

Pulling out a large scroll, he begins unrolling it.

          There must be something here you can use. Let's see . . .

Finding something, he looks up.

          I'm *God of Non-Rectilinear Motion.*

KARION   Of *what?*

HERMES   Of Twisting. Set me by the door, and I'll guarantee
          that your hinges work.

KARION   Twisting is what we need least.
          This is a straightforward mainstream society. *No.*

HERMES

Reading from the scroll.

          Hermes, God of Applied Economics?

KARION   *No.*
          MONEY we have, and we get it wholesale. Why should
          we underwrite *Hermes, God of Retail Resale?*

HERMES   *Hermes, God of Fraud and Double Dealing?*

KARION   *NO!*
          No Fraud! I told you, this is a straightforward place,
          Home of the Single Deal.

HERMES   *I'm the God of Guidance—*
          He Who Shows the Way?

KARION   Well, we have a God
          Who *Knows* the Way—he sees it straight and clear.
          What possible use would we have for a Guide?

Hurt, Hermes rummages in the scroll. Suddenly he straightens up in joy.

HERMES   I got it!
          HERMES, GOD OF COMPETITIVE CONTESTS!
                                          That
          is just what I'll do!

Nothing goes better with MONEY
than games and bouts.

Impresario Hermes, that's me—
Producer of Matches and Meets in Art and Sport!

KARION   A dandy ploy, this nice profusion of epithets.
This fellow's occupation's *found*—not much, but a living.
He's hedged his bets like a juror eager for duty,
who busts his tail getting his name enrolled
on the panels of *all* the courts.

HERMES   That good enough?
Can I go in now?

KARION   I guess so . . . Wait a minute!

He grabs the scroll and speeds through it.

I think you missed one.
Let's see—*here* we are:
Hermes, God of Menial Taskery!
Enter,
and make a quick start on your duties by lugging the tripe
to the well and washing it off—
HERMES THE FLUNKY!

Chuckling, he escorts Hermes into the house. Almost immediately, a distressed Priest of Zeus enters, stage left. He looks around in confusion, then makes an appeal, either to the Chorus, or to the audience, or to both.

PRIEST   Can anyone help me? All I want is an answer,
plain and simple:
Where is Khremylos?

KHREMYLOS

Entering from the house, in expensive formal dress. He is in excellent spirits.

Here,
most excellent Sir. What's up?

PRIEST   *Nothing* is Up.
Everything's *Down.* The moment that MONEY commenced
to see, I became an instant, long-standing victim
of terminal famine.
I don't have a crumb to cram in
my ravenous maw.
I'm *starving*—a stupid fate
for a duly certified Priest of Zeus the Savior!

KHREMYLOS

With complete unconcern.

> Ye Gods.
> > I suppose there's a reason?

PRIEST   The *sa-cri-fi-ces*—
they stopped!
> > Nobody bothers, nobody cares!

KHREMYLOS   And why is that?

PRIEST   *Why*? Everybody's got MONEY—
who needs to be saved anymore? Oh, when they were poor,
we got your Speculator, grateful to be home safe
from a risky venture—always good for a nice,
fat victim.
> > We got your Lucky Defendant, grateful
to save his skin in a lawsuit.
> > > We got your Future-
Shockee, Potential Investor, Nervous Nellie—grateful
to learn what the omens predicted, grateful enough
to invite a Priest for a sit-down dinner.
> > > > But *NOW*?
Nobody dedicates, nobody offers, nobody
even comes to the temple!
> > > Except for the millions
who use the foyer to relieve the calls of nature.

KHREMYLOS   Just doing their bit. I suppose you take a cut?

PRIEST   Well, *I* have said Good-bye, Farewell, and So Long
to Zeus the Savior. *I* intend to stay *here*!

KHREMYLOS   Calm down. It'll all work out. God willing, of Course.
And as for Zeus the Savior—He's there inside.
He got the same idea and joined up on His own.

PRIEST   The way you put it, everything turned out fine!

He starts for the door, but Khremylos catches him.

KHREMYLOS   No, don't go in; you came at just the right time.
The Parade's beginning, the Re-Installation Procession.
We're setting MONEY up at his former location
behind Athena's temple, with its unblocked view
of the Treasury vaults.[32]

---

32. The treasury of the Athenian state, much depleted since the disastrous end of the
Peloponnesian War, was kept in the back room of the Parthenon.

Calling to the house.

> Torches! Light the torches
> and bring them outside!

Lighted torches are produced from the house and
given to him. He hands them to the Priest.

> You take them and lead the Parade,
> directly in front of the God.

PRIEST

In priestly tones.

> It is meet and right
> and fitting that I so do.

KHREMYLOS   Let MONEY be summoned!

A procession-preparing throng [contrasting strongly with the handful
that made the trip to Asklepios' temple] pours out of the house. Among
them are MONEY, who is immediately escorted to his place of honor in
the formation, and the Decayed Gentlewoman, still unsatisfied and without assignment as the Parade assembles. She seeks out Khremylos.

DECAYED   Use me as you will!

KHREMYLOS   Of Course. Well—*Pots*. They're very
important. Can't install a God without *Pots*.

Pots are brought to him, and he holds them out to her.

> You take these *Pots* and *Bear* them. On top of your head.
> And do be serious. Your costume's fine—those clashing
> panels and dots are perfect for the girl who *Bears*
> the *Pots*.

DECAYED   You forgot our agreement.

KHREMYLOS   It's all looked after,
it's already fixed:
> Your gigolo comes at sundown.

DECAYED   Well, all right, if you give me your solemn word
that he'll drop in . . .

Khremylos nods.

> Then I will be your *Pot-Girl*!

She happily piles pots on her head and joins the now-ready procession.
Khremylos draws back to appraise the effect and turns to the audience.

KHREMYLOS   Now, here's a conundrum for you:

How do these Pots

differ from all other Pots?

Give up? It's simple:

In all other Pots, the Icky Scum will rise

to the top of the Pots, you see—but these Pots rise

to the top of the Icky Scum.

What a cunning stunt.

He joins the Parade, which starts off, watched by the Chorus.

CHORUS   *Now the play is over,*
Take we our assigned
Place in the procession,
Following behind.

Marching firmly forward,
Singing loud and clear,
Let us go rejoicing,
Bringing up the rear.

They join the Parade, which moves off stage left, marching and singing, till omnes exeunt.

New Comedy: Menander's *Samia*

The date of *Samia* is unknown, but various allusions suggest a first performance relatively early in Menander's career, probably within a few years of 314 BCE. The play was thus produced after the defeat of Athens and most other Greek city-states by the kingdom of Macedon under King Philip II (338 BCE), the conquest of the Persian empire by Philip's son Alexander, and the death of Alexander (323 BCE), during the struggles between Alexander's generals for control of his empire. Athens was more a pawn than a major player in the events of the day, and aside from a possible suggestion by Demeas that things are difficult in Athens (v. 102, in scene 1.5), the plot does not reflect contemporary politics in any explicit way. The play does, however, reflect important features of Athenian ideology, including the distinction between citizen and noncitizen women, desire for harmony between rich and poor, and the complicated nuances in relationships between fathers and sons.

Although Menander's plays were enormously popular in antiquity, they were not preserved through the Middle Ages in manuscripts. What we have of Menander, therefore, we owe to the dryness of Egypt, which preserved pieces of several plays and one whole play (*Dyskolos,* or *The Grouch*) written on papyrus. The papyrus containing *Samia* includes almost all of the play's third through fifth acts, but only portions of the first two acts. Parker has filled in the missing sections of the play with educated guesses based on the fragments that remain, the rest of the plot, and comparison with other comedies.

The decreasing importance of the chorus evident in *Money, the God* reached a further stage in the plays of New Comedy. The text of *Samia,* like other plays of Menander, preserves no words of the chorus. Instead, we see the word *chorou* ([song] of the chorus) four times to indicate interludes during which the chorus sang and danced. The four interludes divided the play into five acts, the standard structure of New Comedies. Parker further divides each act into scenes, determined by entrances and exits of characters. Although such division into scenes is a modern convention, a look at the structure in terms of both acts and scenes reveals much about the play. Note, for example, the large number of short scenes in the fourth act, reflecting the chaos that takes over as Nikeratos learns about the baby. Note also the many monologues, rarely found in Old and Middle Comedy but ubiquitous in New Comedy.

Verses	Scene	Events
ACT I		
1–57 + missing verses	1.1: Prologue	Moschion tells his story
missing verses +59–60	1.2	Chrysis monologue
61–86 + missing verses	1.3	Chrysis, Moschion, and Parmenon prepare for the return of Demeas
missing verses +87–95	1.4	Moschion monologue

96–119+ missing verses	1.5	Demeas and Nikeratos, returning, agree to marriage of Moschion and Plangon
CHOROU	Choral Interlude	No words preserved
ACT II		
missing verses +120–166	2.1	Moschion persuades Demeas to let Chrysis stay in spite of the baby and gets permission to marry Plangon
missing verses +167–188	2.2	Demeas and Nikeratos arrange for the marriage of Moschion and Plangon
189–205 + missing verses	2.3	Demeas sends Parmenon for wedding provisions
CHOROU	Choral Interlude	No words preserved
ACT III		
missing verses +206–282	3.1	Demeas reports learning that Moschion is the baby's father
283–324	3.2	Parmenon returns with the cook and is interrogated by Demeas
325–356	3.3	Demeas monologue
357–368	3.4	Cook enters and hears commotion
369–398	3.5	Demeas expels Chrysis
399–420	3.6	Nikeratos takes in Chrysis
CHOROU	Choral Interlude	No words preserved
ACT IV		
421–439	4.1	Moschion returns
440–520	4.2	Moschion fails to persuade Demeas to take Chrysis back; Nikeratos learns Moschion is father of the baby
520–532	4.3	Moschion tells Demeas Plangon is the baby's mother
532–539	4.4	Nikeratos has seen Plangon nursing the baby; Moschion flees
540–547	4.5	Nikeratos rushes back into his house
547–556	4.6	Demeas monologue
556–567	4.7	Nikeratos rushes out and then back into his house
568–575	4.8	Chrysis flees from Nikeratos into Demeas' house

575–615	4.9	Demeas persuades Nikeratos to accept birth of the baby
CHOROU	Choral Interlude	No words preserved
ACT V		
616–640	5.1	Moschion monologue
641–669	5.2	Moschion orders Parmenon to get his cloak and sword
670–690	5.3	Parmenon fails to persuade Moschion to stay
690–712	5.4	Demeas makes his case to Moschion
713–737	5.5	Moschion and Nikeratos persuade Moschion to stay; wedding

SAMIA
a.k.a.

Wedding Day

BY
MENANDER

translated by
douglass parker

The Set

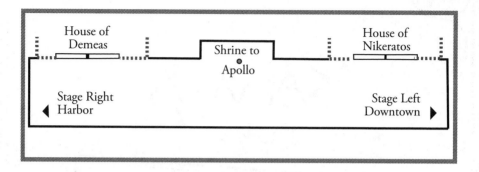

SCENE: A street in Athens. We see the fronts of two houses side by side: stage right, the palatial residence of Demeas; stage left, the quite modest house of Nikeratos. Between them, an altar, with statue, to the god Apollo. Wing exits: stage right, to the harbor; stage left, to the agora.

Dramatis Personae

Speaking Roles:

MÓSCHION,	*a young and perplexed Athenian gentleman, adopted son of Demeas [passionate, slightly spoiled, more likeable than not; æt. 21?]*
CHRYSIS,	*a courtesan from Samos, Demeas' live-in mistress [quite competent, but sorely tried; late 20s or early 30s; genuinely attractive; a good neighbor]*
PÁRMENON,	*slave to Demeas [managing, crafty, not all-powerful]*
DÊMEAS,	*an elderly Athenian gentleman, quite rich [an indulgent authoritarian, if that makes sense]*
NIKÊRATOS,	*an elderly[1] Athenian gentleman, rather poor, neighbor and friend to Demeas, father of Plangon [more reserved than Demeas, but capable of really astounding rages]*
COOK,	*a cook [an independent contractor]*

Mute Roles:

ATTENDANTS TO DEMEAS
COOK'S HELPERS
A SHEEP
A BATHMAN
A MUSICIAN
PLÁNGON, DAUGHTER OF NIKERATOS
EXTENDED FAMILIES OF DEMEAS AND NIKERATOS
TRYPHÊ, FEMALE SLAVE TO DEMEAS

> *Everyone is quite nice, really. No bogeymen or bogeywomen, no unpleasant characters. Unpleasantness, when it comes, results from putting pleasant people in untenable situations.*

---

1. *Mutatis mutandis,* of course. Demeas and Nikeratos may be as ancient as forty or forty-five. [Parker's note]

A Note on the Text

NB: In the following text, *translated* dialogue—that based on existing Greek text—is printed in Garamond, the font you are reading now, thus:

> The logical way to approach this duty should be
> for me to recite you all the ins and outs
> of Daddy. The kind of person he is.

Supplied dialogue—that excogitated to fill in the substantial holes in the text, where the Greek has been lost—is printed in Helvetica, a sans-serif font, thus:

> I'd better tell you my name. It's Moschion. Monster
> lecher, besmircher and worse of the family honor
> of the dearest Daddy that ever adopted a worthless
> ingrate . . .

Occasionally, due to the occurrence of the holes, the two kinds, and hence the two fonts, will be found mingled in the same speech, thus:

> The way I saw it, he really
> should bring her home, and set her up in the house.
> But he was too ashamed, and because of *me*.
> What would my friends say? That's the way he thought.
> Not that he ever let me know it. Daddy,
> well, he *hides* his feelings. Worried or angry,
> you'd never know from the calm, unruffled surface.

Caveat Lector . . .

DSP

SAMIA

ACT I: I.1 [11 vv. + 1–29 + 20–25 vv. + 30–57 + c. 25/2 vv.]²

Moschion enters from Demeas' house, stage right, moves recal-
citrantly down center, and, after a bit of dither, strikes a pro-
logue-making attitude and addresses the audience.

MOSCHION   To start with, I'm adopted . . .

He stops and slumps.

> —Don't think I enjoy this.
> I'd rather be *any* place but here.—

Back to the prologue.

> My daddy,
> my adopted daddy, Demeas, he lives right here.

He indicates Demeas' house.

> He's rich. He's also away. For quite a while.

He stops and slumps again.

> —Oh, god. This is hell.—

Back to the prologue.

> I was adopted quite young.
> Had every advantage, you'd say. But . . .

Another slump.

> —Oh, let's call
> the whole thing off. I am not doing this well.—

Back to the prologue, with clenched teeth.

> I'd better tell you my name. It's Moschion. Monster
> lecher, besmircher and worse of the family honor

---

2. At the beginning of each scene Parker recorded what verses, missing and extant, were
included in the scene. Here, for example, where the heading says [*11 vv.* + 1–29 + *20–25 vv.*
+ 30–57 + *c. 25/2 vv.*], the remains of the papyrus suggest that there are approximately eleven
verses missing, then the extant verses numbered 1–29 in the standard text of the play, then
20–25 verses missing, then verses 30–57 in the standard text, then about twenty-five verses
missing. The "25/2" means that we do not know how many of those final missing twenty-five
verses occurred in this scene and how many in the next. Thus the 25/2 in the heading before
the next scene refers to the same twenty-five verses.

of the dearest daddy that ever adopted a worthless
ingrate . . .

A stab of insight.

—This is no way to do a prologue.
Whatever I am, I'm not a masochist. No.
So what's the point in flogging myself in public?
Admittedly, what I did was awful. I made
a huge mistake, it's not going to go away,
and I have to deal with it somehow, like it or not.

He squares his shoulders and starts again.

The logical way to approach this duty should be
for me to recite you all the ins and outs
of Daddy. The kind of person he is.
                                        I omit
the luxuries lavished on me when I was little.
Not that I'll ever forget them, but I wasn't yet
sophisticated enough to appreciate them.
He brought me up some cuts above the others,
I went first class: no "one-of-the-bunch" cliché . . .
but, just between you and me, by inborn nature
my real genius is being a first-class disaster.
I came of age; what money could do, I did:
I made my mark, and quite a mark it was,
at underwriting the arts, at making donations,
at representing the tribe in the field, in the hunt—
with horses, dogs, and resources Daddy supplied.
I could even come up with the cash, in the right amounts,
to aid and assist my occasional friend in need.
In short, I became a fully *human* being
through Daddy's doing.
                        Don't think I wasn't grateful;
I paid him back in the proper coin by being
a Proper Young Man.
                        It wasn't long after that—
I'll go through the whole relationship; I don't
have anything else to do—well, Daddy fell,
and fell very hard, for a call girl who came from Samos.
I suppose it happens all the time; he's human.
But Daddy felt embarrassment, shame. He tried
to cover it up. He didn't want me to know,
but I figured it out for myself, and I was worried:
It seemed to me that if he didn't make some
really deep commitment, get some grip on this woman,

he'd be fair game for any young stud inclined
to contest his claim. The way I saw it, he really
should bring her home, and set her up in the house.
But he was too ashamed, and because of *me*.
What would my friends say? That's the way he thought.
Not that he ever let me know it. Daddy,
well, he *hides* his feelings. Worried or angry,
you'd never know from the calm, unruffled surface.
(Except, of course, when pressure builds up and he blows.
But let's not think about *that*.)
                          So I went to Daddy,
I actually did, and Told Him How I Felt:
That he was in Love, and I wanted to see him Happy,
and my friends would learn to handle the problem somehow.
And I won him over. You've never seen such a change.
My calm, cool daddy actually *capered*—he did.
I'd made him Happy—and, more important, we'd come
to a great new level of father-son relations:
Perfect Trust.
                   Which makes me feel all the worse
about what I've done, and how I've abused that Trust,
and how . . .

He gets a grip on himself.

                   He moved the Samian in that day,
and suddenly, a woman's touch, with light and air
throughout the house, and, wonder of wonders, *parties*.
Things were perfect!
                   —Till not quite a year ago,
when Daddy's business got *very* active, and he
and his next-door neighbor Nikeratos—that's his house—

He points to Nikeratos' house, stage left.

had to go off on a trip, up to the Black Sea.
They're not back yet.
                   Well, what this meant for me
was the greatly increased responsibility . . .
that goes with Perfect Trust. Oh, god.
                          And among
the usual duties—the house, the farm, the business—
I also found myself specifically charged
with looking after the women next door. His friend
Nikeratos isn't rich. In fact, he's downright *poor*.
Right from the start, I managed very well.
How would Daddy handle it? This was my guide.

I even once broke Daddy's seal on some wheat:
they were getting short over there. I did my best,
and, in the course of checking on things, began
to notice Nikeratos' daughter. Her name is Plangon,
but this'll go better if I just call her *the Girl.*
And the Girl's mother, the rest of the women next door—
they became fast friends with Daddy's Samian woman,
and from then on it was back and forth: She'd spend
a lot of time at their place, and they'd come over
to visit us.

        About ten months ago,
not long after Daddy left, I'd been at the farm
looking after things, and rushed back here, to find
the whole bunch, with other women as well,
assembled at our house, observing Adonis-Fest.
You know how those things go. It's fun for all,
and since I was already there, and they were there,
I followed along, let's say, to observe them observing.
I didn't have a prayer of sleeping, what with
all the noise they were making: lugging the trays
of seeds up topside, dancing, holding an all-night
whoop-it-up jamboree all over the roof.[3]
And then *It* happened—I'd rather not say what.
I'm ashamed, and a hell of a lot of good that does.
but still, I'm ashamed . . .

A difficult pause.

             Well, let me put it this way:
The girl got pregnant. (I guess you can figure it out.)
My behavior was perfectly proper . . . for the situation.
I didn't deny my guilt. Before I did anything else,
I went to her mother, and promised to marry the girl—
pursuant, of course, to my daddy's safe return.
I gave my solemn oath.
         A few weeks ago,
the baby was born. I took it straight to our house.
In the only piece of good luck in this whole affair,
Chrysis—the woman from Samos; we call her Chrysis—
well, Chrysis had a baby, too, not long before,
but it died . . . I know that doesn't sound terribly lucky,
and Chrysis was very upset about it, but think:
She still had her milk. She could nurse the new baby *here,*

---

3. During the annual festival for Adonis, the Adonia, Athenian women placed seeds sown in broken pots on rooftops to commemorate the death and deification of Adonis, a lover of the goddess Aphrodite.

we wouldn't have to ferry it back and forth.
—They certainly couldn't keep it over *there*.
This is a very close-knit community, not
the place for a sudden child to coexist
with an unwed daughter. So Chrysis nurses him here,
and Plangon sees him whenever she wants. That's *lucky*.
It's only a temporary arrangement, of course;
it won't work after we're married.

He takes a very deep breath.

                              If we're married.
I can't see Daddy jumping for joy when I tell him
I want to marry a girl with no dowry at all.
I'll bring him around with my golden tongue.
                                        Oh, god:
I hunt, I ride. I was not raised to *persuade*.
And he's due any time now.
                              Parmenon—the family slave,
our agèd retainer—goes down to the docks every day
to check the arrivals. He's got it all worked out.
I'd better find him. I simply can't handle this.

Moschion exits stage right, to the harbor, just as Chrysis emerges from Demeas' house. She is carrying the baby.

I.2 [c. 25/2 vv. + 59–60]

CHRYSIS   Moschion?
                        Where did he get to?

She moves down center and addresses the audience.

                              The baby's quiet.
I guess I have time to talk.
                              For someone who thought
she'd found, at long, long last, the perfect solution
to life's vicissitudes, waking up has been *rough*.
Kept in the height of style in the home of a patron
who loved me madly and showed no sign of changing,
who showered me with attention, affection, and trust,
who made each day an endless round of devotion . . .
why, this was the answer to a call girl's prayer . . . until
quite suddenly, Demeas went away, and it stopped.
My perfectly ordered life turned accidental.
First off I was running things, and then I was pregnant,
and then I had a baby, and then I didn't,
and now I have a baby again, and my daily

round is just as endless, except that it's feeding
this little thing here.
                              Please don't misunderstand me;
I love the baby, and I'm not complaining.
I simply have no idea of what comes next.

Hearing something, she looks off stage right.

Here's Moschion. Parmenon, too. Rushing home
in ill-suppressed excitement. I'll wait around
and try to see what the conversation's about.

Holding the baby tighter, she presses back against Demeas' house
as Parmenon and Moschion enter stage right, from the harbor.

I.3 [61–86 + c. 21/2 vv.]

MOSCHION   You're sure it's Daddy, Parmenon? Saw him yourself?

PARMENON   That's precisely what I said. Why don't you listen?

MOSCHION   And the man next door?

PARMENON   They're *here*. The two of them. Both.

MOSCHION

Depressed and fearful.

That's great.

PARMENON   A little more masculinity, please?
Bring up the business of the wedding right away.

MOSCHION   But how do I do it? The crucial moment's at hand,
and all I feel is fear.

PARMENON   And what do you mean by that?

MOSCHION   I'm embarrassed to face my daddy.

PARMENON   What about facing
the girl you ruined? What about facing her mother?
And stop that shaking! We certainly do not need
another woman in the house.

CHRYSIS   You'll wake the baby up!
You're really hopeless! Do you have to shout?

PARMENON   Here's Chrysis, too. To answer your stupid question:
Of course I have to shout! I'm shouting because
what I want is a wedding in progress here!
I want this wimp to stop whining outside the door

and remember the oath he swore *inside* the door!
I want him burning a sacrifice, wearing a wreath,
cutting a cake—I want him to *help* a little!
And those are some of the reasons I have to shout!
Are you satisfied?

MOSCHION   I swear I'll do it all.
I can't be clearer than that.

CHRYSIS   Well, I'm convinced.

MOSCHION   Once more to get it straight:
                                    We're letting Chrysis
raise the baby the way she's doing now
and claim it's her very own—that it?

CHRYSIS   That's it.

MOSCHION   Look out for Daddy; he certainly doesn't want
a brand-new baby. He'll have a conniption.

CHRYSIS   Thanks,
but Daddy's conniption won't last very long.
Because he's in love, and just as badly and sadly
as you are. And that's the way love works. It makes
a raging monster sue for peace in an instant.
Besides, there's nothing I won't suffer, sooner
than ship the baby off to a wet nurse somewhere
down in the slums.

MOSCHION   But I don't like to deceive him,
having him think the baby is yours by him
when really it's hers by me.

CHRYSIS   Not bothered at all.
The first one was his by me—or mine by him—
whatever. The gods must be at work in this;
correcting something that worked out wrong the first time.
We've got another chance!

PARMENON   Attention, all!
Cut out the philosophy, please, proceed with the plan:
All right, Moschion: what's your strategy?
How do you bring your daddy around?

MOSCHION   To the marriage?
I haven't the slightest idea.

PARMENON   Then GET the slightest idea!
He's almost here!
                         And DO NOT mention the *rape*!

MOSCHION   Don't call it that.[4]

PARMENON   I'll call it whatever I want!

A wail from the baby.

CHRYSIS   That did it; you woke the baby.

She exits, with the baby, into Demeas' house. Parmenon follows her in, but not without a parting shot at Moschion.

PARMENON   Be a MAN!

Moschion, apprehensive, is left alone.

I.4 [c. 21/2 vv. + 87–95]

MOSCHION   And now I guess it all devolves on me.
                  How do I start my appeal? Maybe like this?
                  "Please, Daddy, I want to grace your family tree
                  with an indigent pauper"? Oh, fine. And he says NO.
                  Then what's my rebuttal? What can I possibly say?
                  "But, Daddy, I'm in love"? A real crusher.

He slumps.

                  Intentions—honorable; motives—truly sincere . . .
                  But grab the first man you meet in the Street; he'll give you
                  a better speech. He won't be racked with shame.
                  Let's face it: I'm the worst possible man for the job.
                  I'd save everyone concerned a terrific amount
                  of grief by hanging myself right now.
                                          —I might
                  do a passable job in support, but as Only Speaker
                  I couldn't convince someone who *agreed* with me;
                  in a one-on-one with Daddy, I'll simply collapse.
                  —Well, no help for it. I'll find a deserted spot—
                  a really deserted spot—and practice. Rehearse.
                  Try, at least, to think up something to say.

---

4. In fact, nowhere in the extant text is Moschion's interaction with Plangon explicitly called "rape," but most members of an Athenian audience would probably have assumed that rape rather than seduction occurred: in other comedies this is made explicit. Some Athenians argued that seduction was a worse crime than rape, as it meant the wronged woman was corrupted. Because the most serious aspect of the rape of an unmarried woman for Athenians was that it soiled the woman, making it less easy for her to marry, rape could be condoned if, like Moschion, the rapist agreed to marry his victim.

He remembers an inspiring quote from somewhere.

It is no middling conflict faces me.

He exits stage left.

I.5 [96–119 + 14/2 vv.]

Demeas and Nikeratos, attended by a train of slaves carrying their baggage (ten slaves for Demeas, one for Nikeratos) enter stage right.

DEMEAS   Even you have to admit that this is a change
              for the better. What a wretched spot that was.

NIKERATOS   Delights of the Black Sea:
                                    Old men, fat and flush.
              Fish. And fish. And *fish*. Strictly business.
              And then Byzantium:
                                    Wormwood. Everything bitter.

He salutes the statue between the houses.

              Thank Apollo we're back where poor folks' food tastes *pure*.

DEMEAS

Following suit.

              Athens, beloved Athens, mayst thou receive
              thy just deserts, and may they trickle down
              on patriots true like us and bless us, too.

He turns to the baggage handlers.

              —Okay! Inside!

The bearers exit into Demeas' house, all except
one who is staring at him openmouthed.

                          —What's this? Paralysis? Lockjaw?

The slave scuttles into Demeas' house.

NIKERATOS   Of all the wonders we saw there, Demeas, the one
              that tickled me most was the mist that used to descend
              and settle over the landscape for days and days
              and make it so dark we couldn't see a damned thing.

DEMEAS   And rightly so. There's nothing there *to* see;
              that gloom is all the light the natives need.

NIKERATOS   I like the way you put it.

DEMEAS   And so let's leave it
for somebody else.
                    —About that other matter
under discussion: What do you think we should do?

NIKERATOS   You mean about your son and the wedding?

DEMEAS   That's it.

NIKERATOS   Well, same as I said before. All that remains
is setting a date and praying we hit it lucky.

DEMEAS   And that's the considered decision?

NIKERATOS   That's it on this end.

DEMEAS   On this one, too. In fact, I was there before you.

NIKERATOS   Drop by and give me a holler later.

DEMEAS   I will. Few details left to settle.

NIKERATOS

Turning to enter his house, then turns back.

                              Oh.

He speaks in high tragic diction.

            What joy, dear friend, to this our native land
            returning, after ten years' sore travail
            at Troy!

With a wave he enters his house.

   DEMEAS   That's close enough.

To the audience, in explanation.

                              —A tragedy fan.
            Myself, I'm more the comic type, and so
            it's Ho for the Happy Ending!
                              Chrysis is waiting,
            and for the moment, the next few moments,
            no business worries, no family obligations.
            Pure bliss.

He looks off stage left.

                  Uh-oh. I'm home; a bunch of drunks.
            I'd almost forgotten. Up north, no drunks on the streets.
            They can't find their way around in all that fog.

Happily, he enters his house. Enter the Chorus as a drunken
group. They provide a **CHORAL INTERLUDE**

ACT II: II.1 [14/2 vv. + 120–166 + 27/2 vv.]

Demeas enters from his house, shocked and surprised, controlling his fury with extreme difficulty.

DEMEAS   How could she do that to me? It was in the agreement!
                And then she goes and lets it happen—and worse,
                she *keeps* it!
                    I don't care how much she loves it. She's nice,
                but she's not *that* nice!
                        I'd be a laughingstock.
                I should go back in right now and . . .
                                            —No, I shouldn't.
                Remember, self-control. I should sit down here,
                and quietly think the catastrophe through.

He sits before his house, his head buried in his hands.
He does not see Moschion enter stage left.

MOSCHION   I'm back.
                Behold the orator, rhetoric honed to a fine edge.
                Behold the warrior, totally . . . useless for battle.
                Rehearsal did not go well. Oh, not that I couldn't
                find a place to be by myself. "Deserted"
                doesn't begin to do it justice. And "empty"
                comes up short as a word to describe my thinking.
                I've wasted all this time *daydreaming*! I've practiced
                Getting Married, of all the stupid maneuvers.
                I should have been running through my concluding remarks
                and polishing all the points I had in mind,
                but *NO*. Somewhere out beyond the suburbs,
                with no other soul for miles, completely alone . . .
                and I was running the ceremony through
                in my head. I worked on the sacrifice, I kept
                inviting my friends to the dinner and dispatching the women
                to fetch the water for the lustral baths. I actually
                choreographed the path to use in passing
                the wedding cake around, and punctuated
                the whole procedure with selected hums from the Hymn.
                I didn't stop until I'd made a champion
                idiot out of myself, and then . . .

He sees Demeas.

Oh god—it's *Daddy*!
I'll bet he heard every word.

In fear and trembling, he advances to Demeas.

He-hello there, Daddy.

DEMEAS

Demeas does not move, or even rise, but stares straight
ahead, mumbling viciously to himself.

Hello there, son.

MOSCHION   D-daddy? Why so ferocious?

DEMEAS   Good question. I thought I had a mistress—that's all.
I've just been informed that she is also my *wife*.

MOSCHION   Your wife? How could she be? I don't understand.

DEMEAS   Somehow, I seem to have become a father.
It's a boy.
          A bouncing, *secret* baby boy,
who now will go, with his mother, out of my house
and straight to hell!

MOSCHION   Oh, no! Oh, never!

DEMEAS   Whatever
does *Never* mean? You certainly can't imagine
that I would devote this house to raising a son
born out of wedlock? I don't do bastards
for *anybody*.

MOSCHION

Quoting from somewhere.

It matters not . . .

DEMEAS   It *what*?

MOSCHION   *It matters not which one of us is trueborn,*
Which is bastard. Humanity's *all that counts.*

DEMEAS

Absolutely thunderstruck, less at the sentiment than its source.

You must be joking.

MOSCHION   I'm not. I'm in dead earnest.
To my mind, no distinctions derive from birth.

> If you really get down to cases, *legitimate* means
> *the virtuous man,* and bastard—and, yes, *slave,* too—
> they're only other ways to say *the bad man.*

DEMEAS Do you have any idea what it is you're saying?
Next thing, you'll tell me *money* doesn't matter.

MOSCHION

Surprised.

> You know, you're right—it doesn't!
> I'll get to that.
> But the question now is birth. It doesn't determine
> a thing. It's *good man, bad man*—that's important.

DEMEAS You mean that good and bad have nothing to do
with family stock?

MOSCHION Oh, no, that's not it at all.
But being legitimate doesn't *make* anyone good.
And no one's evil simply because he's a bastard.
There are lots of virtuous bastards.

DEMEAS Name one.

MOSCHION I can't,
but that doesn't lose the argument. Take me.
You adopted me, made me your *legitimate* son.
But that didn't make me the least bit better.

DEMEAS I hate to admit the point, but you're right.

MOSCHION I am?

DEMEAS I brought you up to be an honorable man.
And that's why you've turned out the way you have.

MOSCHION

Aside, struck by guilt.

> Oh, god.

DEMEAS And so I'll grant you what you ask:
Chrysis can stay, and the baby, too . . .

MOSCHION Daddy!

DEMEAS But I'll be damned if I'm going to *adopt* the baby:
Your point is good, but still it's too far out
for an old man stuck in his ways.

MOSCHION Daddy.
There's one other little item.

DEMEAS	Oh, yes.

You were going to tell me all about *money,* weren't you?

MOSCHION

Feeling his way.

All right, I will.

Well, money doesn't make virtue, either . . .

DEMEAS   It helps a bit.

MOSCHION   . . . and poverty isn't the source of vice.
Just because we're rich, we shouldn't be blind
to the many excellent members of the deserving poor,
and to the fact that archaic marriage customs
keep many an excellent, poverty-stricken virgin
from making an excellent match with a member of, er,
the advantaged classes.

DEMEAS   You interest me strangely.

MOSCHION   To take a purely random example: *Plangon.*

DEMEAS   Who?

MOSCHION   Nikeratos' daughter. The girl next door.
Her father is poor . . .

DEMEAS   Her father is stone *broke.*

MOSCHION   This excel . . . this worthy and virtuous female person
lacks a dowry—a fact of minimal import
which totally bars the darling from contracting
an advantageous alliance with anyone wealthy.

DEMEAS   With whom, for instance?

MOSCHION   Oh, any young man with money.
With me, for instance.

DEMEAS   A purely random example.

MOSCHION   Of course. Well, this young man . . .
                         Oh, Daddy, I can't
conceal it any longer. Yes, I'm the one.
And she's the one I want to marry.

DEMEAS   You really
mean this?

MOSCHION   I certainly do. I'm in love with her, Daddy,
and I'm worried sick that you won't approve of the marriage.

DEMEAS   I didn't expect you to be this effective a speaker.

MOSCHION   She's all I want. Have I been effective enough
           to win your consent? Or does it just seem that way?

DEMEAS   The consensus of the jury is, you're doing well.

MOSCHION   And what does that mean? Yes or no?

DEMEAS   It means
           I have to be sure you're sure. If I ask her father,
           you'll really marry the girl if he says yes?

MOSCHION   Do you have to keep asking questions? Can't you see
           that I'm in dead earnest, and what I need is your help?

DEMEAS   Moschion, look: Dead earnest, no questions asked,
           I see what you're saying. I'm already on my way
           to Nikeratos' house. I'm running, Moschion, running!
           I'll tell him to get the nuptials started *now*!
           And we'll be ready, we'll do our part of the wedding
           just the way you say! I'll be back in a flash,
           and sprinkle myself all over, and pour out the wine,
           and set the incense out . . .

MOSCHION   And I'll go over
           and get the girl.

He starts for Nikeratos' house, but Demeas stops him.

DEMEAS   Oh, no, you won't! Not yet.
           And not until I find out if her father agrees.

MOSCHION   Believe me, he *couldn't* say no.
                                      I shouldn't be here.
           It isn't proper for me to obstruct the arrangements.

He exits, stage right this time.

DEMEAS   Accidents happen. And *Accident* happens to be
           a god, I guess. He must be the god who somehow
           salvages so many desperate situations
           we don't even know exist. Take this example:
           I didn't know my boy had fallen in love
           with the girl next door—what's her name? Plangon.
           The wedding her father and I arranged was, well,
           pure Accident. So was the falling in love. And then
           Accident—god—takes these two Accidents—
           the occurrences—and puts them together, and bang,
           a Coincidence happens. And that's what turns into Fortune,
           or Chance.
                        Or take this baby that Chrysis just had.
           Now, *that* was an Accident. But if Chrysis turned out

to be a freeborn Athenian citizen, *that* would be Chance
or Fortune for her, but Accident for me, I guess.
Unless it developed that she was Moschion's sister . . .
which would be Fortune for her, Accident for him,
and Chance for me . . .

              I don't have it all worked out,
but I do know that the baby was Accidental,
and we need another Accident for this to work,
and I wouldn't adopt him while there's an Accident pending.[5]
But the wedding—what a lovely Coincidence!
Just what *we* want and just what *they* want.

                        But look,
I'm forgetting my duties. Father of the groom, and all that.
Time to set a date with Nikeratos—why not
have the wedding today?

He moves to a point in front of Nikeratos' house and calls out.

II.2 [27/2 vv. + 167–188 fragg.[6]]

DEMEAS   Hello, the house! I have some important business!

Nikeratos appears at his door.

NIKERATOS   Is there some trouble? What's all the excitement for?

DEMEAS   How am I? I'm fine, Nikeratos. Thanks for asking
and a good, good day to *you*.

NIKERATOS   Have you lost your mind?

DEMEAS   You doubtless recall our talking about a wedding?
Well, tell me: Did we happen to set a date?

NIKERATOS   You know we didn't. At least, I didn't set one.

DEMEAS   Then may I, with all respect, suggest *Today*?
I'm really very serious. Be sure of that.

NIKERATOS   *When?* You mean Today, like Today, Right Now?

DEMEAS   The best things, I think, are those that happen quickly:
And thus I repeat, let's have it Now. Today.

---

5. Parker has Demeas allude to a common way dilemmas of New Comedies were resolved: a man is in love with and/or has fathered a child by a woman who, because she is allegedly foreign or not freeborn, is unmarriageable (Athenian law prohibited marriage between citizens and noncitizens); and it is revealed in the course of the play that the woman is in fact a freeborn citizen of Athens but was, for example, captured by pirates as a toddler.

6. The papyrus preserves only the last half of each line in verses 167–88.

NIKERATOS   I still don't understand. Why all the hurry?

DEMEAS   I have just discovered my son is in love with your daughter.
             What's more, I think it's mutual.

NIKERATOS   That's impossible!

DEMEAS   Well, that's what *I* thought, but I didn't have the advantage
             of someone like you to confirm it. But you have *me:*
             It ought to be no strain at all for you to believe.

NIKERATOS   God almighty, so sudden!

DEMEAS   I'd really prefer
             not to spring it on you, but you must admit
             that time is rushing on, and we have to hurry.

NIKERATOS   Before we ask the guests, shouldn't we fix
             some place for the ceremony to, as they say, take place?

DEMEAS   Simple, Nikeratos. Here, right here, in front
             of our mutual houses, on which be the grace of the gods.

NIKERATOS   Are you putting me on? I have no way of knowing.
             I'll simply have to trust my dearest friend.
             Still, tell me clearly: are you in earnest about this?
             I want with all my heart to agree with you,
             but if we're going to fight, let's start it now.

DEMEAS   In earnest? Perspicacious of you to ask.
             I am in the deadest earnest. Will that suit you?

NIKERATOS   Then so am I. Whatever you say, I'm with you.
             Just let me go into the house and get my cloak.

He exits into his house. Demeas looks around.

II.3 [189–205 + 10/2 vv.]

DEMEAS   Parmenon—where are you, boy?—hey, Parmenon!

PARMENON

Emerging from Demeas' house.

             You wanted me? Here I am.

DEMEAS   Go down to the market
             and buy for the wedding! You'd better take the biggest
             basket we have. Buy garlands, and sesame seeds,
             and something to sacrifice . . . and don't come back
             until you've bought them out!

PARMENON   What? Bought them *out*?
Hey, Demeas, cut me some slack. You get so savage
if anyone misses an item.

He nips into the house. Demeas calls after him.

DEMEAS   Chop-chop! And quick!
Like *now*!

Parmenon emerges from Demeas' house, carrying a huge basket. He starts to exit stage left.

                    And one more thing. Bring back a cook!

PARMENON

Parmenon, concerned with getting everything correct, stops.

                                             A cook?
Before I do the shopping, or after?

DEMEAS   After!

PARMENON   I have to get the money. Then off to the races.

He puts down the basket, re-enters Demeas' house. Demeas looks around.

DEMEAS   Are you still here, Nikeratos? Not gone yet?

NIKERATOS First, I'd better go in and tell my wife
to get the house in order. And then I'll follow
your man to the market.

He exits into his house. Parmenon emerges from Demeas'
house, talking over his shoulder to someone inside.

PARMENON   —Don't ask me what he wants.
I've got my orders, and have to bust a gut
to carry them out. I should already be downtown!

He returns to the huge basket, and struggles with it.

DEMEAS   I'll know Nikeratos; bet he tries to use *reason*
and *persuade* his wife.

He calls to Nikeratos' house.

                    —We don't have time to *explain!*

He notices Parmenon fumbling.

          —Hey, boy, you're wasting time!
                    Now run, boy, run!

Crashes and yells from Nikeratos' house.

>   Never use reason. His wife's in a perfect fury.

To Nikeratos' house.

>   —Hello the house! Please, what's holding you up?
>   We've got a wedding out here!

Nikeratos emerges from his house. He carries his cane
and a rather small sack. He is seething.

NIKERATOS   Alas and Woe!
>   I quake aghast at the depths of feminine
>   iniquity!
>   Oh, that woman! I swear to god . . .

DEMEAS   No! No swearing! Not a single word!
>   Now run, don't walk, to market and shop till you drop!

He herds the hobbling Nikeratos off stage left and calls after him.

>   And don't stop off on the way!

He pauses and looks around.

>   Well, it's a start.
>   But there's all this work to do, and nobody knows
>   about it inside.

He rushes into his house, yelling:

>   We're having a wedding! Today!

CHORAL INTERLUDE

ACT III: III.1 [10/2 vv. + 206–248 + 3 vv. + 249–282]

Demeas enters from his house under severe strain, in fact furious, mut-
tering to himself and striving for control. His behavior is in stark contrast
to the ebullient joy with which he entered the house at Act 2's end.

DEMEAS   Yes. Self-control. Triumph over Inner upset.
>   Quietly talk the catastrophe through to the end.

Moving down center, he addresses the audience. He starts quite coolly,
and actually remains collected until, at his monologue's end, he blows into
little pieces—but the careful observer may note the signs of tension: the
odd wiggle or twitch, the occasional superfluous detail in his narrative.

>   Have you ever noticed the fickle nature of the ocean?
>   Completely uncertain. Out of the clearest sky
>   to interrupt the fairest voyage, there often arises

at random a sudden, unpredictable storm
to smash and send to the bottom the sailors—who,
an instant before, were comfortably gliding over
a glassy sea.
        I bring this up because
it happened to me just now. Yes, I who was,
a moment ago, arranging the wedding, performing
the proper oblations, everything rational, fixed
according to plan . . . I suddenly don't even know
if I'm seeing straight. I'm trundled out here on stage,
flattened in a flash by destiny's quick right cross.
It passes belief . . . but that I leave to you:
Am I sane or crazy? Have I condemned myself
to random disaster by failing to ascertain the facts?

He takes a deep breath and pulls himself together.

As soon as I entered the house, propelled by my haste
to start the wedding, I laid it all out to the servants
inside quite simply and gave them clear directions
for everything needed—the cleaning, the cooking, the loading
of the holy basket. Everyone worked with a will,
of course, but the general haste created a certain
confusion, the way it always does. The baby
was bawling, dumped out of the way on a couch, the women
joined in with shouts of "Give me the oil! The flour!
The water! The charcoal!" and I was helping out
and filling these orders, and so, as it happened, I found
myself in the storeroom . . . and there was so much to get
that I had to dig into corners and search and didn't
come out for a while. And while I was there in the back
a woman came down from upstairs and into the room
that's right in *front* of the storeroom.
        —You see, we have
a room for the loom, and you have to go *through* that room
if you want to go upstairs . . . or into the storeroom,
of course.—
        The woman was Moschion's former nurse . . .
elderly, used to be my slave. Free now.
She saw the baby, neglected, bawling away;
she had no clue that I was inside, and so
she figured that she could prattle on in safety . . .
which she proceeded to do, once she'd gone over
to the baby. The standard babble: *"Baby dearest,"*
"Where's Mommy?" and *"Pride and joy,"* the usual kiss,
and she started to tote it around. When it stopped crying,

she said to herself, "*Oh, dearie me! It's only
the other day that I was nursing Moschion himself—
looked just like this baby; oh, did I love him!—
and now he's already got his own little baby,
and here it is, and* I'm quieting it as well."
Well, gentlemen, I was too startled to say a word,
and was wondering what to do, when one of the maids
came in from outside. The old nurse up and said,
"*Give this baby a bath! My goodness, what's
the matter with you? You leave a baby to fend
for itself when its father's getting married?*" The girl
broke in with, "*You are in trouble! Don't talk so loud—
the master's in there!*" "*Oh, no, he can't be! Where?*"
"*Inside the storeroom!*" and then she raised her voice:
"*Mistress is calling you, nurse!*" and whispered, "*Move!
and hurry! He didn't hear a thing. That's lucky.*"
And the nurse said, "*Dear oh dear, I do babble on!*"
and scooted out of there. I don't know where.

The direct appeal.

And I went out exactly as you beheld me
when I came out here just now, so calm and cool
you wouldn't think I'd seen or heard a thing.
And on the way out I see my girl from Samos
holding the baby and offering it her breast . . .
establishing who its mother is, but leaving
up in the air the identity of its father:
Is it me, perhaps, or is it . . . I forbear
to state it, gentlemen. I have no suspicions.
I simply relay to you this absolute hearsay—
which I heard myself.
                    I Am Not Angry.
                              Yet.
You see, I know my boy, and know him well,
by god, and he has ever and always been
decent, dutiful, well behaved, and above all
as respectful as he could be toward myself.
But, on the other hand, when I reflect that those words
were uttered by his former nurse, and then that she
had no idea of my presence, and then look back
at Chrysis, who loves the baby so and who
simply overpowered me into raising it
when I didn't want to . . .

His voice rises to a shriek as he comes unglued.

                    I GO ABSOLUTELY NUTS!

With an effort, but quite successfully, he com-
poses himself and looks off stage left.

> Well, here's luck. It's Parmenon back from downtown
> with the cook and his people. He'd better take them inside.

He pulls back out of the way.

III.2 [283–324]

Parmenon enters stage left, herding the Cook and his entourage—too good a name for it, probably—to Demeas' house for
the wedding. The Cook is, as will appear, quite a talker.

PARMENON   Hey, Cook! I'm damned if I see why you lug those knives
around. You can kill and gut anything in the world
with your naked tongue.

COOK   Another hopeless amateur.

PARMENON   Me?

COOK   I'm sorry, but that's the way I see it.
I ask you for information, the simplest questions—
How many tables of guests? and How many women?
and When will dinner be served? and Will I need
to bring a table-setter? and Does your household
have sufficient dinnerware? and Is the kitchen
open or covered? and What about everything else? and . . .

PARMENON   And what you get, in case it escaped your notice,
dear friend, is me, dispatched and gutted and sliced
into very small bits. By the true professional.

COOK

Not really annoyed???

                                            Damn *you*.

PARMENON   Manners! Damn you first.

He bows and waves the group into Demeas' house.

                         Go right on in.

Cook and entourage go into the house.

DEMEAS   Parmenon!

PARMENON   Someone want me?

DEMEAS   Someone does.

PARMENON   Hi, boss.

DEMEAS   You stow that basket and come straight back.

PARMENON   Fine by me.

He enters the house.

DEMEAS   Nothing, but *nothing*, gets by that man. Nothing
            of the sort in question, at least. If the world contains
            a snoop, it's him.
                                And here he comes. Does he *have*
            to slam the door?

Enter Parmenon who, having closed the door, shouts back through it.

PARMENON   And, Chrysis, be sure to give the cook
            whatever he asks for. And *please* be careful to keep
            the old woman away from the jug!
                                —Well, boss, what's up?

DEMEAS   What's up for you? Come here, away from the door . . .
            A little farther.

PARMENON   Ta-*da*!

DEMEAS   Now, Parmenon, *listen:*
            I swear by all the Olympian gods, all twelve,
            that I have many reasons for preferring NOT
            to flog you within an inch of your life.

PARMENON   To flog me?
            What've I done?

DEMEAS   Conspiracy. You and the others are keeping
            something from me. I found you out.

PARMENON   I never!
            By Dionysos, by that Apollo right here,
            by Zeus—that's Zeus the Savior—
                                by the God of Doctors . . .

DEMEAS   Halt! No swearing. I've got you dead to rights.

PARMENON   If I so much as . . .

DEMEAS   Look me straight in the eye.

PARMENON   I'm looking.

DEMEAS   The baby's mother?

PARMENON   Ooops.

DEMEAS   I'm asking,
Who is the baby's mother?

PARMENON   Chrysis.

DEMEAS   The father?

PARMENON   You are . . . or so she says.

DEMEAS   Oh, dear departed,
you are trying to con me.

PARMENON   I am?

DEMEAS   You are.
I know it, I found it out, in whole and in part:
Moschion's the father, you're a party to the plot,
and Chrysis is raising the child because of Moschion.

PARMENON   Who says?

DEMEAS   *Everybody* says. But answer anyway:
Is all this true?

PARMENON   Yes, boss, it is. But we thought
it might slip . . .

DEMEAS   . . . might slip past me?
To the house.

                                             Bring me a strap!
I have a perjurer here!

PARMENON   I beg you, NO!

DEMEAS   I assure you, YES! What's more, I'll tattoo you!

PARMENON   T-tattoo me?

DEMEAS   And quickly, too.

PARMENON   Say good-bye to the dear departed!

Exit, in terror, stage right, in the direction of the Piraeus.

III.3 [325–356]

DEMEAS

In futility, gazing off-stage right after the departing Parmenon.[7]

                          Where are you going? Come back here and be whipped!

---

7. Parker's typescript says that Demeas gazes off-stage left after Parmenon. I have assumed
that this is a typo, as it contradicts the stage direction just given for Parmenon.

Into a quote from Euripides' *Oedipus*.

> *O Citadel of Cecrops' sacred soil!*
> *O wide-outspreading ether! O . . .*

                                          why the shouting,
Demeas, why? Control yourself! Hang in there,
stupid—Moschion isn't injuring you!

He turns to the audience and addresses them with complete calm.

This judgment, gentlemen, may appear the maddest
conjecture, but actually, true it is. Consider:
If he had committed this . . . act with deliberate intent,
or consumed by passion for her or hatred of me,
he would still be obviously hostile, drawn up to oppose me
to the death.

                   But his complete compliance on hearing
the wedding suggested—*that* blows away any charges.
It isn't love—as I formerly thought—that makes him
so eager to agree; he wants to escape the clutches
of the Helen I keep in that house.

                              And *she* is guilty,
she is the cause of everything that's gone wrong!
Doubtless she sank her hooks into him one day
when he was drinking and wasn't really in control:
the blending of youth with unwatered wine produces
Folly, especially when accompanied by
an accomplished accomplice's help!

                                        I simply refuse
to believe that Moschion, such a peerless paragon
of modest demeanor and self-control toward others,
could have behaved toward me in such a fashion,
were he ten times adopted, or were he my son
by birth! His birth is nothing to me; his *character*,
that's what I prize.

                         But as for that person, that roller
in dirt, that female epidemic—why waste my breath?
She's a loser; she'll never stay the distance.

                                        —Demeas,
now must you be a man. Obliterate your passion!
Cease this lust! Bury the present disaster
as deeply down as you can, for the sake of your son!
And shove that Samian, lovely as she doubtless is,
headfirst out of your house and into hell!
No one can question your motives: she kept the baby!
And every bit of the rest is nobody's business.
Stiff upper! Persist! Survive, and show your stock!

III.4 [357–368]

Demeas is frozen at his peak of resolve by the appearance of the Cook, who emerges from Demeas' house in annoyance. He does not see Demeas, but Demeas sees him.

COOK　　　　　Where is that guy? He's got to be somewhere out here!
　　　　　　　　Boy!
　　　　　　　　　　　Hey, Parmenon!
　　　　　　　　　　　　　　Guess I've been deserted—
　　　　　　　　a hell of a lot of help he was.

Demeas, galvanized into action, races past him into the house.

DEMEAS　　　　　　　　　　　　　　　BACK OFF!
　　　　　　GET OUT OF MY WAY!

He disappears inside in a flash. Slam!

COOK　　　　　　　　　　　　　And what the hell was *that*?

He calls through the door.

　　　　　　　　Hey! Some old madman just ran into the house!
　　　　　　　　—What could it possibly mean? To me, nothing.
　　　　　　　　—Hey! I swear that he's mad!
　　　　　　　　　　　　　　—He looks that way,
　　　　　　　　and gave that enormous yell. It would be a nice touch
　　　　　　　　if he cracked all the dishes I just set out, made instant
　　　　　　　　shards.

A banging at Demeas' door from inside.

　　　　　　　　　　—The door, bang bang. Goddamn you, Parmenon,
　　　　　　　　why'd you bring me here?
　　　　　　　　　　　　　　—Better move.

He moves aside just in time to be missed by a small procession: Demeas driving out Chrysis with the baby.

III.5 [369–398]

Demeas, brandishing his stick, pursues Chrysis with baby and the old woman.

DEMEAS　　　　Hear what I'm saying? *GIT!*

CHRYSIS　　　　　　　　　　　　But where? Oh, dear!

DEMEAS　　　　To hell, but quick!

CHRYSIS　　　　　　　　　　It's awful!

DEMEAS   Sure, it's awful!
And pitiful tears, of course! I'll make you stop,
I can tell you that . . .

CHRYSIS   Stop what?

DEMEAS   Oh, nothing at all!
You've got the kid, you've got the old woman—Get lost!
Get wasted!

CHRYSIS   Because I wouldn't expose the baby?

DEMEAS   That's part of it.

CHRYSIS   And the rest?

DEMEAS   That's part of it.

COOK

Watching with great interest, he interposes an aside.

So *that's* the trouble. My, what a lucid excuse.

CHRYSIS   I don't understand.

DEMEAS   You—uh—couldn't handle affluence.

CHRYSIS   I couldn't?

She is genuinely puzzled, rather than indignant.

Just what in the world are you talking about?

DEMEAS   When you came to my house, you wore a simple shift—
understand?

She doesn't.

—a plain and simple linen shift.

CHRYSIS   You mean that was wrong?

DEMEAS   I mean that when you were
common and low, then I was your Everything.

CHRYSIS   Oh.
And who is now?

DEMEAS   Don't say another word!
I give you your servants, your jewels, your gold. Now leave
my house!

COOK   I see; he's angry. Well, I can fix that.
—Excuse me, sir, but . . .

DEMEAS   Why are you talking to me?

He aims a ferocious slash with his stick, but misses the already retreating Cook.

COOK   Don't bite!

DEMEAS   Another woman will be enraptured
with what I provide. She'll thank the gods.

COOK   *Now* what?

DEMEAS   And now you possess your very own son;
what more could a woman want?

COOK   At least he hasn't
bitten anyone yet.
                    —Consider, sir . . .

DEMEAS   Look, fella, stop talking to me or I'll crush your skull!

COOK   Correct, sir. Look, I'm going . . . I'm gone.

He hurries inside Demeas' house.

DEMEAS   You think
you're something special, but once you're down and out
in the City, you'll see yourself as you really are.
The girls there aren't your style: ten drachmas, tops,
to make the rounds of parties and swill straight wine
until they die, and if they aren't ready and quick,
they starve. But you'll learn as well as any, and then,
I'm sure, you'll know who you were and where you made
your mistake!
                    Stay!

Shouldering his stick, he stomps into the house, leaving Chrysis and company deserted, center.

CHRYSIS   How absolutely awful!

III.6 [399–420]

Nikeratos enters stage left, from downtown, pulling a remark-
ably tiny and scrawny sheep, with which he is fully occupied.

NIKERATOS   Once it's slaughtered, this sheep should fill the bill
for the gods. And goddesses, too. Let's see: now what
about blood? Blood, check. And bladder? Enough. And bones?
Great bones. And spleen—big spleen. That does for Olympos.
And so, what's left? The skin. I'll chop it up
and distribute the bits among my friends. Tasty.

The inventory over, he looks up and sees Chrysis and company.

—Good god, what's this? Is that Chrysis in front of the door
doing all the crying?
                    —Whatever happened to you?

CHRYSIS   Your great friend threw me out. It's obvious, no?

NIKERATOS   Good god! But what friend—Demeas?

CHRYSIS   Yes.

NIKERATOS   But why?

CHRYSIS   The baby.

NIKERATOS   My women told me you'd taken it home
to bring up. Lunatic thing to do.
                              But Demeas
is always so free and easy.

CHRYSIS   He wasn't nasty
to start with, and not for a good while after.

NIKERATOS   Quite recent?

CHRYSIS   One minute he told me to ready the house
for the wedding; the next, he'd charged in, almost raving,
and locked me out.

NIKERATOS   Well, Demeas must be crazy.
I know—it's the Pontos. Not a healthy region.
Come on with me; inside, and see my wife.
It's not so bad. No problem: once he figures
the profit and loss on this madness, he'll be cured.

All, including the sheep, enter Nikeratos' house. **CHORAL INTERLUDE**

ACT IV: IV.1 [421–439]

There is loud female wailing from Nikeratos' house. Nikeratos, furious, enters, speaking back to his wife through the open door.

NIKERATOS   Easy on the torture, woman! I'm already taking steps:
I'll handle him!

He slams the door, and moves downstage.

                    —You simply couldn't pay me enough
to want what's happened to us today to goddamn happen.
Spang in the middle of our wedding, an unlucky omen:
                                             Cast-off
unmarried mother brings baby boy and settles in.
And disorder, and tears, and hubbub among the women.

DEMEAS. EATS. SHIT!
                              Of all the idiotic actions . . .
        I swear he's going to be sorry for this!

Moschion enters stage left, talking to himself. He does not see Nikeratos.

MOSCHION	The sun won't set. Never. And why, I wonder? Night's had a memory loss? What a long afternoon! I'll take another bath. That's three . . . what else have I got to do?
NIKERATOS	Moschion! Good to see you.
MOSCHION	Is it time? Are we starting the wedding? I just met Parmenon down in the market, and he said so. Can I go get your daughter now? Is something wrong?
NIKERATOS	You haven't heard?
MOSCHION	Haven't heard what?
NIKERATOS	What happened here.
MOSCHION	What happened here?
NIKERATOS	Good question. A messy business. Very peculiar.
MOSCHION	Gosh. What was it? I don't know a thing; I just arrived.
NIKERATOS	It's Chrysis. Your father threw her out.
MOSCHION	You can't be serious.
NIKERATOS	That's what happened.
MOSCHION	But why?
NIKERATOS	The baby.
MOSCHION	So where's she now?
NIKERATOS	Inside with us.
MOSCHION	I can't believe what you said. It's awful!
NIKERATOS	If you think *that's* awful . . .

*Nikeratos is interrupted by a chorus of female wailing from Demeas'
house, which is followed almost immediately by the appearance of
Demeas, who bursts from his house and shouts back into it.*

IV.2 [440–520]

Demeas does not see the two on stage. After a take
as he talks, they continue conversing apart.

DEMEAS   STOP!
  Knock off the tears or I'll get a stick and *knock* them out!
  Enough of this nonsense! Go give the cook a little help,
  and that means all of you!
                                  Such an appropriate upswell of grief,
  given the great good worth of the dear departed . . . as attested
  by her recent escapade.

He slams the door and addresses the statue of Apollo.

                              —*O lord Apollo, I greet you in love
  and friendship. Grant that I guide the wedding set for today
  through to its end with great good fortune for all and sundry.*

Demeas addresses the audience.

              —Gentlemen, I fully intend to carry this marriage out
  by choking back my anger.

Back to the prayer.

                              —*And, lord, take care that I show
  my distress to no one, but force me to raise a joyful voice
  in the wedding hymn.*
                          —But what's the point?
                                          —*Let anything happen.*

Nikeratos and Moschion have come to a decision.

NIKERATOS   You'd better go up to him first.

MOSCHION   All right.

He moves to Demeas.

                                          —Why are you doing this,
            Daddy?

DEMEAS   Doing *what*?

MOSCHION   You know very well what. Why has Chrysis
            gone away and left us?

Silence.

                            Come on!

DEMEAS

Aside.

Now someone I know
is sending ambassadors—dreadful!

To Moschion.

—It's nothing to do with you;
Apollo, no! This matter is purely my own affair.
What's all this nonsense?

Aside.

It's *really* dreadful now: Moschion's
joined my enemies!

MOSCHION   You said?

DEMEAS

Aside.

It's plain as day. Why else would he come to plead her case?
Curious. He should be overjoyed that she's left the house.

MOSCHION   Do you have any idea what our friends will say when they find out?

DEMEAS   I rather expect that our friends . . . oh, Moschion, leave this to me.

MOSCHION   If I allow you to do this, I perform an ignoble act.

DEMEAS   You mean you'll prevent me?

MOSCHION   I will.

DEMEAS

To the audience.

You see? He goes beyond
the outer limits. More dreadful than all those other dreadfuls!

MOSCHION   It is not meet to give anger its head completely.

NIKERATOS   The boy
is right.

MOSCHION   Nikeratos, tell her to rush right back to our house.

DEMEAS   Moschion, leave it to me.
Leave it to me, Moschion.
That makes three times I've said that.
And I know everything!

MOSCHION   Everything? What everything?

DEMEAS	Stop talking to me!
MOSCHION	Daddy, I simply have to.
DEMEAS	Have to? I'm not to be the master of all that's mine?
MOSCHION	Then grant me this kindness.
DEMEAS	Sure, kindness. You mean like clearing out and leaving the house to you two? If you have an ounce of sense, you'll leave this wedding to me!
MOSCHION	I will—except that I want Chrysis to be there, too.
DEMEAS	Chrysis?
MOSCHION	I'm eager to have her on your account most of all.
DEMEAS	And what could be plainer or clearer than that? —*I call you to witness, Apollo: My enemies have acquired a co-conspirator . . . and I shall explode into tiny pieces. Woe!*
MOSCHION	You said?
DEMEAS	You really want me to tell you?
MOSCHION	I certainly do.
DEMEAS	Over here.
MOSCHION	Tell me.
DEMEAS	I am. I know the baby is yours. I heard this from a sharer in your deep dark secret, Parmenon. So . . . enough of gamesmanship!
MOSCHION	But in that case, if the child is mine, how can *Chrysis* be causing you harm?
DEMEAS	Who is, then—*you*?
MOSCHION	But, if it's my child, then how is *Chrysis* the guilty party?
DEMEAS	I can't believe you said that. Do you two have no SCRUPLES?
MOSCHION	Why are you shouting?
DEMEAS	Why am I shouting, you shameless scum? Is that your question? Okay, let's see if I'm right: You freely assume the guilt for this action? And you can look me straight in the eye and say so? Have you so utterly cast me off?
MOSCHION	How could that be?

DEMEAS   *How could that be?* You dare to ask *me?*

MOSCHION   It's really not such a cosmically dreadful matter, Daddy.
                 Men in the tens of thousands have done the very same thing.

DEMEAS   God, the presumption!

With a wave at the audience.

                                  I put this question to you in front
                 of witnesses: *Who is your baby's mother?* Or, since you feel
                 it's not so dreadful, go tell Nikeratos; see what he thinks.

MOSCHION   Oh, no! It *isn't* dreadful, but if I tell it to him,
                 it's *very* dreadful! If he learns this, he'll explode in frenzy.

As Demeas tries to digest this bolus, light dawns over Nikeratos, who has suddenly worked out for himself, not the truth, but Demeas' reading of it: that Moschion has fathered a child with Chrysis. It is close enough to incest to scandalize Nikeratos, who is even a more enthusiastic fan of tragedy, and tragic language, than Demeas. Utilizing this, he addresses Moschion.

NIKERATOS   Monster and more than monster! I do begin to suspect
                 the obscene enormity of what has happened here!

MOSCHION   I'm very sure I'm dead.

DEMEAS

To Nikeratos.

                                  I take it you see the problem.

NIKERATOS   Oh, do I not!
                        O dreadful deed! O dastard dread
                 who dwarfs th' incestuous beds of Tereus, Oedipus, Thyestes,[8]
                 and all the rest whose crimes are spread abroad!

MOSCHION   That's me?

NIKERATOS   You dared—I mean, *thou durst* commit this bloody act?
                 Demeas, borrow some good old-fashioned rage from the stage
                 and *blind* him! That's the ticket.

DEMEAS

To Moschion, ruefully.

                                  Why did you make it so clear?
                 He wouldn't know, otherwise.

---

8. Tereus had sex with his sister-in-law, Oedipus with his mother, and Thyestes with his daughter.

NIKERATOS

On the attack, to Moschion.

                                        There's no one you wouldn't harm;
no crime you wouldn't commit—and I'm supposed to marry
my daughter off to you? I swear I'd sooner have
a well-established disaster like Diomnestos[9] at home
(knock wood, and spit in my lap, and pray to the Nemesis-goddess).

DEMEAS   I take some satisfaction in my behavior. Severely
wronged I may have been, but I kept it all to myself.

NIKERATOS   That's the way a slave thinks, Demeas; hide and sneak.
If I were you, and he had dishonored *my* bed, he wouldn't
do it again, and neither would she. I'd be downtown
first light tomorrow to put her on the block and write him
out of my will. I'd start the news, and it would spread through
the market, stuffing the stoas and cramming the barber shops,
and everyone would say Nikeratos really knew
what manhood meant, and that he was perfectly right to bring
a charge against his son for murder . . .

MOSCHION   *Murder*? What murder?

NIKERATOS   Assault with intent to replace another—I call that murder!

MOSCHION   This language dries me out and freezes me stiff as a board.

NIKERATOS   What's worst of all, I've given a place in my hallowed halls
to the woman who perpetrated this reign of terror!

DEMEAS   Nikeratos,
chuck her out. Continue to share my distress in the way
a true friend does.

NIKERATOS   Of course I will. One look at her
and I'd rupture myself.

Starting toward his house, he ups to Moschion and yells.

                        Barbarian! Thracian![10] Slave to passion!
Let a true Greek pass!

He exits into his house. A pause.

---

9. It is not known who Diomnestos was.

10. Thracians had a reputation for savagery.

IV.3 [520–532]

MOSCHION	For god's sake, Daddy, listen!
DEMEAS	No. I'll listen to nothing.
MOSCHION	Not even if not a single one of your suspicions ever occurred? I've figured this out.
DEMEAS	Not a single one? You mean that?
MOSCHION	For starters, Chrysis is *not* the mother of the baby she's bringing up. It's a favor to me, that's all. She's just pretending it's hers.
DEMEAS	What's this you say?
MOSCHION	The truth.
DEMEAS	And why is Chrysis doing you this favor?
MOSCHION	I'd really rather not say . . . but if you learn the real truth, I won't be nearly so guilty, because the fault will be less . . .
DEMEAS	Will you answer my question, please, before you kill me?
MOSCHION	The baby's mother is Plangon, Nikeratos' daughter. The father is me.
DEMEAS	What's this you say?
MOSCHION	I say precisely what happened.
DEMEAS	Look, I'm no bumpkin; no tricks.
MOSCHION	It's easy to prove what I'm saying; what good can I gain by tricks?
DEMEAS	Well, none.

A crash from Nikeratos' house.

Uh-oh . . . the door.

IV.4 [532–539]

Nikeratos, distraught and upset, rushes out of his
house, talking to himself. The two listen.

NIKERATOS	Woe. One vision inside that house, and, raving, out I raced through the door, struck heartsick with sad surprise!
DEMEAS	Quite a preamble.

NIKERATOS   I just now met my daughter inside:
she was breast-feeding the baby.

DEMEAS   Well, what do you know?

MOSCHION   You hear that,
Daddy?

DEMEAS   I do. So you haven't done me any wrong,
but I've wronged you with all my crazy suspicions.

NIKERATOS   Demeas!
Coming right over!

MOSCHION   And away I go.

He starts to exit stage left. Demeas tries to restrain him.

DEMEAS   Buck up.

MOSCHION   No way.
One look at him, and I'm dead.

He slips out, stage left.

IV.5 [540–547]

Nikeratos, still beside himself, has made his way to Demeas.

DEMEAS   What's wrong?

NIKERATOS   I just now met my daughter inside;
she was breast-feeding the baby!

DEMEAS   Maybe she was just playing.

NIKERATOS   It wasn't play! She saw me come in, and passed out cold.

DEMEAS   Maybe she thought that . . .

NIKERATOS   Maybe you'd better stop it! I'll die!

DEMEAS
Aside.

This state of affairs is my fault.

NIKERATOS   What say?

DEMEAS   Your daughter nursing?
I can't believe it.

NIKERATOS   I saw it myself.

DEMEAS   Drivel at best.

NIKERATOS   It's more than a story! I'll go back in and . . .

DEMEAS   Here's an idea;
                hang on a minute, friend.

But Nikeratos has gone back into his house.

IV.6 [547–556]

DEMEAS   He's gone.
                                     That does it. Confusion
                on every side; the end is right at hand. Oh, god.
                When he finds out the truth, farewell to all restraint—
                undiluted fury and screams. He is not nice:
                a rough and rugged type who squeezes grudges and insists
                on absolute freedom of action. Dangerous man. But I,
                yes, I was the one that suspected, damn me to hell.

Screams, yells, and crashes from Nikeratos' house.

                                                      Oh, god,
                my fault. If I died now, it would be perfectly just.

An especially loud scream.

                Hercules, there he goes. And what's he shouting for?
                That's it . . . fire! It's a threat: He says he'll burn the baby.
                Roast grandson, that's what I need . . . Another bang on the door.
                That man is a natural disaster, like lightning, or maybe a cyclone.

IV.7 [556–567]

Nikeratos rushes out of the house.

NIKERATOS   Demeas, there's a plot against me! Everything's dreadful in there!
                And Chrysis is doing it all!

DEMEAS   What's all?

NIKERATOS   She won my wife
                and daughter over, and now they refuse to confirm the story.
                And then *she* took the baby by force and absolutely refuses
                to hand it over. I really may have to kill her; don't be surprised.

DEMEAS   You mean you'll kill your wife?

NIKERATOS   Well, she's got a part in the plot!

DEMEAS   NO, don't!

NIKERATOS   I wanted you to be the first to know.

He zips back into the house.

DEMEAS   He's completely out of control!

                                    And now he's gone back inside.
           How do you handle catastrophe? I've never been
           in a riot this big or this wild!

                                        Maybe reason would work.
           That's it—I'll make a clear and cool presentation of the facts.
           There goes the door again!

IV.8 [568–575]

Chrysis rushes out of Nikeratos' house with the baby.

CHRYSIS   But this is terrible! What can I do? Where can I go!
           He'll take my baby away!

DEMEAS   Chrysis, over here!

CHRYSIS   Who's that?

DEMEAS   Hurry! Get inside!

Chrysis runs towards Demeas' house with the
baby, as Nikeratos enters and calls her.

NIKERATOS   Where do you think you're going?

He sets out after her. Demeas, brandishing his
cane, addresses the statue of Apollo.

DEMEAS   Well, Apollo, I guess it's my day for a duel.

He gets in Nikeratos' way.

                                        Hey, there!
           What's the big idea? Who are you chasing?

NIKERATOS   Demeas?
           Out of my way. I want to hear what the women say
           when I face them holding the baby.

DEMEAS   Oh, no, you don't.

He raises his cane.

                                        En garde!

NIKERATOS   You really intend to *hit* me?

DEMEAS   I do.

To Chrysis.

                                        —Inside, and *hurry!*

NIKERATOS   Well, then, *en garde* yourself!

The two get down to serious belaboring.

DEMEAS

To Chrysis.

                              Get out of here! I can't hold him!

Chrysis, with the baby, nips into Demeas' house, as the battle rages.

IV.9 [575–615]

NIKERATOS   Is there a witness in the house? You started this!

DEMEAS   Only after you raised your cane in assault against
                a freeborn woman!

NIKERATOS   You'd take me to *court?*

DEMEAS   Well, you'd take *me!*

NIKERATOS   Bring out the kid!

DEMEAS   *My* kid? Don't be ridiculous!

NIKERATOS   It's not your kid!

DEMEAS   I said, *my* kid!

He presses his advantage—at which, to tell the truth, he is rather surprised.

NIKERATOS

To the audience.

                              You out there—*help!*

DEMEAS   Your shouts can't help you now!

With a final thrust, he uncanes Nikeratos, who is left defeated but not deflated.

NIKERATOS   It's back to killing my wife—
                that's all that's left.

He starts back to his house.

DEMEAS   And here it comes again—what a mess!

Dropping his cane, he blocks Nikeratos' way.

                    This can't go on.

Nikeratos swerves.

                        Where *now*?

He blocks Nikeratos' way again. Nikeratos swerves again.

                                        Oh, dammit! Just stand still!

He grabs Nikeratos, who roughly brushes him off.

NIKERATOS   Oh, no! Don't you dare touch me!

DEMEAS   Then get a grip on yourself.

NIKERATOS   At last it all comes clear—*you're* out to get me, too!
                  You *co-conspirator*—in on the plot from the very start!

DEMEAS   Then get the facts from *me*. Don't go . . . upsetting your wife.

NIKERATOS   I have been *mulcted*! And by *your* son!

DEMEAS   Oh, don't be silly.
                  He'll marry your daughter. It's not at all what you think it is.
                  Let's go for a little walk. The two of us. Right here.

NIKERATOS   A LITTLE WALK!?

He is about to explode, but Demeas links an arm with
his and starts walking him around in a circle.

DEMEAS   A walk. And will you please simmer down?

As they plod, he waxes reflective.

                  All this is just like a tragedy—don't you think so, friend?
                  You know the one I mean—the actors go on about Zeus,
                  and how he turned to gold, and gushed down into the house
                  through a hole in the roof, and deflowered a virgin they'd shut up
                        safe?[11]

NIKERATOS   So what's your point?

DEMEAS   My point's you never know what's up.
                  Does your roof leak anywhere?

---

11. The mythological king Akrisios locked his daughter Danaë in a tower because of a
prophecy that his grandson would kill him. Zeus, in disguise as a shower of gold, raped
Danaë, who gave birth to the hero Perseus.

NIKERATOS   My roof leaks *everywhere*.
        But what's your point?

DEMEAS   My point is Zeus. One day he's gold,
        next day he's rain . . .
                        See what I mean?
                                This trouble you've had:
        Zeus did it. That didn't take much time to figure out.

NIKERATOS   Things aren't bad enough, but you've got to make jokes . . .

DEMEAS   I *mean* this.
        Who was Akrisios? Some hillbilly king; you're better than he is,
        and look how Zeus glorified his daughter . . .
                                and now, *your* daughter . . .

NIKERATOS   Oh damn, oh damn! Your Moschion made fast food out of me!

DEMEAS   Oh, that. Don't fuss; *he'll marry the girl.*
                                    But here's my point:
        What's happened to her is an obvious case of Divine Intervention.
        Don't think it's at all unusual. Why, I can point out to you,
        right here in Athens, children of gods by the thousands and thousands,
        walking around in plain view!
                            You want an example? Well,
        there's Khairephon . . .

NIKERATOS   The party-crasher?

DEMEAS   That's just my point.
        Mere mortals *pay* for dinner, but Khairephon always eats *free.*[12]
        Doesn't that look like a god?

NIKERATOS   Okay, it looks like a god.
        I won't go to war over trifles.

DEMEAS   Now you're showing some sense.
        —Let's look at granddaddy Androkles.[13] The man is *ancient*—
        but he's always bopping around the town with a spring in his step,
        and poking his nose into everything new. And have you noticed
        the color of Androkles' *hair?* All black; not a hint of grey.
        Not that it matters. His hair could turn dead white, and still
        you couldn't kill that guy with an axe . . . *because*—you see?—
        he's a *god,* right?

---

12. Khairephon was a famous parasite, who kept himself fed by being a perpetual dinner guest.

13. It is not known who Androkles was.

Well, now: burn your incense, and slay your victim,
and pray that that this . . . *situation* . . . comes to a happy end.
My son'll be over shortly to take your daughter home.

NIKERATOS   It's got to be. I guess I've got to accept it.

DEMEAS   That's wise.

NIKERATOS   But if he'd been caught in the act . . .

DEMEAS   No, drop it. Don't get worked up.
Go in and get things ready.

NIKERATOS   You're right.

DEMEAS   And I'll go in
and get things ready here.

NIKERATOS   You do that.

DEMEAS   No flies on you.

Nikeratos enters his house. Demeas looks after
him, then raises his eyes to heaven.

I'd like to give especial thanks to each and every god:
All those suspicions I had, and none turned out to be true.

He enters his house. **CHORAL INTERLUDE**

ACT V: V.1 [616–640]

Moschion enters, not from stage left, where we last saw him exit.
Reconciliation has taken place, the wedding is on again, but Moschion is not completely happy. He feels, in fact, ill used.

MOSCHION   Back when I was first set free of the charge
so falsely lodged against me, I felt quite happy.
I even allowed as how I'd had Good Luck.
But since I've been restored to my senses, and now
I think the matter through and reckon it up,
with reason and logic, I GO ABSOLUTELY NUTS!
My wrath, in fact, is extreme: How could my father
suspect me of such a really disgusting mistake?
Well, all other things being equal—especially Plangon—
and all other obstacles cleared away—my oath,
my love, the time we've spent, our intimacy
(to all of which I am, of course, an absolute slave)—
he'd never get the chance to accuse me again,
not face to face, because I wouldn't be here.
I'd hire out as a soldier, ship out of Athens

to somewhere . . . Bactria, maybe, or Halicarnassus,[14]
and spend my days in feats of arms in the field.
But now, of course, I won't. I love you, oh
my darlingest Plangon, far too much to engage
in acts of courage. I simply couldn't, nor
would Love, who holds my will in chains, permit it.
Sad, but there it is.
                             However:
                                          I must not,
in low or baseborn fashion, let this slight
slip by in blithe and utter disregard
by default, as it were. I must, at the very least,
say something. I intend to frighten him
by stating my imminent departure. And then in the future
perhaps he'll show me some human sympathy, when
he's seen how really important it's been to me.

He looks off, stage right.

—But look, here comes the man I especially want
at the very time when I especially want him.

V.2 [641–669]

Parmenon, overcome with terror at the possible results of his audacity,
enters cautiously stage right. He does not immediately see Moschion.

PARMENON   Zeus best and greatest, here I am to reap the fruits
of a really stupid and wholly contemptible act:
completely blameless, I was so overcome
by fear that I ran away from my master. But why?
What had I done to warrant running away?
Let's take a clear and logical look
at all the possible actions, one by one:
The young master made a slip with a citizen's daughter—
Parmenon, one must presume, did no wrong there.
The daughter got pregnant—Parmenon wasn't the guilty
party. The baby was introduced into our house—
but Moschion brought her; I didn't. A certain person
agreed to say that she was the mother—but what
commission of wrong can be laid at Parmenon's door?
None at all. Why then, if you please, you softheaded
faintheart, did you run away?

---

14. Bactria is in what is now Afghanistan, at the farthest limits of Alexander the Great's conquests. Halicarnassus is a town on the southwestern coast of modern Turkey, known today as Bodrum.

A ridiculous question:
He threatened to brand me. You certainly understand *that:*
Just or unjust torture, the difference is terribly tiny;
whichever way you get it, it's hardly *nice.*

MOSCHION   Hey, you!

PARMENON   . . . And hello to *you.*

MOSCHION   Cut out this nonsense
and get inside on the double.

PARMENON   What for?

MOSCHION   For fetching
a cloak and a sword for me.

PARMENON   For you? A *sword?*

MOSCHION   And quickly, too.

PARMENON   What for?

MOSCHION   Just go inside
and do what I said. In silence.

PARMENON   Something's up . . .
what is it?

MOSCHION   I can always get a strap . . .

PARMENON   No, don't!
I'm on my way.

Parmenon exits into Demeas' house. Moschion yells after him.

MOSCHION   Then why the constant delay?
—Let's see. First Daddy comes up and implores me,
obviously, to stay at home. This fruitless imploring
lasts for a while; it's a must. Then, when I choose,
I let him win me over. I have to make it convincing
that leaving—the thing I absolutely cannot do—
is, in all conscience, the only thing I *can* do.

He starts slightly, then listens at the door.

This must be it. A sound. He's coming out.

V.3 [670–690]

It is, however, Parmenon, not the expected Demeas, who enters
from the house. He is empty-handed, but really quite joyful.

PARMENON   You know, you appear to be completely behind the times
            with events inside. There's nothing you know and nothing you've heard
            for certain, and that's the reason you plunge yourself into flaps
            and total despair.

MOSCHION   My cloak? My sword?

PARMENON   Now look, they're really
            beginning the wedding. The wine's on the mix, the incense burning,
            the innards already blazing away in Hephaistos' fire . . .

MOSCHION   Hey, there! My cloak? My sword?

PARMENON   The only thing lacking is *you,*
            they've waited for you for hours. Go get the girl—why wait?
            Your luck is in, and nothing's wrong! So what's your trouble?

MOSCHION   I need advice from a hooligan?

PARMENON   Owww! Moschion, what
            are you up to?

MOSCHION   You run in there and bring out what I tell you!
            And hurry up!

PARMENON   You split my lip.

MOSCHION   Always the talker . . .

PARMENON   I'm on my way!
                    —God, have I found myself a mess!

MOSCHION   Still more delays?

PARMENON   The wedding really is on, you know.

MOSCHION   More news? Be sure to bring me back the latest dispatches.
            —And shortly, here comes Daddy. But what if he doesn't implore me?
            Suppose he's so sunk in his anger he lets me go? I didn't
            figure on that. But what do I do? He probably won't;
            he wouldn't. But if he does? Well, then it's all up for grabs.
            I'll have to make a right about face . . . Oh god, I can hear
            the laughter already.

PARMENON   So here. One cloak, one sword. They're yours.

MOSCHION   Well, give them here. Anybody see you inside?

PARMENON   Nobody.

| MOSCHION | Nobody at all? |

PARMENON   That's what I said.

MOSCHION   You really mean it?
Oh, damn you to hell!

PARMENON   So go. Anywhere. You make no sense.

V.4 [690–712]

And finally, from his house, Demeas enters, speaking, in the
usual fashion, over his shoulder to someone inside.

DEMEAS   Then tell me where I can find him.

He turns, to see Moschion dressed for the field of battle.

                                        —And what the hell is this?

PARMENON   Now hurry on up.

DEMEAS   My son in uniform? What does this mean?
What's wrong? You're leaving Athens? Don't spare me, let me know!

PARMENON   It's obvious, really. He's already off on his march to glory.
I'd better have a chat inside. I'm already gone.

DEMEAS   I know you're angry, Moschion, and I love you for it.
I'm hardly astonished to find you hurt at an unjust charge.
But do keep this in mind:
                              Just who are you bitter *at*?
After all, I am your father. I took you in when you
were only a baby; I brought you up. Whatever pleasure
or delight has occurred in your short life, you got from me.
And that is why you should have endured whatever pain
you received at my hands and made allowances for my behavior,
as a proper son should.
                              I admit I accused you quite unfairly,
misread you, mistook you, slipped into madness. But think about it:
I went wrong on the rest, but kept your interests uppermost.
I read you wrongly, but kept those readings strictly at home,
refused to furnish your enemies with aid and comfort. But you,
you publish my errors abroad, you solicit witnesses to my folly.
And Moschion, that's not right. Don't memorize that single
day in my life when I slipped but forget the days before it.
There's more, lots more, but that's enough. You don't need me
to tell you that hangdog obedience to father wins no points,
but swift compliance and ready giving in is the real virtue.

V.5 [713–737]

Nikeratos enters from his house, talking over his shoulder to his wife inside.

NIKERATOS   Nag, nag, nag.
                              We're through. It's done: Baths, oblations,
                    the wedding. If the groom ever comes, he can take her away.

He turns, to see Moschion still dressed for the field of battle.

                    —And what the hell is this?

DEMEAS   I don't have the slightest idea.

NIKERATOS   Oh, yes, you do. You see that cloak? This man is planning
                    to take a trip.

DEMEAS   Or so he says.

NIKERATOS   An admitted degenerate,
                    caught in the act? They wouldn't let him. And I won't let him:
                    I'll hog-tie you into marriage, sonny, and soon!

MOSCHION   Please do—
                    And tie me tight!

NIKERATOS   You're addicted to nonsense? You hurry and drop
                    that sword.

DEMEAS   Oh god, Moschion, drop it—don't rile the man!

Moschion gets rid of the sword, and probably the cloak as well.

MOSCHION   Behold it, dropped. The constant stream of imploring requests
                    from you both has won me over.

NIKERATOS   Requests? Get over here!

MOSCHION   You mean I'm fit to be tied?

DEMEAS   Now cut that out!

He turns to Nikeratos.

                                        —And now,
                    bring out the bride!

NIKERATOS   You're sure?

DEMEAS   I'm very sure.

Nikeratos exits into his house.

MOSCHION   Daddy?
If you'd only done this at first, you wouldn't have had
to work so hard at philosophizing a minute ago.

Nikeratos enters again, pushing his shy daughter Plangon in front of him.

NIKERATOS   All right, you go ahead.

The couple stands before him as he says the formula. People from both households cluster around.

In the presence of witnesses here
I grant this girl to you, to have and to hold, to cherish,
to engender a crop of legitimate children, and give as dowry
my estate upon my death—
                                    may it never come to pass,
but may I live forever.

MOSCHION   I have, I hold, I cherish.

DEMEAS   What's left to do?
                                    We need the water for Moschion's bath.
Chrysis, you form the procession: Water boy, women, and flute[15] girl.

Chrysis enters from Demeas' house with the wedding party.

Bring out the torch and garlands, and we'll join in the parade.

A servant enters with torch and garlands.

MOSCHION   And here's the man with the gear.

DEMEAS   Now deck your head with a wreath,
and put your finery on.

MOSCHION   I certainly shall.

DEMEAS   And now,
you beautiful boys, you young men, old men, gentlemen all,
join in hearty applause, the spokesman Dionysos loves.
        May Victory, deathless goddess
        who sits in judgment upon
        this fairest of all competitions,
        incline her mind in favor
        and attend my choruses ever.

Exeunt omnes, singing and dancing in the wedding procession.

---

15. I.e., aulos (see introduction). A female player of the aulos would accompany the wedding procession.

Appendix A: Prose translations of
Peace 775–818 and 1305–1317

In an email he sent in January 2001 to Jamie Masters, who produced the music for productions of Parker's *Peace* by the Thiasos Theatre Company in 2001, Parker wrote regarding these two passages, "I've been stumped for years." Parker planned to produce translations to go with Masters' music in the forthcoming performances, but he never sent those translations, and no translations of these passages have been found with Parker's papers. These are thus the only two passages in the three plays that Parker had not translated and revised before his death.

Peace 775–818

Strophe (1st Semichorus)

Muse, drive off wars and dance with me, whom you love, glorifying the marriages of the gods, the feasts of men, and the festivals of the blessed. For from the beginning these things have been your concern. But if Karkinos comes and begs you to dance with his children, don't listen, and don't go as a helpmate to them, but consider all of them home-born quails, dwarfish dancers with necks like hedgehogs, bits of goat-droppings, producers of contrivances. Indeed, the father, when contrary to expectations he got a chance to stage his play, said a ferret throttled it one evening.[1]

Antistrophe (2nd Semichorus)

These are the kinds of hymns of the Graces with lovely hair, songs of the people, that a skillful poet should sing, whenever the perching swallow murmurs songs of spring with its voice, and when neither Morsimos nor Melanthios gets a chorus. I heard Melanthios crying out in the harshest voice, when he and his brother had a chorus of tragedians. Both of them are polluted grasping Gorgons with armpits like goats, who eat delicacies, watch out for the best fish, and scare old women when they run them off at the fish market. Spit a big fat wad on them, divine Muse, and celebrate the festival with me.[2]

---

1. Karkinos was a tragic poet who had four sons, one of whom was also a tragic poet. All five of them are brought on stage dancing at the end of Aristophanes' *Wasps*. The context for Karkinos making an excuse about a tragedy is obscure.
2. Morsimos and Melanthios were both tragic poets. To "get a chorus" means to have the opportunity to have one's play produced at a festival. Aristophanes elsewhere mocks Melanthios as a lover of fine foods.

Peace 1305–1317

JACK   The remaining job for you who stay here is to devour all these and pound them down, and not drag your oars without effect. But go to it in a manly way, and grind them down with both your jaws. For there's no purpose for your white teeth, worthless fellows, if they don't chew on something.

CHORUS   We'll take care of this. You do well to tell us. Okay, you who are hungry for this, fall upon the hare's meat. It's not everyday you come upon wandering lonely flat cakes. So bite into these, or I say you will soon be sorry.

Appendix B: Douglass Parker, "A Desolation Called *Peace*: Trials of an Aristophanic Translator"

James Constantine Lecture
The University of Virginia, Charlottesville, November 3–4, 1988

Whether I should be giving this address at all is a matter that has caused me no little concern. The transition from the young Turk I once fondly thought I was to the phthisic fuddy-duddy I have inevitably become has been traumatic enough when I have kept it to myself; but washing my linen in public, however clean it may be ["you never know when you'll be hit by a truck," they used to tell me], is almost certain to expose my critical underpinnings—if nothing else—as hopelessly out of date, to show, shall we say, that the bikini briefs I thought I wore are sagging camiknicks in this much more upfront age . . . and, incidentally, to make me wish I'd never got caught in this metaphor. It's unusual to make the following statement in one's first minute of a speech, yet I seem to have managed it: **But I digress** . . .

Let me begin again. Twenty-nine years ago this month, in November 1959, a symposium on the Craft of Translation was held at the place I now hail from, the University of Texas at Austin. The ten addresses given there were published subsequently in a volume I have been conning with a good deal of nostalgia this past month[1] . . . though I was not a participant in that symposium, and, indeed, did not make the scene, physically, anyway, for almost eight years. But my mentor, William Arrowsmith (now of Boston University),[2] together with Roger Shattuck (now Commonwealth Professor of French here at UVA),[3] organized, spoke at, and edited the proceedings of that symposium, and in the process, all those years ago, managed to quote *me* (as I recall, I was going quietly mad in Southern California, wrestling with the parabasis of *The Acharnians*), which makes me, as it were, someone present, if only by proxy, at not so much the founding as the zenith of that great age of translation, classical and other, that marked the sixth and seventh decade of this century in America. What would be known for a bit as "The Michigan Aristophanes" (the U of M Press was the first publisher) was poised to go into print—if only Parker could figure out what he was doing. A new age was upon us, not only in translation in general, but in Aristophanic translation in particular. Things would never be the same again. And, indeed, we sprang on a breathless world in a bare two years, with five plays in a very short time in 1961–62, and two more—mine, inevitably—coming out during the years after that.[4] Aristophanes

---

1. William Arrowsmith and Roger Shattuck (eds.), *The Craft and Context of Translation: A Symposium* (Austin: University of Texas Press, 1961).

2. William Arrowsmith remained at Boston University until his death in 1992.

3. Roger Shattuck later moved to Boston University. He died in 2005.

4. After being published individually, the seven plays appeared together in two volumes published by the University of Michigan Press in 1969: *Three Comedies (Birds, Clouds, and Wasps),* translated by William Arrowsmith and Douglass Parker, and *Four Comedies (Lysistrata, Acharnians, Congresswomen, and Frogs)*, translated by Douglass Parker and Richmond Lattimore.

actually began to be **put on**, to be **staged**, to reach a wider audience. The world was our oyster, and all the months had "R's." . . .

In a way, it would be nice to leave the course of events poised there in the past, transfixed and caught by the perspective lines from now. Ideally, this lecture should give me an opportunity, all passion spent, to look back at a phenomenon now comfortably enthroned in the past, divide my swift mind this way and that, and pronounce upon it, the cricket-like flutings of my geronion voice dispensing measured praise, and blame, and, above all, *judgment.* A *veteran,* that's what I'd be. A *sage,* even, one ideally equipped to assay and assess what had been done, with a *hmph* here, a *tsk* there, and fix everything with the occasional appreciative, albeit quite objective, nod. Instead, I find myself still, or better *again,* engaged in, grappling with, the whole wretched translating process, a Laocoön who, through some inconceivably awkward concatenation of events, finds himself giving a lecture on the present state of herpetology while doing yet one more last tango with Apollo's constrictors. Because it's still going on, you know, and here I am, a generation on, *still* translating Aristophanic plays.

The statement—or, better, the yawps—that I give to you on the state of Aristophanic translation has been somewhat informed by experience, but is more functional than normative, and, as you will see, hopelessly nonobjective. It is, god save us all, *personal,* and may best be considered a series of notes from the trenches, or from underneath the pythons, on how I do, or have done, or would like to do, whatever it is that I do/did/might yet accomplish. William Arrowsmith eloquently summed up a great many of the problems and solutions prospectively in an essay, "The Lively Conventions of Comedy" in the Texas symposium of 1959; what I supply here, in a rather more aphoristic approach, should be taken as variations on parts of that—expansions, or, occasionally, revisions.

It's not that the intervening years passed without anything happening, of course. Let me fill you in a bit. The first seven volumes of the Michigan Aristophanes duly appeared beginning in late 1961. The translators were William Arrowsmith, my mentor, who translated *Clouds* and *Birds,* edited the series, and taught me whatever I know about translating; Richmond Lattimore, who translated the *Frogs;* and me/I, Douglass Parker, who brought out four: *Acharnians* and *Wasps* in 1962, *Lysistrata* in 1964, and *The Congresswomen,* my name for the play entitled in Greek *Ekklesiazousai,* in 1967. There, incidentally, the series stuck; the remaining four plays were never published; in fact, only one, Tim Reynolds' version of *Peace,* was submitted for publication in 1968, but in the meantime that phenomenon known as the Sixties had begun to happen, and that translation was deemed too activist by the University of Michigan Press, setting in motion a more than mildly insane chain of events which culminated in the cessation of the series. It was fitting, somehow, that this most political of playwrights should still be arousing upset 2,400 years after his birth.

What surprised me, however, was the fact that I, due more to the luck of the draw than anything else, had translated the one play that really grabbed the sixties counterculture—or, if you prefer, mainstream—*Lysistrata.* Make Love Not War, and all that. It was first produced at the University of California at Davis twenty-four years ago this month,[5] and has been going steadily ever since. I've been informed

---

5. That is, November 1964.

of at least 150 productions over the years, and that may be just a fraction. As I say, this had very little to do with me—but as I look back, I see that it won me, for a while, a modest reputation as a political activist, which caused me a little trouble. I was accused of starting the Berkeley riots of late 1964, for example—admittedly, only by one person, who had just been passing through Davis when the play opened, but she did go to the trouble of writing UC's president, Clark Kerr, citing me as an example of "moral rot" in the faculty; and I was co-opted by some students at UC–Riverside in early 1967 to take a part in a concert reading of a new, Aristophanes-type play being put on to raise money for a new student organization on campus. As it turned out, I was playing the LBJ role in Barbara Garson's notorious Macbeth parody, *MacBird!* in benefit of a bunch going by the interesting name of "Students for a Democratic Society." The most unpolitical of types—I was, as I recall, a California Republican at the time—I rather felt like the Chaplin character who sees a red warning flag fall off a passing truck, picks it up, and waves it to catch the driver's attention as he walks—only to have a mob of anarchists materialize behind him, and thus be charged with inciting a riot. The trouble was minimal, but my astonishment was extreme.

There my interest in Aristophanes held on, though not my curious affinity for radical causes, until 1984, when I received a Guggenheim and set about translating two other of Aristophanes' comedies—*Plutus* [which I call *Money*] and *Peace* [which I call *Peace*]. I finished the first, and have been struggling with the second for some time.

Now Read On: the aphoristic approach. I'll double back in a moment, but this will do for a start.

On Translating the Classics: It should be unnecessary to make this statement, but let me do it anyway: The classical translator is favored, I hold, by what some translators may actually consider a disadvantage—the fact that there are, and will very likely continue to be, other versions in the field. He/she is thus not compelled to be concerned with the asymptotic approach, vectored ever and ever nearer some impossible standard of literal accuracy. Were his to be the only Aristophanes ever, this would not be the case. His audience, and his responsibilities, would be quite different. As it is, he can choose one of a number of possible aims.

On Translating Aristophanes: There are many possible goals to putting a classic into closer reach of a larger public. I don't believe, as I look back, that there was any particular overarching motive. We—certainly I—didn't see the sixties coming, and want to help it, or them, along. I think our motives were at once simpler and more complex. We saw something there that we thought other translations didn't convey, and wanted to show this to others. What, then, was the object of the Michigan translations—as I will continue to call them? Originally, to create on the page, for the Greekless, something like the experience of **seeing and hearing the play** for the first time. That is, we were trading across media, among other things, and, odd though it seems, we, or at least I, had very little hope—or not so much hope as *idea*—that they would actually be *put on*. It was not an unusually puritanical place, the United States of the middle and late fifties when the translations were in progress, but it was one where the open, *public* performance of, say, *Lysistrata* was almost inconceivable. There had been the Gilbert Seldes version put on around 1930, but that was really quite sanitized and muted.[6] I recall, while the translation was still being worked out, sometime around 1960, watching a couple of students run through the really quite tame tease scene between husband Kinesias and wife Myrrhine, and thinking that it might be put on in the dark, somehow; a shadowed stage, maybe; have Myrrhine go in and out of a tent, or something, where her eager spouse was waiting. . . . How nice it would be, I wished, to see it put on *somehow;* wouldn't that be great?

A funny time to live in, that writing time was. Production didn't really seem in the cards. I saw a performance of Arrowsmith's version of the *Clouds* (that play which makes so much out of *not* being obscene), in [Washington] D.C. in 1961 or early 1962, and even it was quite sanitized in production: For example, *So the gnat has a bugle up its ass* had been bowdlerized to *So the gnat has a trumpet up its rump*—a victory of assonance over principle. Certainly nothing in it made me think that any of the more obscene plays might be put on.

Perhaps it was just as well. If possible had been foremost, initially at any rate, we might, necessarily, have been more circumspect, more guarded in translating obscenity—or else we might have bit the bullet and charged ahead to even greater heights or depths. I particularly regret the pigs.

Let me explain this a little more fully. What seems to have been a stock shtick in Old Comedy was based upon a happy linguistic accident, the use of the Greek word for "piglet"—*khoirídion*—as slang for the human female genitals. Happy accident for Greek comic writers, that is; not so good for English translators. Especially translators of Aristophanes' earliest extant play, where an entire scene is based on that equivalence, as the hero Diakaiopolis goes round and round in an extended verbal maneuver which might be called "the whirling double entendre," with a visitor from the neighboring city-state of Megara, based on the premise that the Megarian is *so* poor that he has brought his daughters to market and dressed them as pigs, intending to sell, or swap, them for food.[7] "Is that a piggie?" "No, that's not a piggie; that's a piggie." Very funny—if you understand the equivalence. Heaven knows I tried, loading the context, having them do everything but give a dictionary definition—but I don't think it would play without a footnote—however, I didn't think it would play anyway, not in the late 1950s when I was doing it. Had I thought it might go on to a stage, of all things, I might have seriously considered changing the small girls' trick-or-treat costumes to those of cats. "Pussy" would have worked beautifully for the puns, but would have involved so much incidental falsification in establishing the premise—did the Greeks eat cats? sacrifice them to Demeter? cook them on spits? Not a chance—that it would have been impossible, of course. No way. Not a chance. Never in that world. And yet . . . Anyway, as it was, I seriously compromised there a basic principle.

Principle: More often than not in Aristophanes, the simple *fact* of a pun—that there is one there, I mean—is more important than its specifics. This is often the case in geographical puns, where the author specifies something in the ballpark, as it were, and it is up to you, not to translate exactly what he said, but something along its lines.

---

6. Gilbert Seldes (trans.), *Aristophanes' Lysistrata: A New Version* (New York: Farrar & Rinehart, 1930).

7. *Acharnians* 729–817.

There should be a pun, of course, but it need not, in fact, almost *cannot* be the same one. The translator learns very early that English is not Greek.

But, let me say, occasionally, just occasionally, you win one. *Trouvailles,* we call them, or, if we're being very Texan, *Birds' nests on the ground.* Those little bits of intimation, when the stars are right, and Greek and English seemed to have planned a happy rendezvous, when you are suddenly assured that the gods were with you, when you can get all the particulars into the English that the Greek demanded—or, even better, pick up something that the Greek might have demanded, had it only been English. When, as it were, the solution is there just waiting to be picked up. Some god or other of language—maybe Hermes the Twister—was being openhanded when I arrived at *Lysistrata* line 1080, when the Athenian chorus-leader has just noted that the Spartan delegates to the Peace conference have arrived in a pitiful state of sexual excitement, and remarked on it somewhat as follows:

> *Well, I'll be damned. A regular disaster area.*
> *I imagine the temperature's somewhat intense?*

Now, in the Greek, the Spartan replies *Aphata. ti ka legoi tis. (Unspeakable. What could anyone say?),* but Hermes, or whoever, pointed and there was the English version of what someone *did* say, what Aristophanes might well have said, had he only had the good fortune to write in English:

> *Hit ain't the heat. Hit's the tumidity.*

The fact of **obscenity**, however, varies from play to play. It is necessary in *Lysistrata,* rare in the *Clouds,* and a supersaturated solution in parts of the *Ecclesiazusae,* which I translated as *Congresswomen,* and throughout *Peace,* with which I continue to struggle. It has to be dealt with in those latter plays, in the almost sure knowledge that it will get put on stage. Let me give you, in these hallowed halls, one tiny fragment of the last, where our hero, Jack the Reaper, is trying to present to the Board of Governors who supervise the play an allegorical female figure who goes by the name, in this version, of Jamboree.[8] He goes by double entendre, working Sport for all the quibbles he can.

> *BUT THAT'S NOT ALL! Tomorrow morning,*
> *now that you have Jamboree, it's the Best In Sport!*
> *It's WRESTLING, all-in and all-out, on a natural mat*
> *where riding time counts, catch-as-catch-can, the quick*
> *reverse with the left leg over, the flex, the drop*
> *to the knees, and then, your muscles shiny and slick*
> *with body-rub, slide into a full spread-eagle*
> *and throw her the pin!*
>   *(Freestyle, no holds barred,*
> *score with a hard cross above, a jab below.)*

---

8. *Peace* 894–904 (Syzygy III).

BUT THAT'S NOT ALL! Day after tomorrow, it's RACING!
Back in the Saddle Again:
                              The frantic jockeying
nose-to-nose, the sudden upsets of sulky
on sulky as, puffing and blowing, the bangtails bang
away at each other, bunched for a flat-out thrust
in the final stretch to drive home and Win by a Head!
And the other jocks, in shock, their colors still flapping,
their steeples still chaste, lie littered around the offtrack,
losers who skidded, who stuck in the pack and Came Short.

There's a certain thoroughness in Aristophanic dedication to a basic trope which commands fascination and, indeed, emulation.

On the "Intruded Gloss": A central demand on any Aristophanic translation that aims to be more or less freestanding—that is, at least potentially capable of performance—is to produce, in the audience, the entirely erroneous, and in fact impossible, impression that they **understand what is going on**. This must be done without footnotes, Brechtian labels on the scenes (though I'd rather like to see this tried), or an onstage expositor like Gower in *Pericles, Prince of Tyre*. The demand arises partly from basic cultural difference, and partly from the immense body of knowledge of trivia and ephemera and rhopographical twaddle, much of it the detritus of daily life that tragedy spares us, that the original audience had at their fingers' ends, but is known, and that very imperfectly, only to specialists among moderns. What results is often cutting, on the grounds that it only gets in the way. But, if the translator's aim precludes cutting, then he will perforce resort to any number of more or less nefarious devices to further what, in its basic essence, is a scam—beneficial and in the ultimate interests of truth, but a scam nevertheless.

Central to this is what I called, in an unhappy hour, **the Intruded Gloss**. That is, the absolutely necessary piece of information, assumed or better presumed by the original text as part of the audience's shared knowledge and hence not needing to be said, is bootlegged into the translation, but, of course, subtly, so that the modern audience will (a) acquire the desired facts relatively painlessly, without (b) ever suspecting that they are being told anything. Sometimes such a process can go with relative ease, as in this example from the *Acharnians:* The demagogue Kleon was a person of whom Aristophanes most emphatically did not approve. Slug in the occasional bad epithet—*nefarious*, say—when the Greek merely says "Kleon." Write a verbal sneer into the lines in which he occurs. This is relatively painless, and no harm done, not really. The explanation is not only inserted, but it occupies its slot seamlessly, with no hint of its essential schoolmarmish function.

The trouble begins, however, when the reference is rather more recondite. In the *Wasps,* the reprobate father is explaining to his son the advantages of being a juror, and remarks that men of place and power wait/defer to him: even a man like Theoros, who (and I quote) "is a man no less than Euphemios," takes a sponge and wipes off the jurors' sandals.[9] The point of the joke, and it is a joke, though not much of

---

9. *Wasps* 599–600.

one, would appear to be that in actuality neither are important at all. It would help, of course, if we (or, indeed, the scholiasts, who think it might be not Euphemios but Euphemides, about whom they know nothing either) had the slightest idea who Euphemios was. Here, then, the translator's problem. Now, the father, who's trying to make the impression, can scarcely gloss Euphemios or Theoros by any epithet indicating terminal obscurity. The son, because of the formal nature of the passage (long speeches punctuated at regular intervals, of which this is not one, by crossfire), can't really interpose, and the point is minor at best. The translator's result is to make something out of ignorance, not the audience's, but the son's pretended ignorance. In the translation, the father prattles on:

> "Or take Theoros. He's Important . . . You know Theoros?

A negative silence from the son.
> Why, everyone knows Theoros! He's like Euphemios—
> that Big!
> You do know Euphemios?

Another negative silence.
> Well, take Theoros—"

Not, as it happens, the world's greatest solution, but it was *something,* and something is what I was after.

Where the problem breaks out most acutely is where a lot of knowledge is desired in a hurry. At the very beginning of the *Acharnians,* the displaced farmer Dikaiopolis is recalling the few joys he has had, among them

> "The five talents that Kleon vomited up.
> That made me happy, and I love the Knights
> for doing that."[10]

We are spang in the middle of a scholarly hassle, without much hope of getting out. Let us say that there are roughly two alternatives. Either this was a real trial, and a real, quite staggering fine, imposed upon the demagogue Kleon, or it was a scene in a play, probably *The Banqueters,* produced by our author here the year before. Now, the scholar can afford to argue the question judiciously, weigh the alternatives in what is still an undecided question. But the translator is only at line 6 out of more than 1,200; if he stops here, the audience will probably have to stay until noon the next day. He must therefore come down on one side or another, and, moreover, smuggle his decision into his version:

> ". . . when I saw Kleon fairly caught in that comedy
> by Aristophanes, compelled to belch up those five talents.
> That was a tonic. The Knights won my inexpressible
> love for managing that. . . ."

---

10. *Acharnians* 6–8.

Relatively painless, and not overly much space employed. Of course, our audience doesn't yet know who Kleon is (except that he's someone or something that our hero, if it's our hero, doesn't like much), and how much a talent is worth (or possibly not even that it's an amount), and they may be hazy on who or what Knights were (armor? chain mail? in ancient Greece?), but they have been fobbed off with something, and will know more about Kleon, by osmosis, very shortly. And so the translator can sprint ahead for the next line and a half until he has to tell them something about revivals of Aeschylean tragedy, and the quality of a playwright named Theognis, and . . .

No one ever claimed that exposition was easy, of course. But, as you can see, it is often the Aristophanic translator's bane. The parabasis—that section of the comedy, generally in the middle, where Chorus addresses the audience directly on questions of the day, usually for, and sometimes in the person of, the author—well, the parabasis is where the facts flow especially fast and thick. And, if it's a self-referent parabasis, there is even more trouble. At line 626 of the same play, the leader of the Chorus of Old Men from the deme Acharnae (don't ask), having decided the results of the debate, remarks, *all' apodyntes tois anapaistois epiomen* ("Let's undress and go to the anapests").

I must admit that I was tempted, given the general lack of knowledge among moderns about metrical terminology, to leave it at that. The fantasy still haunts me— shamelessly unclad oldsters, out for a night on the town, battering at the door of the sly, kohl-eyed, sinuous, seductive Anapests, those ancient daughters of joy who rivaled the slim-fingered Dactyls in the *maison* next door . . . But no; a translator must be made of sterner stuff. The audience must be made to know, somehow, that this is a reference to the parabasis, which was normally in the anapestic meter (though mine will not be, except by the luck of the draw), and further, given some idea of what a parabasis is, which is to say, a traditional part of any well-appointed Old Comedy. The impulse, though? Well, a sort of familiar contempt is assumed, as of the seasoned chorus that this one certainly is:

> *"Places, Men! It's time for the ANAPESTS.*
> *Off with those cloaks—let's get this atrophied ritual on the road!"*

The word *parabasis* will be coming along shortly—though not in the Greek, which is, and can afford to be, content with playing around with the verb that term is derived from, to be dealt with in its turn, plus the word *didaskalos* "teacher [of the chorus], producer" but also "instructor in other things as well," plus a host of other items basically so unknown to the audience that the first impulse is, as always, to stop the action, stop everything, and EXPLAIN. Since that is precluded, however, five lines of Greek become seven and one half of English, or the original, quite literally translated,

> *Since our teacher first had charge of comic choruses,*
> *he never yet* advanced *on the audience to say he was clever;*
> *but, slandered by enemies to the Athenians, quick to decide,*
> *[saying] that he ridicules our city and insults the people,*
> *he now asks to reply to the Athenians, who change their minds . . .*

becomes, in my English,

> *Gentlemen, our Playwright is a modest man. Never in his career*
> *has he written his ego into the script, or prostituted his Parabasis*
> *to declare his genius. But now that genius is under attack.*
> *Before the people of Athens (so notorious for their snap decisions),*
> *his enemies charge that he degrades the City and insults the Populace.*
> *And thus our Poet requests this time to defend his Art*
> *before the people of Athens (so illustrious for their reasoned revisions*
> *of their snap decisions).*

It may be difficult to excuse this sort of approach, redolent of the Cyclops—or do I mean the Læstrygonian?—episode in Joyce's *Ulysses;* overall, thirty-three lines of anapestic tetrameter in Greek will have ballooned to fifty-one six-beat lines of English, and even that was cut by at least a third. But the rationale, even at the distance of a generation, is easy enough to see, if not forgive: Necessary information is sneaked in, under the guise of rhetoric, which then creates a need for more rhetoric as a balance in those parts which needed no glossing, which may in turn require yet more rhetoric to polish things off, as it were, and, by the time the fine tuning is done, the dainty parabasis waddles around grotesquely, *topologically* equivalent to the original, as I once protested from California to my mentor when he exploded in Texas, but only topologically. I admit he had a point on that particular occasion, since I had translated six short anapestic Greek lines into fifty-six English skeltonics. I eventually trimmed it back to eight lines of English, which, given my usual practice, was Spartan self-restraint:[11]

> *Let the crafty Kleon forge and frame*
> *each fell, nefarious plot.*
> *My aide is Justice; my adjutant, Right—*
> *I defy such scheming! I'll not*
> *be caught!—But his charge of perversion and fear*
> *could lead to arresting ends . . .*
> *since the versatile Kleon turns tail to our Foes—*
> *and repeats the maneuver for Friends.*

The intruded gloss is necessary, very necessary for any direct, seamless reading or production of an Aristophanic play, but it should not be the only basic principle of translation. On the other hand, it is sometimes difficult to decide what the hierarchical order should be. I still bear the scars of an uncomfortable time spent between the rock and the hard place, when form and gloss contended mightily for mastery. At line 1189 of the *Lysistrata,* the Semichoruses of Men and Women reunite and address the audience, not in a second parabasis, where they might try out ritualized insults on the audience, but in a sort of Indian-giving (if that can be said without offending Native Americans), where they promise that audience all sorts of goodies, only to snatch said goodies away in the last line or so of a recitative. They do this four times. It is, I believed, and still believe, desirable that the modern audience know what sort of thing is going on, or rather is *not* going on. I felt it so strongly that I inserted this information,

---

11. *Acharnians,* 659–664.

or rather, expanded on it considerably, in the first offering-cum-snatch-back. Unfortunately, it worked the first time. I had decided to use a modified Burns stanza, short lines, lots of rhymes, AABCCB, etc., etc., so:

> We're not about to introduce
> the standard personal abuse—
> the Choral Smear
> of Present Persons (usually,
> in every well-made comedy,
> inserted here).
> Instead, in deed and utterance, we
> shall now indulge in philanthropy
> because we feel
> that members of the audience
> endure, in the course of current events
> sufficient hell.
> Therefore, friends, be rich! Be flush!
> Apply to us, and borrow cash
> in large amounts.
> The Treasury stands behind us—there—
> and we can personally take care
> of small accounts.
> Drop up today. Your credit's good.
> Your loan won't have to be repaid
> in full until
> the war is over. And then, your debt
> is only the money you actually get—
> nothing at all.

The misfortune was, as I say, that it worked, and worked pretty well as these things go, in the first of the series, intruded gloss and all. It had a form to it, four six-line stanzas, AABCCB, etc., and it accommodated the bootlegged information with ease. What a fine achievement, I thought . . . and then realized with complete horror that I had committed myself to use that same twenty-four-line form THREE MORE TIMES, when each unit, not needing the explanation, the intruded gloss, contained only enough material for sixteen of those very short lines at most. Somehow, maintaining that form became the important thing. I stretched. I padded. I diffused. I suffused. My rhythms became looser, my logic more tortured. It took weeks, and I was on the rack throughout. My rhymes weakened, and finally verged on the assonantal—what I call "rock rhymes" today—a thing I hate, but eventually, battered and bloody, I emerged, the four sequences finished. I had my pride, by heaven! I had also finished by rhyming "own" with "home." My birthright had been sold for one lousy gloss.

One learns early that Choices Breed, which is to say that a strategy adopted to solve a current problem will create others down the line somewhere. To take an example from the *Peace:* I decided, against all counsel, to get what initial tension I could in the play's prologue by having the two slaves, dressed as cooks, engage in kitchen

Franco-American, the while they are preparing and serving, to a dung-beetle, cakes of his excrement of choice . . . and then drop out of the dialect when not in the cooking phase of their action. (I have changed the beetle to a cockroach, by the way; to get an instantaneous reaction of disgust from the audience—not that they won't have one already):[12]

1ST SLAVE	*Vite, vite! Pass me a patty cake for ze cockroách!*
2ND SLAVE	*Voilà.*
	Serve eet to 'eem, zat espèce d'espèce,
	weez compliments from ze chef an' ze weesh zat 'ee
	weel nevair taste a sweetair patty zan zat!
1ST SLAVE	*Anozzair! Ze special!*
2ND SLAVE	*Ze special? Ze donkey shit*
	al burro?
	Voilà encore.
	What 'appen to ze patty
	you take 'eem jus' now? 'Ee should 'ave gobble eet down.
1ST SLAVE	Gobble? *Eet eez to laugh! 'Ee reep eet away*
	from ze plattair, 'ee geeve eet a queeck pirouette or two
	on all zose toes, an' Chomp!—'ee surround *ze patty!*
	—Plus vite! 'Ee want beaucoup—arranged in layers!
	An' mind ze texture!
2ND SLAVE	

Turning to the audience and dropping the dialect entirely.

> An appeal to sanitary engineers:
> Will you PLEASE get on with your job and haul this away?
> Unless you'd prefer an unobstructed view of me
> in terminal asphyxiation.

1ST SLAVE	*Anozzair! Anozzair!*
	An' use ze gay shit!
2ND SLAVE	*You mean ze turnovair?*
1ST SLAVE	*Oui.*
	'Ee want ze fine grind zis time. 'Ee don' like lumps.
2ND SLAVE[13]	*Voilà.*
	—Well, gents, I've got to admit this job
	has one advantage. No one's going to accuse me
	of sneaking nibbles off *this* cake.

---

12. *Peace* 1–17.

13. In the final version of Parker's translation the second slave (Xanthias) adds here, *An ordure like zat eez hard to feel. But steel . . .*

1ST SLAVE   *Yeeuch! Anozzair!*
            —An' steell anozzair!
                        —Anozzair yet!
                                    —Grind more,
an' keep zem coming—vite!

At some point in this jolly badinage the 2nd Slave quits in disgust:

2ND SLAVE   *Zut! Merde alors!*
            —I'm quitting. I can't take this shit.

You may get some inkling of the trouble ahead when I point out that the same slave (at least in my assignment of parts) is shortly to indulge in literary criticism in a direct address to supersubtle types in the audience, with particular reference—conceivably—to natural philosophers from Ionia, who do speak in dialect in the Greek; a close prose version of his remarks would run thus: "Already one of the audience, a young man who seems bright to himself, may be saying: 'What is this business? What's the point of the beetle?' And then an Ionian, sitting next to him, says, 'In my opinion, it's a riddle about Kleon, saying that he's eating runny crap in Hades.'"[14] But, thinking of certain tendencies in modern, or rather postmodern literary criticism, plus the previous assignment of a sort of French to the cooks, my version goes off on its own:

2ND SLAVE   Already among you some bright self-referent youngster
            is making a sign to be heard. And what's he saying?
            "Decode this text and expose the roach's deep structure!"
            Beside him, a deft deconstructionist, newly arrived
            from across the Sea to the East, speaks up:
                                    "Zat's easy:
            Ze cockroách configuration prefigures ze figure of KLEON.
            We commence wis ze eating-codes, ze unblushing ingestion
            of sheet, both solid an' runny. . . ."

I have an unreasoning affection for that solution (as one might say), but it may have created more problems than it solves. And, heaven knows, it will date rather swiftly; at the rate I'm going, it may, structuralist and poststructuralist, be dead before the play sees print.

One of the most engaging features of your basic bipartite Aristophanic comedy—and one of the most disturbing, back in the New Critical 1950s and certainly before that—is a certain potential prodigality or austerity, what might be called its *extensibility/collapsibility index*. With its first part reserved to setting up the problem and its solution, and its second given to developing the ramifications of that solution, it comes as no great shock to observe that such development, such ramifications, could be multiplied greatly without, it seems, doing the play any particular damage. By the same token, it is possible to conceive of an Aristophanic work experiencing cuts and yet being

---

14. *Peace* 43–48.

as much of a whole as it was before. Oh, we would doubtless miss the bits—but the Unity of the work, that Golden Calf to which we did obeisance in those far-off years, would not suffer especially.

It is not surprising, then, that earlier critics, bothered by what may seem a rather slapdash method of approach to a dramatic problem, denied any dramatic unity to the comedies of Aristophanes at all.

What is especially fascinating here, and important for the translator, is the undoubted fact that, in the face of this seemingly random unity, the plays possess a tight *formal* structure that leaves the basic Greek tragedy looking positively splayed, creating the necessity for, say, rhyme that I have touched on earlier, and should like to have had time to develop. But what is important for the structure of this address to you this evening is that it, like an Aristophanic play, is collapsible or extensible at will—which means I can now quickly jump to my coda and no harm done.

To conclude: Translation is, as I see it, a Protean endeavor, wherein the translator turns in two senses, one transitive (the turning of the work into the target language) and one intransitive (the turning of oneself into the original author). The second sounds strange, but it is no more strange, and no less true, than the first.

My feelings on this subject I put, years ago, into a version of a section from an errant Church Father, the acerbic Montanist Tertullian. Tertullian was talking about something else, of course, but to me he was talking about what I do, and I entitled his words on the Chameleon, *Translator at Work*:[15]

> Chameleon: *Living Epidermis.*
> *Such head as he has, jammed straight to spine; neck, lacking—*
> *making reflection a strain . . . but not circumspection:*
> *Stalked eyelets go a stalking, spinning spots of light.*
> *Stupefied, sluggish, he barely lifts from earth,*
> *his gait a stunned struggle at progress;*
> *his pace suggested, not displayed.*
> *Observe: He fasts forever, never starves.*
> *He feeds with a yawn, digests with a shudder: Food from the wind.*
> *Chameleon, yet, can utterly alter . . . if nothing else.*
> *One color alone is his own, but every encounter imbues its hue upon him.*
> *Only to him is it granted to take his fun—as runs the popular phrase—*
> *out of his very own hide.*

All the elements of what the translator, at least this translator, must necessarily go through are there. Especially, not so much the sluggishness, but the bit about the hide.

It may be objected, of course, that, for all his twistings and turnings, the translator of ancient literature remains, willy-nilly, him- or herself, ever recognizable, in style, strategies, and rhythms, through whatever set of crepe whiskers and blue spectacles he/she has chosen to represent his victim of the moment, and it may be that the masking is more a mental set than an actual assumption, and that this set is perceived by the

---

15. *De pallio* 3.3.3–5.

subject but not by his observers, even as a line of S. J. Perelman bespeaks that master, no matter whom he happens to be parodying at the moment. Be that as it may, the fact remains that the translator's experience of the text is inevitably personal, and that he/she may often recall any portion thereof in terms of the pain it cost him. Which has been, I'm afraid, the case tonight. Your speaker is one who sees, not so much the Aristophanic corpus, but his own, covered with wounds which in any other long-past endeavor might have healed, but here, due to his still being engaged in the pricking on the plaine, are nearly as fresh and bleeding as on the days when they were incurred. He sees history (we might term it that) in terms of his disasters, like Belloc's old soldier who "lost a leg at Waterloo, / and Quatre-Bras, / and Vigny, too." A series of battles in which he lost, conceivably, three halves of his sanity.

Or, to arrive finally at the reason for the rather curious title of tonight's lecture. Calgacus, we are assured by the Roman historian Tacitus, was a sturdy Briton, otherwise unknown, who warned his compatriots of Roman scorched-earth policies in the first century AD, when Tacitus' father-in-law was leading Roman troops in Great Britain. Calgacus must have been a fiery orator in the original Celtic; his words come across into Tacitus' Latin with sufficient force to win a place in dictionaries of quotations 1,900 years later: Beware the Romans, he says, because, *ubi solitudinem faciunt, pacem appellant.*[16] "They make a desolation and they call it Peace." There are thus two reasons for my choosing to echo Calgacus:

First, I am at present still wandering around, lonely, in the desolation of what I call *Peace,* because that's its name, the name of the Aristophanic play I'm still translating.

And second, because I am among those who think that Tacitus made at least the speech up, if not its speaker Calgacus—and, after what I have said tonight, you will see how I descry a kindred soul in a translator who may have turned a non-existent text into good rhetoric.

Thank you very much.

---

16. *Agricola* 30.5.